# Fine-tune Your English

*For competitive Examinations* 

## K.J Tom

# Fine-tune Your English

by

K.J. Tom MA, BEd.

Main topics covered:

| | |
|---|---|
| 1. **Essential grammar aspects** | 11. **Spot mistakes in sentences** |
| 2. **Synonyms** | 12. **Redundant words** |
| 3. **Homonyms** | 13. **Important idioms** |
| 4. **Antonyms** | 14. **Letter writing** |
| 5. **Important phrasal verbs** | 15. **Biodata writing techniques** |
| 6. **Formal & Informal English** | 16. **Job/Exam interview strategies** |
| 7. **Foreign words in English** | 17. **Job application writing** |
| 8. **Commonly used English terms** | 18. **Reading strategies** |
| 9. **Confusing English terms** | 19. **Essay writing techniques** |
| 10. **Correct the grammatical errors** | 20. **Group discussion** |

**This book covers English topics which are commonly asked for in the following competitive examinations**

1. Civil Services Examination (UPSC)
2. Various MBA admission tests such as CAT, XAT, GMAT, etc.
3. Indian Economic Service Examination (IES)
4. Staff Selection Commission Examinations (SSC)
5. Common Law Admission Test (CLAT)
6. Combined Defence Services Examination (CDS)
7. Law School Admission Test (LSAT)
8. National Defence Academy Examination (NDA)
9. Food Corporation of India Examination (FCI)
10. Various Bank tests
11. Railway Board Examinations
12. Reserve Bank Tests
13. Various State Recruitment Examinations
14. Forest Department Examinations
15. Teacher/lecturer eligibility tests like NET, CTET, SET, etc.
16. International English tests like IELTS, OET, TOEFL, PTE, etc.
17. For students of various professional courses (*wherein English is part of the syllabus*)
18. For professionals such as IT professionals, teachers, English language trainers, lawyers, journalists, etc. who want to fine-tune their English.

Book is available only in the E-commerce platforms such as
Amazon, Flipkart and Notion Press web store.

# Contents

---xxx---

# Useful English data



--xxx---

# 1. Sentence (Main division)

<u>**Kinds of sentences**</u> (*on the basis* of the ***structure** of the sentence*)

**1. Simple sentence:** A sentence which has only one subject and one verb is known as a simple sentence. Only subject and verb are compulsory in a sentence and the other parts of speech such as adjective, adverb, preposition, etc. may or may not be there.

        **e.g.**: Williams speaks French quite well.

**2. Compound sentence:** A sentence which is made up of two or more co-coordinating clauses (*clauses of equal rank*) is known as a compound sentence.

        **e.g.**: Maria is very clever but she is lazy.

**This sentence has two parts/ clauses.**

        a) Maria is very clever.

        b) Maria is lazy.

Each of the above clauses is fully independent and can stand by itself. Both are of the same rank or status. Such clauses are called co-*coordinating clauses.*

**3. Complex sentence:** A sentence which is made up of **one main** or **principal clause** and **one** or **more subordinate clauses** is  known as a complex sentence.

        **e.g.**: You can win the race if you run fast.

        The above sentence has two parts.

|  A  |  B  |
| :---: | :---: |
| <u>**principal** or **main clause**</u> | <u>**subordinate clause**</u> |
| You can win the race | if you run fast |

The clause under **group-A** makes sense by itself and is totally independent. Hence, it is called a **principal clause.**

The clause under **group-B** does not make sense by itself and is dependent on the principal clause for its full meaning.

Hence, it is called a **subordinate clause.**

<u>**Certain important terms:**</u>

i)   **Phrase:** A group of words which makes some sense but not complete sense is called a phrase.

        **e.g. :**  i) <u>In my view,</u> hard work is the key to success.

ii) **Clause:** A group of words which forms part of a sentence and contains a subject and a verb is known as a clause.

        **e.g.**: i) <u>We cannot start the match</u> while <u>it is raining.</u> (2 clauses)

iii) **Principal clause:**  The clause which is independent and on which other clauses depend is known as the principal or main clause.

        **e.g. <u>This is the village</u>** where I was born.

1

iv) **Subordinate clause:** A clause which depends on the principal clause and does not make sense by itself is known as a subordinate clause.

   **e.g.** This is the village **where I was born.**

v) **Coordinate clause:** Clauses of the same rank or status are known as coordinate clauses.

   **e.g.:** The audience listened attentively while the chief guests poke.

vi) **Kinds of sentence** (*on the basis of nature*)

   i) Assertive sentence: Expresses a fact.

   **e.g.:** Today is a sunny day.

   ii) Interrogative sentence: Asks a question.

   **e.g.:** Could I meet the director of this company?

   iii) Imperative sentence: Expresses a command, order, request, etc.

   **e.g.:** Complete the assignment on time.

   iv) Optative sentence: Expresses a wish, a prayer, etc.

   **e.g.:** May you have a happy married life.

   v) Exclamatory sentence: Expresses sudden feelings.

   **e.g.:** What a fantastic scenery!

---xxx---

## Useful data

# 1. Portmanteau words

(A portmanteau is a word that blends the sounds of two words and combines their meanings to form a new word. The meanings of these words are quite obvious. The use of such words has become quite common in modern English.)

| | | | | |
|---|---|---|---|---|
| 2. Biopic : | (biography + picture) | 3. Bollywood : | (Bombay + Hollywood) |
| 4. Brexit : | (Britain + exit) | 6. E-commerce: | (electronic + commerce) |
| 7. Edutainment: | (education + entertainment) | 8. E-mail: | (electronic + mail) |
| 10. Hi-tech : | (high + technology) | 11. Infotainment : | (information + entertainment) |
| 12. Intercom : | (internet + communication) | 13. Internet: | (international + network) |
| 14. Interpol : | (international + police) | 16. Joypad: | (joystick + pad) |
| 17. Medicare : | (medical + care) | 18. Motorcade: | (motorcar + cavalcade) |
| 20. Multiplex : | (multiple + complex) | 21. Netizen: | (internet + citizen) |
| 22. Newscast : | ( news + broadcast) | 23. Parasailing : | (parachute + sailing) |
| 24. Paratroops: | (parachute + troops) | 25. Sci-fi: | (Science + fiction) |
| 26. Smog : | (smoke + fog) | 27. Telecast: | (television + broadcast) |
| 28. Telecom : | (telephone + communication) | 29. Vlog: | (video + log) |
| 30. Webinar : | (Web+ seminar) | | |

# 2. Basic order of words in a sentence

(Normal sentence pattern in English)

The following is the basic order of words in a **simple sentence**.

| subject | verb | object/complement | modifier |
|---------|------|-------------------|----------|
| Robertson | bought | a new car | last year. |
| Maria | hung | a picture | on the wall. |

This basic order should be maintained, as far as possible, in all **simple sentences** except in the following three main situations:

i) When we begin a sentence with adverbial terms such as **today, nowadays, consequently, thus, perhaps, fortunately, when,** etc.

    **e.g.:** <u>Today, the Indian economy</u> is one of the fastest growing in the world.

        *Adverb       sub*

ii) When we use **linking terms** or **connectives** *(words that connect parts of a sentence together)* such as, *in my humble view, to begin with, to conclude, to put it in a nutshell*, etc.

    **e.g.:** <u>In my humble view, globalization</u> has affected everyone of us.

        *Linking term       sub*

iii) When we use  adverbs of **time** *(There should be a comma after such words.)*

    **e.g.:** <u>From 2000 to 2010</u>**,** <u>the sale of laptops </u>went up dramatically.

        *time adverb       sub*

<u>**Improper placing of subject**</u> is a common grammatical error. Complements, modifiers, prepositions, clauses, etc. should not be placed, as far as possible, before the subject.

    **e.g.:**  Pune, a city in Maharashtra, is <u>my hometown</u>. **(X)**

        *sub*

    <u>**My hometown**</u> is Pune, a city in Maharashtra. (✓)

    *sub*

<u>**Notice the wrong placing of subject:**</u>

1. Today is my birthday.**(X)**

   <u>My birthday</u> is today.(✓)

    *sub*

2. In my hometown a number of sky-kissing apartments have come up recently.**(X)**

   <u>A number of sky-kissing apartments</u> have come up in my hometown recently.(✓)

    *sub*

3. To meet an old friend I went to Chennai a few days ago. **(X)**

   <u>I</u> went to Chennai a few days ago to meet an old friend. (✓)

*sub*

3

# Modifier

A modifier tells about **the manner, place** and **time** of action.

A modifier shows

| | | |
|---|---|---|
| **How** was the action done? | : | **Manner** of action |
| **Where** was the action done? | : | **Manner** of place |
| **When was the action done?** | : | **Manner** of time |

A modifier generally consists of a prepositional or adverbial phrase.

**Prepositional phrase**: A prepositional phrase is a group of words which starts with a preposition but may end with a noun or a preposition.

**Examples:**

| | |
|---|---|
| by the roadside | on the way |
| in the market | in the evening |
| at home | in the town, etc. |

A modifier can also be **adverbs** or **adverbial phrases**.

**Examples:**

| | |
|---|---|
| the following day | previous night |
| this morning | last night |
| yesterday | tomorrow, etc. |

## 1. <u>The position of modifier in a sentence</u>

The modifier should be placed after the object/complement.

> **Sub + verb + complement/object + modifier**

**E.g.:** i) <u>Mr. Singh</u> <u>speaks</u> <u>English</u> <u>quite fluently</u>.
      **sub**     **verb**    **object**   **modifier**

    ii) <u>Sham</u> <u>met</u> <u>one of his friends</u> <u>in the supermarket</u>.
    **sub**  **verb**    **object**      **modifier**

<u>Special Note:</u>

Do not confuse modifier with adjective. An adjective says something more about the noun while a modifier says something about the **place, time** and **manner** of action.

    **e.g.:** Maria sang a <u>sweet</u> song during the cultural programme of the school.
               **adjective**

        Maria sang a song <u>sweetly</u> during the cultural programme of the school.
               **modifier**

## Modifier

*** Wrong placing of modifier is a common mistake in English.**
<u>Examples</u>

> i) <u>**Yesterday**</u> I met one of my former college friends.**(X)**
>
> (*'Yesterday'* *is misplaced. It should be placed after the object.*)
>
> I met one of my former college friends <u>**yesterday**</u>.(✓)
>
> ii) I shall <u>**now**</u> tell you an interesting story. (**(X)** *because of the improper placing of the modifier 'now'*)
>
> I shall tell you an interesting story **now**.
>
> iii) <u>**In my town**</u> there are many modern facilities.**(X)**
>
> There are many modern facilities <u>**in my town**</u>.(✓)

<u>Kinds of modifiers:</u>

i)<u>**Modifier of manner**</u>: Modifier of manner tells how the action was done.

> **e.g.:** The newly appointed manager looked <u>very smart.</u>
>
> *modifier of manner*

ii) <u>**Modifier of place:**</u> Modifier of place tells where the action was performed or done.

> **e.g.:** I bought an interesting novel <u>from the book fair.</u>
>
> *modifier of place*

iii) <u>**Modifier of time**</u>: Modifier of time tells about the time of an action.

> **e.g.:** The musical programme got over <u>late at night.</u>
>
> *modifier of time*

## 2. <u>**Position of different  modifiers**</u>

If there are more than one modifier in a sentence, the following order should be followed. (**MPT order**: *Manner-Place-Time*)

modifier of **manner**- modifier of **place**- modifier of **time**

> **e.g.** <u>Sham</u> <u>drove</u> <u>the vehicle</u> <u>very carefully</u> <u>during the driving test</u> held <u>last month.</u>
>
>    *sub*    *verb*    *object*    *manner*    *place*    *time*

## 3. <u>**Exception to the rule of modifier**</u>

3. We may place modifiers, particularly the modifier of time, before the subject for the sake of emphasis. But there should be a <u>**comma**</u> after the modifier in written form and a different pitch in speech.

> **e.g.:** <u>**This morning,**</u> I am happy to welcome our honourable chief guest to our midst.

Modifier

### 4. <u>Position of different modifiers of time</u>

If there is more than one modifier of time, the following order should be followed:

---

Most immediate **first - second** immediate next, and **so on.**
**hour-day-date-year:** at 8.30 pm., on Sunday, 15th March, 2023.
Specific time-general time : **at 4.30 in the evening**

---

**e.g.: i)** You are hereby invited to the birthday party of our eldest son which will be held
in our house at 7.00 p.m., on  Saturday, October 14, 2023.
*place       hour                 day           date      year*
ii) The cultural programme will commence at **10.00 in the morning.**

### 5. <u>Arrangement of different modifiers of manner</u>

Whenever possible, modifiers of manner should be arranged according to length with the shortest preceding the others.
**e.g.:**  The chief guest spoke sincerely, meditatively and frankly.
The chief guest spoke **frankly, sincerely and meditatively**.

# Exercise

Place the modifiers in their appropriate places:
1. Last week I bought a new storybook from the bookstall.
2. Today the meeting took place an hour late.
3. My mom is now preparing dinner in the kitchen.
4. Tonight I shall go for a movie with my friend.
5. My dear students, now I shall tell you an interesting story.
6.  I saw a fight in the market between two men.
7. In Karachi, the Indian cricket team played quite well in the one-day series.
8. On the way to the shopping mall Tom met one of his old friends.
9. Day before yesterday there was a fire in our apartment.
10. The chairs were arranged in the auditorium in a haphazard manner.
**Answers:**
1. I bought a new storybook *from the bookstall **last week.***
2. The meeting took place *an hour late **today.***
3. My mom is preparing dinner *in the kitchen **now.***
4. I shall go for a movie with my friend *tonight.*
5. My dear students, I shall tell you an interesting story *now.*
6. I saw a fight between two men *in the market*.

Modifier

7. The Indian cricket team played *quite well in the one-day series **in Karachi.***
8. Tom met one of his old friends *on the way to the shopping mall.*
9. There was a fire *in our apartment **day before yesterday.***
10. The chairs were arranged *in a haphazard manner **in the auditorium.***

—xxx—-

<u>**Useful data**</u>

# 2. Uncommon adjectives

| | | | | |
|---|---|---|---|---|
| Monkey/Ape | : | Simian | Bees : Apian |
| Bird | : | Avian/Ornithic | Cow : Bovine |
| Horse | : | Equestrian, Equine | Fish : Piscine |
| Dog | : | Canine | Sheep : Ovine |
| Elephant | : | Pachydermic | Forest : Sylvan |
| Aging/aged | : | Geriatric | Eye : Optic |
| Farewell | : | Valedictory | Marriage : Nuptial |
| Flesh | : | Carnal | Night : Nocturnal |
| Bishop | : | Episcopal | Heart : Cardiac |
| Money | : | Pecuniary | Heaven : Celestial |
| Memory | : | Mnemonic | Brother : Fraternal |
| Sister | : | Sororal | Hearing : Auditory |
| Disease | : | Pathological | Kidneys : Renal |
| Coins | : | Numismatic | Cooking : Culinary |
| Devil | : | Diabolic | Dress : Sartorial |
| Weather | : | Meteorological | Tooth : Dental |
| Governor | : | Gubernatorial | Sound : Acoustic |
| Church | : | Ecclesial, Ecclesiastical | |

# 3. Noun

**Kinds of Nouns:**

| | | |
|---|---|---|
| i) Proper noun | : | **e.g.:** Maria, Raja, Kolkata, India, etc. |
| ii) Common noun | : | **e.g.:** girl, boy, dog, man, etc. |
| iii) Collective noun: | | **e.g.:** class, team, committee, etc. |
| iv) Material noun | : | **e.g.:** wood, gold, coal, etc. |
| v) Abstract noun | : | **e.g.:** honesty, truthfulness, beauty, etc. |

**Nouns: Number**

| | | |
|---|---|---|
| i) Singular number | : | **e.g.:** an apple, a book, a table, etc. |
| ii) Plural number | : | **e.g.:** apples, books, tables, etc. |

Generally, plurals of nouns are formed by adding **'s'**, **'es'** or **'ies'**.

Some nouns are changed into plural by a change of the vowels or by a different term.

| Singular | | Plural |
|---|---|---|
| i) foot | : | feet |
| ii) tooth | : | teeth |
| iii) man | : | men |
| iv) woman | : | women |
| v) mouse | : | mice |
| vi) louse | : | lice |
| vii) goose | : | geese |
| viii) child | : | children |
| ix) ox | : | oxen |

<u>**Special note:**</u>

* The plural of **mongoose** is **mongooses** (*not mongeese*)
* The plural of **German** is **Germans** (*not Germen*)
* The plural of **man-eater** is **man-eaters**. (*not meneaters*)
* The plural of **alumna** (*former female student*) is **alumnae** (*not alumnas*)
* The plural of **precis** is **precis** (*not preces*)

**Nouns: Gender:** There are four genders:

i) Masculine gender (*denotes male*: **e.g.:** *boy, father, brother, etc.*)

ii) Feminine gender (*denotes female*: **e.g.:** *girl, mother, sister, etc.*)

iii) Common gender (*denotes both male and female*: **e.g.:** *teacher, cousin, artist, etc.*)

iv) Neuter gender (*denotes neither male nor female*: **e.g.:** *wood, gold, rice, etc.*)

**Noun**

## <u>Some important genders and their opposites</u>

| <u>Masculine</u> | : | <u>Feminine</u> | <u>Masculine</u> | : | <u>Feminine</u> |
|---|---|---|---|---|---|
| sir | : | madam | bachelor | : | maid/spinster |
| gentleman | : | lady | brother | : | sister |
| uncle | : | aunt | nephew | : | niece |
| son | : | daughter | husband | : | wife |
| prince | : | princess | villain | : | vamp |
| bridegroom | : | bride | hero | : | heroine |
| monk | : | nun | widower | : | widow |
| man-servant | : | maid-servant | step-father | : | step-mother |
| horse | : | mare | dog | : | bitch |
| bullock | : | heifer | fox | : | vixen |
| stag | : | hind | cock | : | hen |
| boar | : | sow | bull | : | cow |
| peacock | : | peahen | he-goat | : | she-goat |

**Common gender:** Nouns denoting either sex are of common gender (*Most nouns referring to professions belong to the common gender.*)

| | | | |
|---|---|---|---|
| artist | author | cook | doctor |
| editor | engineer | foreigner | lawyer |
| magician | magistrate | professor | writer |
| student | lecturer | teacher | parent |
| baby | pupil | friend | bird |
| person | servant | spouse | cousin |
| principal | | | |

**E.g.:** i) He is a principal.   ii) She is a principal.

**Neuter gender:** Lifeless things have no sex. In other words, they are neither male nor female.

    **e.g.:** book, pen, table, knife, pen, chair, etc.

**Noun**

**Special note:**

i) Currently terms such as *businessman/ businesswoman, salesman/saleswoman, spokesman/ spokeswoman* are less used. Terms such as **businessperson, salesperson, spokesperson,** etc. are more used than the former terms.

ii) **'Cousin brother** 'and **'cousin sister'** are not considered correct terms. Use only **cousin** which stands for male or female person.

      **e.g.:** i) He is my cousin.    ii) She is my cousin.

iii) The feminine forms *authoress, poetess, directress, inspectress,* etc. are no longer used. Nowadays terms such as **poet, director, inspector,** etc. are used both for male and female persons.

iv) Masculine gender is generally used with nouns showing strength, valour, chivalry, toughness and superiority. Nouns such as ***sun, summer, thunder, winter, storm, death, fear, war, wind, etc.*** are considered masculine.

      **e.g.:** Death spreads his wings everywhere.

v) Feminine gender is generally used with nouns showing beauty, grace, gentleness, fertility, inferiority, love, affection. Nouns such as ***moon, earth, one's country, peace, hope, spring, cars, nature, justice, mercy, liberty, charity, truth, fame, ship, etc.*** are considered feminine.

      **e.g.:** Nature is at her best during spring.

**Special note:**

* One's country is considered feminine gender and hence the usage of the term 'motherland.' Germans, however, refer to their nation as fatherland, and not motherland.

## Useful data

# 3. Dictionary abbreviations

| | | | | | |
|---|---|---|---|---|---|
| 1. abbr. | : | abbreviation | 11. pt. | : | past tense |
| 2. adj. | : | adjective | 12. prep. | : | preposition |
| 3. adv. | : | adverb | 13. C | : | countable noun |
| 4. conj. | : | conjunction | 14. U | : | uncountable noun |
| 5. det. | : | determiner | 15. sb. | : | somebody |
| 6. n. | : | noun | 16. sth. | : | something |
| 7. pl. | : | plural | 17. pp. | : | past participle |
| 8. v. | : | verb | 18. opp. | : | opposite |
| 9. sing. | : | singular | 19. NAmE | : | American English |
| 10. pron. | : | pronoun | 20. BrE | : | British English |

# Nouns: Countable and Uncountable

**Main division of Nouns:**

        i) Countable nouns (*also called count nouns*)

        ii) Uncountable nouns(*also called non-count nouns*)

**i) Countable nouns:** Count nouns are those nouns which can be counted. *Examples*: toys, books, students, etc.

**ii) Uncountable nouns:** Non-count nouns are those nouns which cannot be counted. Generally, liquid items, abstract ideas, qualities, etc. belong to this category of nouns. *Examples:*  advice, ink, wisdom, etc.

<u>**Some important uncountable nouns**</u> *(given in alphabetical order)*

| | | | |
|---|---|---|---|
| accommodation | advice | agriculture | aid *(help)* |
| alcohol | beef | bread | business |
| confidence | cooperation | coordination | crockery |
| data* | deadlock | debris | destruction |
| determination | devastation | education | enjoyment |
| equipment | evolution | expenditure | experience |
| exploitation | faith | fame | feedback |
| filth | firewood | fitness | food |
| furniture | greenery | health | homework |
| illness | information | jewellery | joy |
| knowledge | literature | love | luggage |
| meat | money | music | news |
| poetry | pollution | population | power |
| pride | progress | salt | sand |
| scenery | space | starvation | stationery |
| success | technology | time | traffic |
| violence | wealth | wisdom | work, etc. |

* *Data* is an uncountable noun; it can be ***used with singular/plural verb:*** data is/are:

# Problems associated with the use of uncountable nouns

i) Uncountable nouns cannot be used with ***a/an*** because *a/an* has the sense of **'one'**.

| | | |
|---|---|---|
| **not** *an* advice | but | ***a piece of*** advice |
| **not** *an* information | but | ***a bit/piece of*** information |
| **not** *an* attention | but | ***a moment/minute of*** attention |

# Nouns: Countable and Uncountable

ii) Uncountable nouns *cannot be made plural* by adding **'s'**, **'es'** or **'ies'**.

| | | |
|---|---|---|
| **not** sceneries | *but* | a lot of scenery |
| **not** informations | *but* | a great deal of information |
| **not** advices | *but* | lots of advice |

iii) We cannot use cardinal numbers such as **one, two, three**, etc. with uncountable nouns.

| | | |
|---|---|---|
| **not** one news | *but* | **a piece of** news |
| **not** two advices | *but* | **some** advice |
| **not** three works | *but* | **much** work |

iv) Many uncountable nouns such as *time, experience, food, character, technology,* etc. can also be used as countable nouns in certain situations.

    **e.g.:**  i) How much *time* does the effect of this painkiller last?

            You have been warned many *times* not to talk loud in the ward.

        ii) I have three years' *experience* in the nursing field.

            I have had some bitter *experiences* during the first few days of my duty in the psychiatric ward.(*The term 'experiences' here means incidents, situations, etc.*)

## 1. Method of giving **singular sense to** uncountable nouns

If you want to specify a particular item of uncountable nouns, use the following collective terms suitably:

| | |
|---|---|
| *a piece of* (**advice, information, news, work, etc.**) | *a blade of* (**grass**) |
| *a bit of* (**news, advice, information,** etc.) | *a lump of* (**sugar**) |
| *a bar of/cake of* (**soap**) | *a sheet of* (**paper**) |
| *a bottle of* (**milk, ink, water, blood,** etc.) | *a block of* (**ice**) |
| *a set of* (**furniture, belief,** etc.) | *a speck of* (**dust**) |
| *a heap of* (**sand, ruins, debris,** etc.) | *a drop of* (**water, oil,** *etc.* |
| *an item of* (**information, news, clothing,** etc.) | *a loaf /slice of* (**bread**) |
| *a grain of* (**sand, salt, rice, truth,** etc.) | *a tuft of/strand of* (**hair**) |
| *a pinch of* (**salt**) | *a sum of* (**money**) |

Examples

    i) This **piece of medical equipment** must be sterilized before use.

    ii) There is **a strand of hair** on your uniform. Let me rub it off.

    iii) Please add **a pinch/a bit of** salt to the salad.

# Nouns: Countable and Uncountable

## 2. Method of giving **plural sense** to uncountable nouns
(We cannot make them plural by adding 's' , 'es' or 'ies'.)

To give **plural sense** to uncountable nouns, <u>use uncountable noun determiners</u> or common determiners: (*determiners are words that go before nouns and help determine their meanings*)

| Countable noun determiners | Uncountable noun determiners |
|---|---|
| **many**(*many-more-most*)<br>a large number of<br>several, both,<br>few, a few, the few<br>fewer ... than<br>one of the | **much** (*much-more-most*)<br>a large amount of<br>a good amount of<br>little, a little, the little<br>less... than<br>a  piece of |
| **Common determiners (can be used with countable + uncountable nouns)**<br>*some, more, most, a lot of, lots of, all, enough, any,* etc. | |

 **e.g.:** *some* students     *some* scenery
    *a lot of* people    *a lot of* information
    *none* of the examples  *none* of the luggage ...etc.

    many sceneries**(X)**   **much scenery**
    one of the news **(X)**  **a piece of news**
    much people**(X)**    **many people**

**e.g.:** i) My friend gave me **much** information regarding the wonderful job
   opportunities in Canada.
  ii) **Some** of the medical equipment of this ward **needs** replacement.

3. Certain uncountable nouns when used as a phrase become countable.

| | | |
|---|---|---|
| to have a weakness for | to have a pain | to have a fascination for |
| to light a fire | to have a taste for | to have a good time |
| to have a chance | to make a noise | to have a knowledge of |
| to have a fancy for | to be in a rage | to have a thirst for |
| to run a temperature | to have a headache, etc. | |

4. It is a serious error to use terms such as '**many, few, a few, fewer, a large number of, one of the,** etc.' <u>with uncountable nouns</u>.

| | | |
|---|---|---|
| **not** *many* news | but | **much** news |
| **not** *few* informations | but | **some** information |
| **not** *many* works | but | **much** work |

# <u>Golden rule regarding uncountable nouns</u>

5. All uncountable nouns take <u>**singular verbs**</u> ((*am/is/was/has/verb+s*)**.** Even when plural determiners such as ***some, most, a lot of, lots of,*** etc. are used, the verb is **singular.**
   * In other words, all uncountable nouns are <u>**Third Person Singular**</u> (*He/she/it*)in most situations.

    **e.g.:**  i) This piece of news **is**....(*singular sense*)

          ii) A lot of news **is** ...(*plural sense*)

          iii) This piece of news **shows**.......(*singular sens*e)

          iv) A lot of news **shows**....(*plural sense*)

| |
|---|
| **Singular** means *am/is/was/has/ verb + s* |

The scenery **is**..../scenery **was**.../scenery **has**.../scenery **shows**...

**.... plays** (*Subject is singular*)    : He <u>**plays**</u> football.    **Noun + S= plural noun** (books)

**.... play** (*subject is plural*)    : We <u>**play**</u> football.    **Verb +S = Singular ver**b (speaks)

| |
|---|
| **Plural** means *are/were/have/ verb without 's'* |

students are.... students were.... students have.... students speak....

6. # <u>Exception on Data</u>

Data is an uncountable noun.

**But** we can say:-

        Data  **shows/show**                  This data **shows.....**

        Data  **is/ are**                      All the data **show....**

        Data  **was/were**

        Data  **has/have**

        One of the data (✓)

# Nouns: Countable and Uncountable

To speak of an item of data, it is better to say

> **a piece of data**

But we can never say or write:

| DATAS (X) | BACTERIAS (X) | MASS MEDIAS (X) | STAFFS (X) |
|---|---|---|---|

With these words verb can be **singular/plural:**

| DATA is/are | BACTERIA is/are | MASS MEDIA is/are | STAFF is/are |
|---|---|---|---|

7. The following nouns in English are generally used as **plural.**

### Important[always]  plural nouns

| | | | |
|---|---|---|---|
| people | women | police | children |
| criteria | staff | phenomena | personnel |
| annals | scissors | shorts | spectacles |
| thanks | trousers | deaf | billiards |
| cattle | clergy | contents | alms |
| wages | gentry | goods | jeans |
| pyjamas | measles | mumps | remains |
| odds | proceeds | repairs | riches |
| alumni | armament | arms | bacteria |
| doldrums | pants | premises | bona fides |
| havoc | poultry | valuables, | clothes, etc. |

* **Singular:** people-person, children-child, police-policeman, clergy-clergyman/woman, criteria- criterion, phenomena-phenomenon, staff- staff member, faculty-faculty member, bacteria-bacteria, women-woman, etc.

    * It is wrong to say **childrens, peoples, womens, gentlemens, staffs, criterias,** etc.

    * To speak of one individual of the staff, say **'a member of the staff'/a staff member/ one of the staff/ a member of the faculty/ a faculty member, etc.**

        One staff **(X)**....................      **one of the staff**

        Staffs of my college **(X)**.....      **staff of my college**

        Faculties of the college **(X)**.      **faculty of the college**

# Nouns: Countable and Uncountable

One criteria **(X)**.............  one of the criteria/one criterion
Every staff **(X)**.............  everyone of the staff
Every people **(X)** ............  everyone of the people/ every person
Every children **(X)**............  everyone of the children/ every child

* **alumnus** (*male singular*) : **Alumni** (plural: former male students)
 **alumna** (*female singular*) : **Alumnae**(plural : former female students)
* **Bacteria** can be used both as singular /plural: **one bacteria/several bacteria.**
* **Faculty** means staff while **faculties** means abilities.
 **e.g.** Our college has several new **faculty/ faculty members**.
  We human beings have several **faculties**.
* The term **'peoples'** can be used in a comparative situation.
 **e.g.:** The **peoples** of India are different from the **peoples** of America.
* The term **cloth** refers to the material.
  **clothe** means to wear.
  **clothes** means the different items that we use for wearing.
  **clothing** refers to those items of clothes used to protect against heat, cold, water or machinery, etc.
* The term **'clothes'** is always plural. To talk about one particular thing that you wear, say *a piece/ item of clothing.*
 **e.g.:** I bought some new clothes for the trip.**(X)**
  I bought some new **clothes** for the trip.(✓)
  This **piece/item of clothing** is quite expensive.
 **e.g. :** i) The **police** <u>have</u> caught the thief after a long chase.
  ii) All my **cattle** <u>have</u> been affected by some new type of ailments.
  iii) The **people** <u>have</u> dispersed after the meeting.
  iv) The **arms** discovered by the police <u>were</u> of foreign origin.

8. The following nouns in English have the *same singular and plural forms.*

| | | | |
|---|---|---|---|
| **innings** | **means** | **public** | **series** |
| **sheep** | **fish** | **apparatus** | **aircraft** |
| **deer** | **species** | **precis** | **noise** |
| **agenda** | **data** | **media** | **bacteria** |
| **swine** | **bison**, etc. | | |

 **e.g.:** i) This **data** is completely wrong.
  ii) These **data** are completely wrong.(never say *'datas,* can say *one of the data*)
  iii) **One bacteria** is found in this drop of blood.
  iv) **Several bacteria** are found in this drop of blood.

# Nouns: Countable and Uncountable

### 9. <u>Some confusing plural forms</u>

| <u>singular</u> | <u>plural</u> |
|---|---|
| boy-friend | boy-friends |
| take-off | take-offs |
| break-down | break-downs |
| in-law | in-laws |
| touch-me-not | touch-me-nots |
| mother-in-law | mothers-in-law |
| grant-in-aid | grants-in-aid |
| man-of-war | men-of-war |
| passer-by | passers-by |
| runner-up | runners-up |
| woman servant | women servants |
| man servant | men servants |
| man-eater | man-eaters (**not** *men eaters*) |
| mongoose | mongooses (**not** *mongeese*) |
| two | twos (**not** *two's*) |
| p | p's |
| t | t's |
| 5 | 5s or 5's |
| 1980 | 1980s or 1980's |
| M.A. | M.As or M.A's |

* The current trend is to use a small **s** for the plural form of abbreviations or acronyms and use **'s** for possessive form.

### 10. <u>Plurals of some foreign words</u>

| <u>singular</u> | <u>plural</u> | <u>singular</u> | <u>plural</u> |
|---|---|---|---|
| agendum | agenda | appendix | appendices |
| alumnus | alumni | alumna | alumnae |
| analysis | analyses | axis | axes |
| basis | bases | crisis | crises |
| criterion | criteria | datum | data |
| index | indices | hypothesis | hypotheses |
| monsieur | messieurs | oasis | oases |
| phenomenon | phenomena | parenthesis | parentheses |
| tableau | tableaux | thesis | theses |
| bacterium | bacteria | corrigendum | corrigenda |
| erratum | errata | ovum | ova |

| | | | |
|---|---|---|---|
| stratum | strata | bacillus | bacilli |
| stimulus | stimuli | virus | viruses |
| genius | geniuses | ellipsis | ellipses |
| diagnosis | diagnoses | synopsis | synopses |
| metropolis | metropolises | precis | precis |

**Points to note:**

i) Nowadays **agenda** and **data** are used both as singular and plural. **Agendum** and **datum** are not much used.

**ii) Alumnus** means former male student; and its plural is <u>alumni</u> while **alumna** means former female student and its plural is <u>alumnae</u>.

iii) **appendix** : a part of the stomach ( its plural is : appendixes )

                     : an extra part of the book (its plural is : appendices)

## 11. <u>Nouns having two plural forms</u>

| <u>singular</u> | <u>plural</u> | <u>plural</u> |
|---|---|---|
| aquarium | aquaria | aquariums |
| stadium | stadia | stadiums |
| curriculum | curricula | curriculums |
| medium | media | mediums |
| forum | fora | forums |
| symposium | symposia | symposiums |
| ultimatum | ultimata | ultimatums |
| memorandum | memoranda | memorandums |
| terminus | termini | terminuses |
| cactus | cacti | cactuses |
| focus | foci | focuses |
| stylus | styli | styluses |
| syllabus | syllabi | syllabuses |
| radius | radii | radiuses |
| nucleus | nuclei | nucleuses |
| antenna | antennae | antennas |
| vertebra | vertebrae | vertebras |
| formula | formulae | formulas |

**Points to note**:

The **'s'** form of the plural is more used than their **'a'** forms.

(**e.g.:** curriculums, stadiums, forums, etc.)

The **'uses'** form of the plural is more used than their **'i'** forms.

(**e.g.:** syllabuses, radiuses, terminuses, etc.)

The **'s'** form of the plural is more used than their **' ae'** forms.

(**e.g.:** antennas, formulas, vertebras, etc.)

# Nouns: Countable and Uncountable

## 12. Plurals of titles

| | |
|---|---|
| Mr | Messrs |
| Mrs | Mesdames |
| Miss | Misses |
| Madam | Mesdames |

**<u>Special note:</u>**

Nowadays stop or period [.] is not used after titles:

  i) Mr  b) Mrs  iii) Ms  iv) Dr  v) Rev, etc.

## 13. <u>Use of apostrophe</u> (*possessive case*)

1. Generally an apostrophe is used only with animate items and not for inanimate things.
    - **e.g.:** Mathew's umbrella (✔)  Maria's books (✔)
    - Table's leg**(X)**  leg of the table (✔)
2. When the noun is plural and ends in 's', the possessive is formed by **adding only an apostrophe.**
    - **e.g.:** boys' hostel  ladies' washroom
    - horses' tail  students' tiffin-boxes, etc.
3. When a person's name ends in 's', only apostrophe is put.
    - **e.g.:** Toms' shop  Mathews' spectacles
4. When two nouns are closely connected, **the apostrophe is added to the latter only.**
    - **e.g.:** John and his brother's shop.
    - Shankar and Son's business.
5. When two or more connected nouns implying separate possessions are used, **the apostrophe is added to both nouns.**
    - **e.g.:** Karim's house and Satish's house have been destroyed.
    - Raj's and Sen's books have been highly appreciated.
6. When two nouns are in apposition (*the noun which follows another noun close by*), the **apostrophe is added to the latter only.**
    - **e.g.:** Alexander the **Great's** legacy has been forgotten.
    - Mr. Robert, our **principal's** office is situated close to the staff room.
7. The use of **double possessives should be avoided.**
    - **e.g.:** My <u>**uncle's friend's** daughter</u> got married a few days ago.**(X)**
    - The daughter of my uncle's friend got married a few days ago. (✔)
8. Use 's' with the last word of a combined word.
    - **e.g.:** My father-in-**law's** wish.

9. Use apostrophe with the **expression of time.**

    **e.g.:**  an hour's work, a week's holiday, etc.

10. The following items, though inanimate, take apostrophe.

    conscience' call, goodness' sake, a day's march, hair's breadth, razor's edge, etc.


### Common  errors in the use of nouns
*(Take note of the errors in the incorrect sentences)*

1. The sceneries of Ooty are indeed enchanting.

    **Ans:** The **scenery** of Ooty is indeed enchanting.

2. I have many works to do before I leave for England.

    **Ans:** I have **much work** to do before I leave for England.

3. The news of his accident are true.

    **Ans:** The **news** of his accident **is** true.

4. Lia is one of the best student in her class.

    **Ans:** Lia is **one of the best students** in her class.

5. Bob has obtained full mark for computer science.

    **Ans:** Bob  has obtained **full marks** for computer science.

6. My grandfather is much fond of vegetable.

    **Ans:** My grandfather is fond of **vegetables**.

7. Sham cannot continue his study any more due to ill-health.

    **Ans:** Sham cannot continue his **studies** any more due to ill-health.

8. My father gave me many good advice before I joined college.

    **Ans:** My father gave me **much good advice** before I joined college.

9. Mr. Williams has sold all his furnitures.

    **Ans:** Mr. Williams has sold all his **furniture**.

10. The little kid has learnt the alphabets within a short time.

    **Ans:** The little kid has learnt the **alphabet** within a short time.

11. Take care of your luggages while travelling by train.

    **Ans:** Take care of your **luggage** while travelling by train.

12. Would you be kind enough to give me fooding and lodging here for a few days?

    **Ans:** Would you be kind enough to give me **food and lodging** here for a few days?

13. What is the cost of this pen?

    **Ans:** What is the **price** of this pen?

14. My brother bought a few articles of clothes for me.

    **Ans:** My brother bought a few articles of **clothing** for me.

15. Sam is a man of bad characters.

    **Ans:** Sam is a man of bad **character**.

16. Most people have black hairs.

    **Ans:** Most people have black **hair**.

17. Two-third of the news can be considered true.

    **Ans:** <u>**Two-thirds**</u> of the news can be considered true.

18. What is your date of birth?

    **Ans:** What is the <u>**date of your birth**</u>?

19. Kindly put the sign here.

    **Ans:** Kindly put the <u>**signature**</u> here.

20. Our English teacher is a European.

    **Ans:** Our <u>**teacher of English**</u> is a European.

# Exercise

**1. Correct the following sentences**

1. Many of the luggages have been lost in the flood.
2. Some of the given bio-datas are wrong.
3. The police is searching for the culprit.
4. The beaches on Goa offers a lot of unforgettable sceneries.
5. Nowadays the price of breads are going up.
6. My uncle has lost many of his hair.
7. Tom and John's houses are situated quite close-by.
8. The number of students who passed the test this time were quite few.
9. Two-thirds of the work are completed.
10. The syllabi of class XII science has been changed this year.

**Answers:**

1. **Much** of the luggage has been lost in the flood.
2. Some of the given **bio-data** is wrong.
3. The police **are** searching for the culprit.
4. The beaches of Goa offers a lot of unforgettable **scenery**.
5. Nowadays the price of **bread** is going up.
6. My uncle has lost **much** of his hair.
7. **Tom's** and John's houses are situated quite close-by.
8. **The number** of students who passed the test this time **was** quite few.
9. Two-thirds of the work **is** completed.
10. The syllabi of Class XII science **have** been changed this year.

—xxx—

# 4. Articles

'**A**', '**An**' and '**The**' are  known as articles in the English language.

<u>Types of articles:</u>

1. <u>Definite article</u>: **The:**   *The* is called the **definite article** because it points to some particular person or thing.

   **e.g.:** Give me **the book** which is over there. *(a particular book)*

2. <u>Indefinite article</u>: **a/an:** *A* and *an* are called **indefinite articles** because they do not point out any particular person or thing.

   **e.g.:** Give me **a book** which is over there. (It *could be any book over there.*)

## 1. '**A**' is used:

i) before countable singular nouns beginning with a consonant.

   **e.g.: a** car, **a** table, **a** student, etc.

ii) before a word starting with a vowel letter but has a consonant sound,

   **e.g.: a** European, a uniform,  **a** one-rupee coin, etc.

iii) before a noun representing a species or a class.

   **e.g.: A** triangle has three sides.

iv) before a verb used as a noun.

   **e.g.:** My father goes for **a** walk every morning.

v) before a noun which takes the meaning of a common noun.

   **e.g.:** My friend thinks he is **a** Sachin Tendulkar.

## 2. '**An**' is used before:

i)  **An** is generally used before vowels: **A E I O U**

   **e.g.:** an orange, an apple, an umbrella, etc.

ii) It is also used before a word starting with a consonant but has a vowel sound.

   **e.g.:** an honest man, an hour, an honour, etc.

# Special use of 'a/an'

The use of <u>**a/an**</u> is determined by the initial sound of the word. If the word begins with a consonant sound, use ' **a** ' and if the word begins with a vowel sound, use '**an**' .

i) Use article '**a**' before certain words starting with a vowel but having a consonant sound.

| | | |
|---|---|---|
| **a union** | **a European** | **a unicorn** |
| **a university** | **a uniform** | **a unique** |
| **a utensil** | **a useful** | **a usual** |
| **a unit** | **a universal** | **a utility** |
| **a eunuch** | **a united** | **a utilitarian** etc. |

.......because of the  long sound of 'u' having a sound of '**yu**'.

**Special note:**

> **a year**    even though the initial sound appears to be 'e' sound.

ii) **'a'** is used before the term **'one'** as it has a **'w'** sound. (*consonant sound*)

>**a one-way street**     **a one-eyed man**
>
>**a one-year course**     **a one-rupee note,** etc.

iii) Use **'an'** before a consonant having vowel sound:

>**an hour,  an honest man,     an honour,**
>
>**an honourable, an heir,** etc.
>
>...... because of the vowel sound of **'o'** ; the **'h'** sound is silent.

If the **'h'** is silent, **an** has to be used. But if **'h'** is stressed or not silent, then such words would take **'a'** before them.

>a **hotel,** a **historical novel,** a **humble boy,** etc.

iv) **an** is used before a number having a vowel sound.

>**e.g.: an** eight-year old boy, **an** eighty-year old man, etc.

v) **'An'** is used before acronyms (*words formed from the first letter of a group of words*) and abbreviations beginning with **F, H, I, M, N,  S, X** because these consonants have a slight vowel sound of **'e'.**

> | | | | |
> |---|---|---|---|
> | 1. **M***(em)* | 2. **S** *(es)* | 3. **F***(ef)* | 4. **H***(eich)* |
> | 5. **I***(el)* | 6. **X** *(eks)* | | |

>**an M.P.**          **an M.A.**          **an SMS**
>
>**an M.L.A.**        **an N.C.C.**        **an ex-M.P.**
>
>**an S.I. of police   an SOS message   an X-ray machine,** etc.

## Use of definite article-**'the'**

**'The' is used**

1. To denote a particular person or thing or one already mentioned.

>**e.g.:  The chair** on which you sit is broken. (*The chair mentioned here refers to a particular chair and not all chairs in the world*)

2. Before a singular noun which is used to represent a whole class.

>**e.g. The horse** is a noble animal.

**special note:**

>When **'man'** is used as a generic noun, article is not put before it.
>
>>**e.g.:** Man is mortal.

3. Before adjectives to represent a class of people. The use of 'the' makes these nouns generic or class nouns.

>**The** young, **the** rich, **the** well-to-do, **the** sick, **the** injured, etc.

4. Before an adjective to denote quality.

  **e.g.: the** good, **the** beautiful, **the** evil, etc.

5. Before both countable and non-count nouns (*singular/plural*) that are made definite.

  **e.g.:**  i) **The** boy who stole my box has been caught.

  ii) **The** information that you gave me is false.

6. Before adjectives in the comparative degree when **'of the two'** is used or when **double comparatives** are used.

  **e.g.:**  i) Shankar is **the** taller of the two boys.

  ii) **The** higher we go, **the** cooler it gets.

7. Before a noun when there is only one of its kind.

  **e.g.: The** earth, **the** moon, **the** sky, etc.

8. Before the names of municipal or government departments, big business houses, industrial concerns, banks, etc.

  **e.g.: The** ministry of defence, **the** public stadium, **the** cooperative bank, etc.

## 9. Before the names of

1. Gulfs- The Gulf of Mannar, the Arabian Gulf, etc.
2. Seas- The Arabian Sea, the Lakshadweep Sea, etc.
3. Oceans- The Pacific Ocean, The Indian Ocean, etc.
4. Rivers- The Periyar, The Ganges, etc.
5. Mountain ranges- The Himalayas, The Alps, etc.
6. Groups of islands- The Lakshadweep Islands, the Coral islands, etc.
7. Plural names of countries- The U.S.A., The U.K., etc.
8. Trains- The Coromandel Express, The Kerala Express, etc.
9. Sacred books- The Bible, The Quran, etc.
10. Newspapers- The Hindu, The Telegraph, etc.
11. Musical instruments- the veena, the flute, etc.
12. Historical events- The First World War, The French Revolution, etc.
13. Nationalities- The Indians, The Russians, etc.
14. Well-known buildings- The Taj Mahal, The Red Fort, etc.
15. Titles- Akbar the Great, Timur the Cruel, etc.
16. Ordinals- the first, the second, the fourth, etc.
17. Directions and sides- the east, the west, the right, the left, etc.
18. Before superlatives- the best, the cleverest, etc.
19. Before inventions- the telephone, the computer, etc.
20. Before parts of one's body - the hands, the shoulders, etc.
21. Before articles of clothing- the tie, the shirt, etc.

## **<u>Omission of 'the'</u>**

**<u>The</u>** <u>is omitted</u>

1. Before singular lakes- Lake Geneva, Lake Chilka, etc.
2. Before singular mountains- Mount Everest, Mount Vesuvius, etc.
3. Before planets and constellations- Venus, Mars, Earth, Orion, etc.
4. Before schools, colleges, universities when the phrase begins with a proper noun- St. Stephen's College, William's Art School, Mahatma Gandhi University, etc.
5. Before cardinal numbers after nouns - World War II, Chapter Three, etc.
6. Before countries preceded by New or an adjective such as a direction- New Zealand, South Africa, North Korea, etc.
7. Names of countries with one word only- France, Sweden, Venezuela, etc.
8. Before continents- Europe, Africa, South America, etc.
9. Before states- Kerala, Tamil Nadu, Ohio, California, etc.
10. Before sports- baseball, basketball, etc.
11. Before abstract nouns- freedom, happiness, honesty, etc.
12. Before the names of languages, arts and science and subjects- English, history, etc.
13. Before names of relatives - father, mother, aunt, uncle, etc.
16. Before school, college, church,  hospital, market, prison, etc. when they are visited by those who work there, etc.
17. Before titles coming before proper nouns- Lord Krishna, Poet  Laureate of England, etc.
18. Before names of meals and articles of food- breakfast, lunch, rice, etc.
19. Before names of diseases - influenza, diabetes, measles, etc.
20. Before names of substances used in a general sense- iron, gold, etc.
21. Before words such as president, king, queen , pope, principal, etc. if the name follows the word-Pope John Paul II, Queen Victoria, etc.

**<u>Special note:</u>**

For the sake of emphasis or stress, we can use the article *'the'* before a noun, before which *'the'* is not generally used.

> **e.g.:**　I took **breakfast** at 8.00 a.m. today.(*before meals 'the' is not generally used.*)
>
> 　　　　**<u>The breakfast</u>** which I took today was delicious.(*'the' used for emphasis*)

# <u>Some important rules</u>

1. We use **'the'** whenever we want to stress or emphasize or particularize an object or a noun. We do not use 'the' when we say something in general.

    **e.g.:** i) **Nurses** have wonderful job opportunities all over the world. *('the' is not required here because the subject 'nurses' is used in a general way.)*
    **The nurses** in India are not paid well.(*'the' is used here because the subject is particularised.)*

    ii) **Children**, in general, are naughty. (*subject is used in a general way.*)
    **The children** in my area are quite naughty. (*subject is particularised.*)

2. 'The' is normally pronounced (*thee*) before a vowel sound and (*tha*) before a consonant sound. However, *thee* sound is used before any noun whenever the word is stressed or emphasized.

    In other words, **'tha'** sound is used wherever the article **'a'** is used and **'thee'** sound wherever **'an'** is used.

    **e.g.:** i) The ice (***thee*** ice)
    ii) The table  (***tha*** table)
    iii) The hour (***thee*** hour: *because of vowel sound 'o'*)
    iv) The M.L.A. (***thee*** M. L. A: *because of vowel sound 'e'*)
    v)  The European (***tha*** European: *because of consonant sound 'yu'*)

3. We should not pause after the articles, prepositions, conjunctions and auxiliaries. We should always pause before them.

    *correct pause*    *wrong pause*

    **e.g.:**  i) My sister works  in a  multi-specialty hospital.
    ii) I come  from  Chennai.
    iii) My teacher said  that  she would be absent the following day.

**<u>Repetition of articles:</u>**

4. When the article **'a/an/the'** is used only once even though there are two nouns or adjectives, it refers to one item but if the article is repeated before each noun or adjective, it refers to two items.

    **e.g.:**  i) I saw **a red** and **black car** parked on the roadside. *(one car which is red and black in colour)*
    ii) I saw **a** red and **a** black car parked on the roadside. *(two cars)*

5. When two or more adjectives refer to the same thing or person, we use the article only before the first adjective.

    **e.g.:**  i) Mr. Dev is **a** tall, clever, and smart person.
    ii) It is **an** old, tall, and impressive building.

6. Certain differences in meaning occur when articles are used:

    1. Maria goes **to school**. (***means....****went as a student*)

     Maria goes **to the school.** (***means....****went as an outsider*)

    2. Arjun went **to bed.** (***means.....****went to sleep*)

     Arjun went **to the bed.** (***means.....****went up to the bed*)

    3. Mr. Raj has **a lovely son** and **daughter.** (***means...****both are lovely*)

     Mr. Raj has **a lovely son** and **a daughter.** (***means...*** *only the son is lovely*)

    4. There is **little hope** of his recovery. (***means...****not much hope*)

     There is **a little hope** of his recovery. (***means ...*** *some hope*)

    5. Mahesh **went to play** with his friend. (***means ..*** *to play games*)

     Mahesh **went to the play** with his friend. (***means...*** *went to see a drama*)

# Exercise

### 1. Correct the following sentences with proper articles:

1. Jim called Tom fool.
2. One should always and everywhere speak truth.
3. My father went out for walk
4. Mr. Rao was neither a poet nor philosopher.
5. Mr. Raj works in an European company.
6. We enjoyed breakfast that Angeline gave us.
7. The English is becoming an international language.
8. There is no higher peak in the world than the Mount Everest.
9. This is a news for all of us.
10. Would you be kind enough to give me hundred rupees?
11. The teacher advised his students not to make noise in the class.
12. Late Shri. Abdul Kalam is considered to be one of the best presidents India had.
13. My uncle and his family lives in U.S.A.
14. Fire broke out in our flat a few days ago.
15. I bought an uniform costing rupees two hundred.

### 2. Add or omit articles wherever necessary:

1. -bag which I bought from— supermarket is quite expensive.
2. My brother studies in —Mahatma Gandhi University.
3. —Lake Chilka is an important lake in the state of Orissa.
4. Mr. Roberts studies-English and— history.
5. —Witness told that he had seen— incident.
6. My friend's father is in— hospital since Monday.
7. —First World War started in the year 1914.
8. Andrews plans to go to —United States soon after his studies in India.
9. —University of Calicut has fewer colleges than Mahatma Gandhi University.

10. Mr. Swaminathan is— M.L.A.

11. What did you eat for —breakfast this morning?

12. My mom bought— utensil yesterday.

13. There is —new professional college near my home.

14. Could you give me —cup of coffee, please?

15. —gentleman who came to see me yesterday met with an accident.

**Answers**

**1. <u>Correct the following sentences with proper articles:</u>**

1. Jim called Tom **a** fool.

2. One should always and everywhere speak **the** truth.

3. My father went out for **a** walk.

4. Mr. Rao was neither a poet nor **a** philosopher.

5. Mr. Raj works in **a** European company.

6. We enjoyed **the** breakfast that Angeline gave us.*(the term ' **breakfast'** is particularised here)*

7. **English** is becoming an international language.

8. There is no higher peak in the world than Mount Everest.

9. This is **news** for all of us.

10. Would you be kind enough to give me **a** hundred rupees?

11. The teacher advised his students not to make **a** noise in the class.

12. **The** late Shri. AbdulKalam is considered to be one of the best presidents India had.

13. My uncle and his family lives in **the** U.S.A.

14. A fire broke out in our flat a few days ago.

15. I bought **a** uniform costing Rs 200.

**2. <u>Add or omit articles wherever necessary:</u>**

1. (*The bag.... the supermarket*)

2. (no *articles required* because no article is used before proper noun)

3. *(no **The** before Lake Chilka because it is a singular lake)*

4. *(no* articles required because before names of subjects *the* is not put)

5. (*The witness... the incident*)

6. *(no articles required* because before names of institutions *the* is not required.)

7.(***The** First World War*)

8. (***The** United States*)

9.(***The** University of Calicut*)

10.(***an** M.L.A. because of the vowel sound 'e'* )

11. (breakfast: *no article required before meals*)

12. (***a** utensil*: a is used because of the consonant sound of *yu'*)

13. (***a** new professional college*)

14. (***a** cup of coffee*)

15. (***The** gentleman*: because the term is particularized)

# 5. Tenses

## A. Present Tense

## 1. Present simple/indefinite

| | |
|---|---|
| I write a letter | We write a letter. |
| You write a letter. | You write a letter. |
| He, she, it writ**es** a letter. | They write a letter. |

Form: | **sub + verb***(in the present tense form)*

**e.g.:** Martin **speaks** German quite fluently.

<u>Uses of present simple:</u>

1. To express a habitual action/repeated action.

**e.g.:** My father **goes** for a walk every morning.

2. To express a universal/general truth.

**e.g.:** The sun **rises** in the east.

3. To express a future event that is already planned.

**e.g.:** I **plan** to go abroad soon after my studies.

4. To introduce quotations. (*past tense also can be used*)

**e.g.:** Robinson **says**, "Money is what money does."

5. To express a fact.

**e.g.:** Today India's population is about 1.4 billion.

6. To speak of major past historical events or personalities.

**e.g. :** The Second World War **is** one of the greatest events of world history.

Martin Luther King is reckoned to be one of the great personalities of America.

7. To show ownership or belonging

**e.g.:** Today India has one of the largest pools of IT professionals.

8. To speak of theories and principles.

**e.g.:** Light **travels** faster than sound.

9. To speak of phrases, idioms and proverbs.

**e.g.:** Charity **begins** at home.

10. To announce news/newspaper headlines.

**e.g.:** The Prime Minister of India **visits** the injured victims of the train accident.

11. To speak of natural or inherent qualities.

**e.g.:** A mother **loves** her child.

12. To speak of professional activities.

**e.g.:** A baker **bakes** bread.

13. To give running commentaries.

> **e.g.:** Ronaldo takes the ball and dashes forward to the goalpost.

14. With stative verbs (*verbs that indicate a state)* of **perception/feeling/emotion/ recognition/thinking**, etc. (*see, doubt, taste, know, love, like, think, remember, etc.*)

> **e.g.:** I **love** my family. ( **not** *I am **loving** my family.*)

**Very important note: 1**

### Third Person 'S' rule

With **third person singular** (*he/she/it/uncountable nouns*) the verb in **present tense** must have **'s', 'es'** or **'ies'**.

> **e.g.:** i) My friend **works** in a private firm near his home.
>
> ii) Bill **speaks** French like a native speaker.

i) If there is an auxiliary verb between the singular subject and the verb, there will **be no 'S' rule.**

> **e.g.:** i) My friend **will come** a week later.
>
> ii) Jill **can sing** better than his friend.

ii) If there are adverbial words such as **always, never, hardly, seldom, sometimes, etc.,** between the singular subject and the verb, there **will be the 'S' rule.**

> **e.g.:** i) My friend **never comes** on time for duty.
>
> ii) The principal **hardly scolds** any student.

iii) If an auxiliary verb and an adverbial word come together in between the singular subject and the verb, there **will no 'S' rule.**

> **e.g.:** i) The patient **can hardly stand** straight.
>
> ii) We **must always speak** the truth.

iv) If the auxiliary **'does'** begins a sentence, there **will be no 'S' rule.**

> **e.g.:** i) **Does** she **sing** like her elder sister?
>
> ii) **Does** Hari **speak** English quite fluently?

v) If an uncountable noun such as *scenery, news, information, pollution,* etc. is the subject, there **will be the 'S' rule.**

> **e.g.:** i) The **scenery** of this hill station **looks** really charming.
>
> ii) **Pollution increases** day by day all over the world.

vi) Even if an uncountable noun is used in a plural sense with the help of plural determiners such as *some, most, a lot of,* etc., there **will be the 'S' rule.**

> **e.g.:** i) **All** the scenery over there **appears** to be mesmerizing.
>
> ii) **Some** of the jewellery in this shop **looks** really good.

> I belongs. **(X)**        I **belong**...(✓)
>
> The news show... **(X)**      The news **shows**..(✓)

| | |
|---|---|
| My family stay... **(X)** | My family **stays**.....(✓) |
| The work start... **(X)** | The work **starts**...(✓) |
| The graphs indicates... **(X)** | The graphs **indicate**...(✓) |
| I doesn't understand. **(X)** | I **don't** understand. (✓) |
| He don't know me. **(X)** | He **doesn't** know me. (✓) |

**Auxiliary:**

| | | | |
|---|---|---|---|
| Present tense **singular** | : Does | Present tense **plural** : do | |
| Past tense **singular** | : did | Past tense **Plural** | : did |

| | |
|---|---|
| She **does** not know me. | I **do** not know you. |
| He **did** not do it. | They **did** not do it. |

**Very important note: 2**

We should use **present simple** or **present continuous tense** for actions that are pre-planned or arranged to do in the future. Do not use **will/shall** for such actions. In such situations use terms such as *'going to, intend to, plan to* or **verb+ ING + time. Will/ shall** is generally used for actions which are *purely future in nature*.

$$\boxed{\textbf{ING + Time = Will}}$$

e.g.: I **will watch** a movie tonight. **(X)**
I **plan to/hope to/intend to watch** a movie tonight. (✓)
**OR**
I **am going to watch** a movie tonight/ I **am watching** a movie tonight. (✓)

**Very important note: 3**

For fixed timetables, routine programmes, official programmes of high dignitaries, etc. we should not use **will/shall**. Use instead **simple present tense**.

e.g.: i) The match will start at 5.30 p.m. this evening. **(X)**
The match **starts** at 5.30 this evening. (✓)
ii) The special class will begin at 10.00 this morning.**(X)**
The special class **begins** at 10.00 this morning. (✓)
iii) The President **will leave** for Russia tonight. **(X)**
The President **leaves** for Russia tonight. (✓)

**Very important note: 4**

When we speak of a dead person or a past event which occupies a significant place in history, **simple present** should be used. This is known as **historical present.**

    **e.g.:**   Abraham Lincoln **was** one of the great personalities of our times.**(X)**
               Abraham Lincoln **is** one of the great personalities of our times. (✓)

<u>Choose the correct word from the brackets:</u>
1. The issue that I spoke about (*needs/need*) serious consideration.
2. My friend's plans (*vary/varies*) according to his moods.
3. The political party which (win/wins) an election through money and muscle power will not last long.
4. The parliament (*do/does*) its work according to certain procedures.
5. Nothing (*work/works*) like hard work.
6. The subject-matter of these books (*appears/appear*) ambiguous.
7. The terms of this contract (*get/gets*) over on the last day of this month.
8. The topic of election reforms (*requires/require*) serious study by all parties concerned.
9. The newly appointed clerk can hardly (*write/writes*) well.
10. The lines in the graph (*indicate/indicates*) an upward swing.

**<u>Answers:</u>**
    1. The issue that I spoke about **<u>needs</u>** serious consideration.
    2. My friend's plans **<u>vary</u>** according to his moods.
    3. The political party which **<u>wins</u>** an election through money and muscle power will not last long.
    4. The parliament **<u>does</u>** its work according to certain procedures.
    5. Nothing **<u>works</u>** like hard work.
    6. The subject-matter of these books **<u>appears</u>** ambiguous.
    7. The terms of this contract **<u>get</u>** over on the last day of this month.
    8. The topic of election reforms **<u>requires</u>** serious study by all  parties concerned.
    9.  The newly appointed clerk can hardly **<u>write</u>** well.
    10. The lines in the graph **<u>indicate</u>** an upward swing.

# 2. Present continuous tense

I am writing a letter.          We are writing a letter.
You are writing a letter.        You are writing a letter.
He/she/it is writing a letter.   They are writing a letter.

Form:  | **sub + am/is/are + verb** in **ING** form |

**e.g.:** The maid **is preparing** the dinner now.

<u>Uses of present continuous</u>

1. To express an action that is going on at the time of speaking.
   **e.g.:** I **am writing** a letter to my brother now.
2. To express an action that has already been pre-planned or arranged to do in the
   **near future.** (*not distant future*)
   **e.g.:** My friend **is flying** to the UK next month.

**Very important note: 5**

The present continuous form should be used only for actions which are going on at the
time of speaking and not for any general type of continuous activity. Do not use the term
**'coming'** while speaking about one's place of birth.
   **e.g.:**  I am coming from Kochi, a city in Kerala. (***incorrect*** *because the action is
              not taking place now.*)
   I **come** from Kochi, a city in Kerala.

| I **hail from**..../ I **am from**..../ My family **resides at**..../ My family **is stationed** at.... I was **born and brought up** at...../ I am a **native of** .../ I **belong to**../My **residence is at** ../ My family **stays** in a place called ...My family is **located at**...., etc. |

**Very important note: 6**

<u>Verbs which are not **usually** used in **ING** form</u>

The following stative verbs *(verbs which show a state rather than action)*of *feeling/ emotion/
thinking/ recognition/ possession, etc.* **are not generally** used in **ING form.**
   i) **Verbs of perception**        : *see, hear, smell, taste, notice,  recognize, doubt,
                                         wonder, intend, realize, etc.*
   ii) **Verbs of appearing**        : *appear, look, seem, imagine, depend, fit, involve,
                                         etc.*

| | |
|---|---|
| iii) **Verbs of emotion** | : *want, wish, desire, feel, like, dislike, love, hate, enjoy, promise, please, hope, satisfy, surprise, concern, refuse, prefer, matter, adore, assume, expect, measure, weigh, fear, astonish, impress, etc.* |
| iv) **Verbs of thinking** | : *think, suppose, believe, agree, disagree, consider, trust, remember, mean, mind, know, understand, need, forget, deny, etc.* |
| v) **Verbs of possession** | : *have, own, lack, possess, belong to, contain, consist of, exist, deserve, etc.* |

These verbs should be used in their **present simple/past tense** forms but not in ING forms.

> **E.g.:** i) **My** brother is **having** an expensive new car. **(X)**
>
> My brother **has** an expensive new car.
>
> ii) Hearing a loud noise outside, I went out of the room. (✓)
>
> *present participle*
>
> Loving friend...(✓)  ..Yours lovingly (✓)

Try to avoid the over-use of **ING** form.

i) What are you **doing**? **(X)** (*What do you do nowadays?*)

ii) How are you **feeling**? **(X)** (*How do you feel?*)

iii) Where are you s**taying**? **(X)** (*Where do you stay?*)

iv) I am **wishing** you a Merry Christmas. **(X)** (*I wish you a Merry Christmas.*)

v) I am **feeling** very tired today. **(X)** (*I feel very tired today.*)

vi) I am **having** severe headache. **(X)** (*I have a severe headache.*)

Exceptions:

1. **'Having'** can be used when it refers to taking meals or a sense of enjoyment.

> **e.g.:** We are **having** our meals now.
>
> She is **having** a great time.

2. **'Feeling'** can be used in the medical sense.

> **e.g.:** Maria is not **feeling** well these days.

3. **'Seeing'** can be used when it refers to an interview or meeting.

> **e.g.:** Shankar is **seeing** his advocate in his chamber.

 Ways of giving a progressive sense to stative verbs:

1. **Can** is often used with verbs such as, **'see, hear, feel, taste, smell, understand, remember'** etc. to give a kind of progressive meaning.

> **e.g.:** i) I **can see** a beautiful house in the distance.
>
> ii) We **can understand** your problem quite well.

2. We can use the term **'always'** to give a sense of continuity to stative verbs.

    **e.g.:** i) I <u>**always remember**</u> my friend.

          ii) We <u>**always consider**</u> your points.

## <u>Correct the following sentences:</u>

1. This box is containing several costly items.

2. Parents are loving their children as never before.

3. My friend is looking tired and worn out.

4. The little boy is wanting to play.

5. That umbrella is belonging to my friend.

6. Most people are believing in God.

7. My uncle is having several shops in the town.

8. I am sorry, I am not remembering your name.

9. I am feeling very cold here.

10. Maria is desiring to become an air-hostess.

## <u>Answers:</u>

    1. This box **contains** several costly items.

    2. Parents **love** their children as never before.

    3. My friend **looks** tired and worn out.

    4. The little boy **wants** to play.

    5. That umbrella **belongs** to my friend.

    6. Most people **believe** in God.

    7. My uncle **has** several shops in the town.

    8. I am sorry, I don't remember your name.

    9. I **feel** very cold here.

    10. Maria **desires** to become an air-hostess.

# 3.  Present perfect tense

| | |
|---|---|
| I have written a letter. | We have written a letter. |
| You have written a letter. | You have written a letter. |
| He/She/It has written a letter. | They have written a letter. |

Form: | **sub + has/have + verb** in the past participle |

        **e.g.:** We **have seen** the movie *'Da Vinci Code'*.

<u>Uses of present perfect:</u>
1. To express an action that began in the past and is completed in the present.
    **e.g.:** I **have just come** in.
2. To express an action just now completed.
    **e.g.**: I **have just completed** the construction of my house.
3. To speak about an action that began in the past and continues until the present time.
    **e.g.:** John **has lived** in the house for twenty years. (*John is living in that house up to now.)*
4. To express a recent past action whose time is not given and not definite.
    **e.g.:** I **have done** the job as per your instructions.
5. To speak about an action that happened more than once in the past.
    **e.g.:** My friend **has seen** this movie more than three times.
6. To describe past actions with certain implications and results in the present.
    **e.g.:** I **have finished** my work. (*so I am free now*)
7. To say that a finished action or event is connected with the present in some way.
    **e.g.:** I can't go on a holiday because I **have broken** my leg.
8. It is often used with words such as *since, for, ever, just, before, never, yet, recently, lately, already,* etc.
    **e.g.:** Mahesh **has already** submitted his assignment.
9. To announce news of recent events.
    **e.g.:** Argentina  **has** won the Football World Cup-2022.

**Very important note: 7**

### **The Past Participle Rule**

The past participle rule involves the following four aspects:
    i) If a verb is used with **has/have/had,** it  must be in the **past participle** form of the verb ($V_3$).
        **e.g.:**  The patient *has broke* the bottle of medicine. **(X)**
        The patient **has broken** the bottle of medicine. (✓)
    ii) In active voice, past participles of verbs cannot be used alone without <u>**has/have/ had**</u>.
    In passive voice they are used without **has/have/had.**
        **e.g.:**  i) The stranger rang the doorbell several times.**(X)**
        The stranger **has/had rung** the doorbell several times. (✓)
        ii) A letter was **written** by me. (*passive voice*)

iii) **'Has'** is used for singular subjects and **'have'** is used for plural subjects.

| He<br>She **has**<br>It | Tom **has...**. My friend **has...**Pollution **has...**<br><br>The news **has...**The quality **has...**<br>*Anything singular* |
|---|---|
| I<br>You **have**<br>We | The questions **have...**Boys **have...**<br><br>The issues **have...**The speeches **have**<br>They<br>Anything plural |

My family **have. (X)**... My family **has...**(✓)    I has....**(X)**......I have....(✓)
My friend **have.(X)**.... My friend **has** ...(✓)    They has.**(X)**They have (✓)
The facilities **has.(X)**... The facilities **have**...(✓)  News have.**(X)**News has (✓)
This have ..**(X)**............This has (✓)    That have **(X)**...That has (✓)
These has**(X)**............. These have(✓)    Those has **(X)**..Those have (✓)

> **Everybody have  (X) .........Everybody has (✓)**

iv)  After an auxiliary verb, **'has' cannot be used...**but only **have** can be used.
**e.g.:** Someone **must has** done it. **(X)**        Someone **must have** done it. (✓)
He **will has** come.**(X)**        He **will have** come. (✓)

**Very important note: 8**

<u>Use of **'has had / have had'**</u>

A sentence that has **'has had** or **have had'**, *has* or *have* acts as an auxiliary verb while
*had* acts as the past participle of the verb **has/have** like any other verb.

| present | past | past participle |
|---|---|---|
| **Be** (am/is/are)<br>**Has/Have** | was/were<br>had | been<br>had |

| **Present simple** | **Present perfect** |
|---|---|
| 1. Mr. Sanjay **is** a teacher. | 1. Mr. Sanjay **has been** a teacher. |
| | (*'has'* acts as an auxiliary) |
| | (*'been'* is the past participle of 'is') |

| **Present simple** | **Present perfect** |
|---|---|
| 2. Miss Jaya **has** a new car. | 2. Miss Jaya **has had** a new car. |
| (**verb**) | They **have had** a new car. |
| | (*'has/have'* act as an auxiliary) |
| | (*'had'* is the past participle of the verb 'has/have' ) |

**Very important note: 9**

### The past time rule

*Present  & past perfect* **should not be used** with adverbs of past time such as:

> *yesterday*                    *last night*
> *previous night*              *day before yesterday*
> *some time ago*              *a few years ago*
> *or with any past time such as* **ago**, **last, past,** etc.

Use instead **simple past** with any mention of past time.

However, with **since** *past time* can be used.

**e.g.:**  i) I **have** met my friend  in the town **yesterday**. **(X)**

I **met** my friend in the town yesterday. (✓)

ii) Sham **has** been working here for the **last two years**. **(X)**

Sham  **has** been working here for two years. (✓)

iii) This factory **has been closed** from **1998 to 2003.(X)**

This factory **was closed** from 1998 to 2003. (✓)

With **since** mention of past time is allowed:

iv) I have been suffering from cold **since yesterday.**

v) Sathyan has been abroad **since last January.**

                          1. **Conjunction** (*I cannot come to class **since** it is raining.*)

**Since** is mainly used as:

                          2. **Preposition** (Raj has been working here **since** 1990.)

**i) Since:**

Since should be used with **a starting point of time.**

It marks the beginning of a period. Since means *'from the mentioned point to the time of speaking'*. The time mentioned with since should be specific.

> Since + **starting point of time**

| | |
|---|---|
| since **2000** | since **morning** |
| since **yesterday** | since his/her **birthday** |

> **Since**-Specific time     **Since/For** goes well with **has/have**
> **For** -general time       **From** goes well with **am/is/was/are/were.**

**e.g.:** i) It is/was raining since morning.**(X)**
It **has been** raining **since** morning. (✓)
It is/was raining from morning. (✓)
ii) I **have been** working as a computer engineer **from** 2010.**(X)**
I **was** working as a computer engineer **from** 2010 to 2014. (✓)
OR I **have been** working as a computer engineer **since** 2010. (✓)

**Since** as a **preposition:**

i) Since as a preposition should be used with the **starting point of time.** (It has a sense of 'from the starting time up to now'.)
**e.g.:** It has been raining **since** this morning.
ii) We cannot use **general time** with **since.**
**e.g.:** I have been sick **since** two days. **(X)**
I have been sick **for** two days. (✓)
**OR** I have been sick **since** day before yesterday. (✓)
iii) **Since** is generally used in present perfect tense only *(has/have)*. It should not be used with present simple/present continuous or past simple/past continuous.
**e.g.:** Maria **is** absent from class since yesterday. **(X)**
Maria **has been** absent from class since yesterday. (✓)
iv) **Since** can be used only with one date. Hence, if there is a break in one's service, we should not use **since.**
**e.g.:** I have been working as a staff nurse **since 2000 to 2005. (X)**
I worked/was working as a staff nurse **from** 2000 to 2005. (✓)
v) Try to avoid using since at the beginning of a sentence. If we use **since** before the subject, there should be a comma.
**e.g.: Since 2000,** there has been a dramatic rise in the sale of computers.

**ii) For:**

For should be used with **<u>a general period of time</u>**.

For + **general period of time**

for **a few days**        for **thirty minutes**

for **a month**        for **three hours**

**e.g.:** My friend has been absent from class **for** ten days.

**iii) Already**

<u>Already</u> usually appears between the auxiliary and the main verb.

Sub + has/have + **already** + verb in the past participle

**e.g.:**  i) The students **have <u>already</u>** completed their assignments.

       ii) Marie **has <u>already</u>** submitted her application for the principal's post.

**iv) Yet**

<u>Yet</u> has a **negative sense** if it is used at the ***<u>end of a sentence.</u>***

Sub + has/have + **not** + verb in the past participle + **yet**

**e.g.:** i) I **haven't** watched the famous movie 'Avatar' ***yet.***

**Yet** has a **<u>positive sense</u>** if it is used after ***<u>has/have</u>***

Sub + has/have + **yet** + verb in infinitive

**e.g.:** I have **yet** to watch the famous movie 'Avatar'.

*****Yet** as a conjunction has a  different meaning (*yet* has the meaning of *but, still, etc.*)

**e.g.:** John is quite sick; **yet** he wants to appear for the interview.

**v) Just/Just now**

The word 'just' is mainly used in the sense of **'a recent past'** and it is mostly used in present perfect.

Sub + has/have + **just** + verb in past participle

**e.g.:**  i) Tom has **just** left the place.

       ii) My brother has **<u>just</u>** returned from a tour of Europe.

When we use  the term **'just now'** to mean a moment ago, **<u>past simple</u>** is to be used.

Sub+ past simple + **just now**

**e.g.:** My brother **came back** home **just now**. *(**not** has come back)*

<u>The term **'just'** can  also be used in other tense forms.</u>

**e.g.:**  i) Inflation fell to **just** over 4 per cent this year.

ii) It's **just** what I wanted.

iii) Rani is **just** as smart as her sister.

# 4. Present perfect continuous tense

I have been writing a letter.

You have been writing a letter.

He/She/It has been writing a letter.

We have been writing a letter.

You have been writing a letter.

They have been writing a letter.

Form: **Sub + has/have + been + verb** in **ING** form

**e.g.:** We <u>**have been discussing**</u> this matter for some time.

<u>Uses of present perfect continuous tense</u>

1. To show an action which began sometime in the past and is still going on in the present.

**e.g.:** The kids **have been cycling** for an hour.

2. To express actions and situations which have just stopped but have present results.

**e.g.:** I **have been waiting** for you for some time now.

3. It is mostly used with time expressions such as *'since, for, recently, lately, this  week'*, etc.

**e.g.:** Mr. Dave **has been working** in this firm **since** 2000.

# B. Past Tense

# 1. Past simple /indefinite

| | |
|---|---|
| I wrote a letter. | We wrote a letter. |
| You wrote a letter. | You wrote a letter. |
| He/She/It wrote a letter. | They wrote a letter. |

Form: | **Sub + past tense** of the verb

**e.g.:** India **signed** a nuclear agreement with the USA in March 2006.

Uses of past simple:

1. To express an action completed in the past 'at a definite' point of time.

    **e.g.:** Saritha **left** college last year.

2. To express a past habit.

    **e.g.:** I always **watered** my flower plants in the morning.

3. Past simple is generally used with *past continuous* and *past perfect.*

    **e.g.:** i) I **met** my friend as he **was walking** on the road.

        ii) After the patient had taken the medicine, his condition **became** worse.

4. For a past action when the time is clearly mentioned.

    **e.g.:** Hari took me to his house **yesterday**.

5. It is used in conditional sentences.

    **e.g.:** If you **worked** hard, you **would** pass the test.

**Very important note: 10**

> **Simple past** must be used *with adverbs of past time* such as
>
> | | |
> |---|---|
> | *yesterday* | *previous night* |
> | *last night* | *day before yesterday* |
> | *a few days ago* | *some time ago*, etc. |

**Do not use present** or **past perfect tense** when there is an indication of **past time.**

    **e.g.:** I had watched a movie yesterday.**(X)**

        I watched a movie yesterday. (✓)

# Important points regarding past simple

1. We cannot use double past simple clauses in a complex sentence. The first action has to be in past perfect, and the second action has to be in past simple.

    **e.g.:**  i) After I **completed** my assignment, I **went to** bed.**(X)**

          After I **had completed** my assignment, I **went** to bed. (✓)

**<u>Exception</u>**

We can use double simple past clauses in a complex sentence when the action is simultaneous or is a statement or a thinking process.

    i) As I **opened** the door, I **slipped and fell** backward. *(correct because it is a simultaneous action.)*

    ii) I **knew** that my friend **loved** me deeply. *(correct because it is a thinking process.)*

    iii) The teacher **said** that she **would** come late to the class the following day. *(correct because it is a statement.)*

2. In a complex sentence, a past simple clause can be followed by a **past continuous clause.**

    **e.g.:** When I **watched** television, my little brother **was sleeping**.

3. In a complex sentence, a past simple can be followed by a past perfect clause.

    **e.g.:** I **watched** television after I **had completed** my assignment.

4. In a complex sentence, a past simple can be followed by a past perfect continuous clause.

    **e.g.:** I **completed** my assignment after I **had been reading** a story book.

5. With any mention of past time such as **yesterday, last night, ago, past, last, etc.** only **simple past** can be used and **not present perfect**.

    **e.g.:**  i) I **have** met you **last week.(X)**

          I **met** you last week. (✓)

6. Whenever we use simple past there should be past time words.

    **e.g.:**  i) I watched a movie. (***not-so-correct***)

          I **watched** a movie **yesterday**/ last Saturday/ a month ago, etc.

# 2. Past continuous tense

| | |
|---|---|
| I was writing a letter. | We were writing a letter. |
| You were writing a letter. | You were writing a letter. |
| He/She/It was writing a letter. | They were writing a letter. |

Form: | **Sub + was/were + verb** in **ING** form

**e.g.:** My friend <u>**was playing**</u> cards when I saw him.

<u>Uses of past continuous:</u>

1. To talk about an action that was going on for some time in the past.

   **e.g.:** Satish **was reading** a novel named '*Da Vinci Code*'.

2. To talk about something that was already in progress when something else happened.

   **e.g.:** Rehman **was returning** home late when a dog bit him.

3. Past continuous is mainly used in combination with simple past.

   **e.g.:** My friend **was waiting** for me when I **reached** home.

## Important points regarding past continuous

1. In a complex sentence, a past continuous clause can be followed by a past simple clause.

   **e.g.:**  When I **was watching** television, the telephone **rang**.

2. A past continuous clause can be followed by another past continuous clause.

   **e.g.:**  As I **was walking** along the road, one man **was coming** towards me.

3. A past continuous clause cannot be followed by a past perfect clause.

   **e.g.:** When Priya **was reading**, her friend **had come** in.**(X)**

   When Priya **was reading**, her friend **came** in. (✓)

4. In a complex sentence, a past continuous clause cannot be followed by a past perfect continuous clause.

   **e.g.:**  When I **was watching** television, my mother had been preparing dinner. **(X)**

   When I **was watching** television, my mother **prepared dinner/ was preparing** dinner. (✓)

5. We cannot use static/stative verbs such as *see, hear, taste, smell, look, wish, have, know, understand, own, consist, contain, desire, love, like,* etc. not only in present continuous but also in past continuous tenses.

   **e.g.:**  I **was looking** at a man walking on the road.**(X)**

   I **looked** at the man walking on the road. (✓)

## 3. Past perfect tense

| | |
|---|---|
| I had written a letter. | We had written a letter. |
| You had written a letter. | You had written a letter. |
| He/she /it had written a letter. | They had written a letter. |

Form:  | **Sub + had + past participle** |

**e.g.:** After the patient **had taken** the medicine, his condition **became** worse.

<u>Uses of past perfect:</u>

1. It is used to denote an action in the past which had been completed at a certain point of time in the past.

   **e.g.:** The patient **had died** before the doctor **reached** the ward.

2. To talk about something that happened before another action in the past.

   **e.g.:** The train **had left** when I **reached** the station.

3. Past perfect is usually used with **before, after, when,** etc.

   **e.g.:** i) The minister **had left** the place **before** the crowd dispersed.

   ii) <u>**After**</u> John **had gone** to the supermarket, he **went** home.

# Important points regarding past perfect

1. A past perfect clause can be followed by a past simple clause.

   **e.g.:** After Sonia **had reached** home, she **watched** television for some time.

2. A past perfect clause cannot be followed by a past continuous clause.

   **e.g.:** After I **had completed** my assignment, I **was taking** my dinner.**(X)**

   After I **had completed** my assignment, I **took** my dinner. (✓)

3. A past perfect clause cannot be followed by another past perfect clause.

   **e.g.:** After Priya **had visited** her friend, she **had returned** home. **(X)**

   After Priya **had visited** her friend, she **returned** home. (✓)

4. A past perfect clause cannot be followed by past perfect continuous clause.

   **e.g.:** After I had completed my studies, I had been working in a private company.**(X)**

   After I had completed my studies, I worked in a private company. (✓)

5. When there are two actions of the past, the first action should be in **past perfect,** and the second action should be in **past simple**.

   **e.g.:** The patient <u>**had died**</u> before the doctor <u>**reached**</u> the ward.

   **1st action - past perfect        2nd action - past simple**

   OR

   Before the doctor <u>**reached**</u> the ward, the patient <u>**had died.**</u>

   **2nd action - past simple            1st action - past perfect**

6. For a single past action, try not to use past perfect. Use instead past simple.

   **e.g.:** I <u>**had watched**</u> a movie yesterday.(*not-so-correct*)

   I **watched** a movie yesterday.

# 4. Past perfect continuous tense

I had been writing a letter.      We had been writing a letter.
You had been writing a letter.      You had been writing a letter.
He/She/ It had been writing a letter.      They had been writing a letter.

Form: | **Sub + had been + verb** in **ING** form |

**e.g.:** Mr. Singh **had been travelling** around the world for a month.

<u>Uses of past perfect continuous tense:</u>

1. It is used to express an action that began in the past and was continued for a  considerable period of time in the past itself.

   **e.g.:** John **had been reading** the novel for two hours.

2. It is used with **since** or **for** to talk about an activity that started at a time further  back in the past.

   **e.g.:** Miss Linda **had been living** here since 2005.

# Important points regarding past perfect continuous

1. In a complex sentence, a past perfect continuous clause can be followed by a simple past clause.

   **e.g.:** After I **had been writing** an essay, I **watched** a movie.

2. A past perfect continuous clause cannot be followed by a past continuous clause.

   **e.g.:** When I **had been watching** television, my younger brother was studying. **(X)**

   When I **had been watching** television, my younger brother **studied**. (✓)

3. A past perfect continuous clause cannot be followed by past perfect.

   **e.g.:** After I **had been watching** television, I **had taken** dinner. **(X)**

   After I **had been watching** television, I **took** dinner/I **had** my dinner. (✓)

4. A past perfect continuous clause cannot be followed by another past perfect continuous clause.

   **e.g.:** After I **had been watching** a movie, I **had been taking** my dinner. **(X)**

   After I **had been watching** a movie, I **took** my dinner. (✓)

# C. Future Tense

## 1. Future simple/indefinite

I will write a letter.　　　We will write a letter.
You will write a letter.　　You will write a letter.
He/she/it will write a letter.　They will write a letter.

Form :　| **Sub + will/shall + verb** in present form |

　　**e.g. :** Sham **will** move to the UK next week for his higher studies.

<u>Uses of future simple:</u>
1. To express actions in the future, i.e., actions that are still to take place.
　　**e.g.:** I <u>**shall go**</u> home soon.
2. To express habitual actions in the future.
　　**e.g.:** The monsoon **will come** at the usual time.
3. To express the speaker's opinions or assumptions about the future. Verbs such as *think, probably, sure, believe, expect, hope, suppose, etc.* introduce such opinions.
　　**e.g.:** I <u>expect</u> he **will do** better next time.

## <u>Important points regarding future simple</u>

1. We cannot use double will clauses.
　　**e.g.:**　When I **will** have time, I **will** visit you. **(X)**
　　　　　When I **have** time, I **will** visit you. (✓)
2. We cannot use **'if'** and **'will'** together in the same clause as 'if' has already a touch of future.
　　**e.g.:**　If I will pass the IELTS, I will go to Australia. **(X)**
　　　　　If I pass the IELTS, I **will** go to Australia. (✓)
3. The following verbs are **generally** followed by a clause expressing a future sense.

| **Probably, sure, wonder, think, believe, expect, hope, suppose,** etc. |

　**e.g.:**　i) We **hope** the examination <u>**won't**</u> be postponed. (*will + not = won't*)
　　　　ii) I **think** my friend <u>**will**</u> pass the test this time.
　　　　iii) I **believe** India **will** become a fully developed nation within a few years.

4. Use of certain terms such as *if, unless, when, while, as, before, after, until, by t h e time, as soon as, so long as, till*, etc. in **present simple** gives a sense of future to the sentences.

      **e.g.:**  Wait for me here **until I will** come back. **(X)**

             Wait for me here **until I come back.** (✓)

**Very important note: 11**

  **Will/Shall** is generally used for actions which are *futuristic in nature* and not for actions that are pre-planned or arranged or fixed or is part of a timetable.

      **e.g.:**  i) I **will** meet my friend <u>tomorrow.</u> **(X)**

             I **plan to/hope to/intend to meet** my friend tomorrow. (✓)

             *OR* I am going to meet my friend tomorrow/ I am meeting my friend tomorrow. (✓)

             ii) The conference **will start** at 10.00 a.m. today.**(X)**

             The conference **starts** at 10.00 a.m. today. (✓)

<u>Different methods of showing future without using **will/shall**</u>

**<u>Future time can be expressed in the following ways:</u>**

1. **By using present simple:** (*intend to/plan to/hope to/ present simple terms, etc.*)

      **e.g.:**  i) I will meet my friend tonight.**(X)**

             I **intend to/plan to/hope to** meet my friend tonight. (✓)

             ii) The programme will begin at 4.30 p.m. this evening. **(X)**

             The programme **begins** at 4.30 pm this evening. (✓)

2. **By using present continuous tense:** (*ING + time = will*)

      **e.g.:**  i) My brother will fly to the UK next month. **(X)**

             My brother **is flying** to the UK next month.(✓)

3. **<u>By using certain terms</u>**: The use of certain terms such as *if, unless, when, while, as, before, after, until, by the time, as soon as,* etc. in **<u>present simple</u>** gives a sense of future to the sentences.

      **e.g.:**  i) Let us wait for him here <u>till </u>he will finish his work. **(X)**

             Let us wait for him here **till he finishes** his work.(✓)

4.**<u>By using 'going to'</u>**: The term **'going to'** expresses future time. This form is used for actions that are likely or expected to take place.

      **e.g.:**  i) We will visit Goa next week.**(X)**

             We are **going to** visit Goa next week.(✓)

             ii) I am **going to** speak to my director tomorrow. (*future action*)

5. **<u>By using infinitive</u>**: am/is/are + **infinitive** gives a touch of future.(infinitive means  to + verb)

       **e.g.:**  i) Harish **is to take** the test next week.

             ii) Angeline **is to meet** her friend day after tomorrow.

**Very important note: 12**

**Use of will/shall**

| | |
|---|---|
| $1^{st}$ person<br>$2^{nd}$ person /$3^{rd}$ person | + **will**    shows promise/determination/assurance.<br>+ **shall** |

       **e.g.:**  i) I will do it as soon as I can.

             ii) You shall do it as early as possible.

             iii) The criminal shall be taken to jail immediately. (*'shall' is used for legal orders*)

| | |
|---|---|
| $1^{st}$ person<br>$2^{nd}$ Person /$3^{rd}$ person | + **shall**    shows pure future.<br>+ **will** |

       **e.g.:**  i) I shall meet you soon.( *less emphatic*)

             ii) You will meet me tomorrow.

             iii) My friend will come today.

**Very important note: 13**

**Uses of would** (Main uses)

i) Past tense of will

       **e.g.:** My friend **said** that he **will** accompany me to the railway station. **(X)**

           My friend **said** that he **would** accompany me to the railway station. (✔)

ii) To show equal probability with a touch of future.

       **e.g.:**  I **would go** to Australia next year.

iii) Used in conditional clauses.

       **e.g.:**  If I were you, I **wouldn't** do it.

49

## 2. Future continuous tense

I will be writing a letter.      We will be writing a letter.
You will be writing a letter.      You will be writing a letter.
He/She/ It will be writing a letter.      They will be writing a letter.

Form:    | **Sub + will/shall + be + verb** in **ING** form |

**e.g.:** Our college team **will be playing** a cricket match against the university team.

<u>Uses of future continuous:</u>

1. To express an action that will continue for a period of time in  the future.
    **e.g.:** Jill **<u>will be meeting</u>** his friend soon.
2. To express future without intention.
    **e.g.:** Bob **won't** (*will+ not*) **be** taking the test.
3. To ask somebody about their plans or intentions.
    **e.g.: Will** you be flying tonight or tomorrow?

## 3. Future perfect tense

I will have written a letter.      We will have written a letter.
You will have written a letter.      You will have written a letter.
He/She/It will **have** written a letter.      They will have written a letter.

Form:    | **Sub + will/shall + have  + past participle** |

**e.g.:** We **will have taken** the test by tomorrow.

**<u>Special note:</u>**

*After will/shall* **'has'** *cannot be used; only* **have** *can be used.*

<u>Use of future perfect</u>

    i) To talk about a future action which will be completed by a given time in future.
    **e.g.:** The students **<u>will have completed</u>** their assignments by next week.

## 4. Future perfect continuous tense

I will have been writing a letter.  We will have been writing a letter.
You will have been writing a letter.  You will have been writing a letter.
He/She/It will have been writing a letter.  They will have been writing a letter.

Form: | **Sub + will/shall + have been + verb** in **ING** form

**e.g.:** Mr Dev **will have been teaching** English for the next twenty years.

Use of future perfect continuous:

i) To express actions which will be in progress over a considerable period of time in  the future. Hence it is generally used with specific expressions of time.

**e.g.:** Mr Raj **will have been completing** one year in this institute by  next month.

# Sequence of tense

**Sequence of tense:** The principle according to which the tense of the verb in a subordinate clause follows the tense of the verb in the principal clause is called the **sequence of tense.**

**Rule 1: Present** or **future tense** in the principal clause may be followed by **any tense** in the subordinate clause.

**Principal clause** means a clause that can stand by itself.

**Subordinate clause** means a clause that cannot stand by itself and is dependent on the principal clause.

**Principal clause**        **Subordinate clause**

**e.g.:  I know/will know** that my friend **works** hard.     (present simple)

**I know/ will know** that my friend **has worked** hard. (present perfect)

**I know/will know** that my friend **worked** hard.    (past simple )

**I know/ will know** that my friend **had worked** hard. (past perfect)

**I know/will know** that my friend **will work** hard, etc. (future simple)

## **The Past Sequence Rule**

**Rule 2:**  A **past tense** in the <u>principal clause</u> must be followed by a **past tense** in the subordinate clause except in the cases of universal truth and comparative **'than'**.

### **Principal clause   subordinate clause**

| | |
|---|---|
| I **knew** | that my friend **worked** hard. |
| I **knew** | that my friend **was working** hard. |
| I **knew** | that my friend **had worked** hard. |
| I **knew** | that my friend **had been working** hard. |
| I **knew** | that my friend **could work** hard. (*'could'* is the past form of *'can'*.) |
| I **knew** | that my friend **would work** hard. (*'would'* is the past form of *'will'*) |
| I **knew** | that my friend **might work** hard. (*'might'* is the past form of *'may'*) |
| I **knew** | that my friend **should work** hard. (*'should'* is the past form of *'shall'*) |

**Exceptions:**

1) A past tense in the principal clause may be <u>followed by a present tense in the subordinate clause</u> when the subordinate clause expresses a **universal truth/ general truth**.

> **e.g.:**  i) The sage **remarked** that man **is** mortal.
>
> ii) The teacher **said** that honesty **is** the best policy.

2) A past tense in the principal clause may be followed by any tense in the subordinate clause if the subordinate clause is introduced by **than**.

| **Principal clause** | **Subordinate clause** |
|---|---|
| He **loved** me | more *than* he **loves** you. |
| He **loved** me | more *than* he **loved** you. |
| He **loved** me | more *than* he **will love** you. |

Examples:

> i) David said that he will meet Robert in the evening.**(X)**
>
>    David **said** that he **would** meet Robert in the evening. (✓)
>
> ii) The police officer asked the young lady what she wants. **(X)**
>
>    The police officer **asked** the young lady what she **wanted**. (✓)

## **1. Correct the sequence of tense in the following sentences:**

1. My friend said that he can do it.
2. Martha said that she has finished cooking the dinner.
3. The clerk told the accountant that the manager wishes to see him.
4. The new recruit ran away because he is afraid.
5. My teacher said that hard work led to success.
6. The minister said that he will visit his constituency shortly.
7. I asked my friend if he has a plan to join the college soon.
8. Sanjay went to England in order that he may become a doctor.

9. I asked the stranger what his name is.

10. I heard that tomorrow is a holiday.

**Answers:**

1. My friend **said** that he **could** do it.

2. Martha **said** that she **had finished** cooking the dinner.

3. The clerk **told** the accountant that the manager **wished** to see him.

4. The new recruit **ran** away because he **was afraid.**

5. My teacher **said** that hard work **leads** to success.

6. The minister **said** that he **would visit** his constituency shortly.

7. I **asked** my friend if he **had** a plan to join the college soon.

8. Sanjay **went** to England in order that he **might** become a doctor.

9. I **aske**d the stranger what his **name was.**

10. I **heard** that tomorrow **would be** a holiday.

**Tenses combined (***all 12 forms***)**

| | |
|---|---|
| 1. Present simple | : Jill **speaks** English quite fluently. |
| 2. Present continuous | : Jill **is speaking** English quite fluently. |
| 3. Present perfect | : Jill **has spoken** English quite fluently. |
| 4. Present perfect continuous | : Jill **has been speaking** English quite fluently. |
| 5.Past simple | : Jill **spoke** English quite fluently. |
| 6. Past continuous | : Jill **was speaking** English quite fluently. |
| 7. Past perfect | : Jill **had spoken** English quite fluently. |
| 8. Past perfect continuous | : Jill **had been speaking** English quite fluently. |
| 9.Future simple | : Jill **will speak** English quite fluently. |
| 10. Future continuous | : Jill **will be speaking** English quite fluently. |
| 11. Future perfect | : Jill **will have spoken** English quite fluently. |
| 12. Future perfect continuous: Jill **will have been speaking** English quite fluently. | |

# Tenses in short form

| Tense | Indefinite | Continuous | Perfect | Perfect  Continuous |
|---|---|---|---|---|
| **Present** **Past** **Future** | I play I played I will play | I am playing I was playing I will be playing | I have played I had played I will have played | I have been playing I had been playing I will have been playing |

## THE GOLDEN POINTS OF TENSES

1. # In general, do not mix up the tenses.

2. **Past tense** will not go with **present tense** or **future tense**.

3. **Present tense** and **future tense** can go together.(If you study well, you will pass.)

4. Tense rules of **simple sentence** are also applicable to **compound sentence**.

5. For **simple** and **compound** sentences, use the **different forms of the same tense** throughout.

**Simple sentence:**
    **e.g.:** I went home yesterday. On reaching home, I watched television for some time. Thereafter I was reading a story book. Then I had gone to visit my friend in the hospital. *(Past tense is used but different forms of past tense are used.)*

**Compound sentence:**
    **e.g.:** I went home yesterday **and** watched television for some time. Thereafter I was reading a story book **but** I could not complete it. **Although** I had read only a few chapters *yet* I was much impressed by the story outline.(*Past tense is used but different forms of past tense are used.)*

**Complex sentence**:
6. **For complex sentences,** follow strictly the compatibility of tenses of the clauses i.e., which clause will go with which clause.

## 1. Compatible clauses *(clauses that will go together)*

| principal clause | | subordinate clause |
|---|---|---|
| 1. Past simple | ✓ | Past simple *(if simultaneous/thinking process/ statement)* |
| | ✓ | Past continuous/ past perfect/past perfect continuous |
| 2. Past continuous | ✓ | Past simple/past continuous |
| 3. Past perfect | ✓ | Past simple |
| 4. Past perfect continuous | ✓ | Past simple |

## 2. Incompatible clauses (*clauses that will not go together*)

| principal clause | | subordinate clause |
|---|---|---|
| 1. Past simple | **X** | Past simple (*if actions are different*) |
| 2. Past continuous | **X** | Past perfect/past perfect continuous |
| 3. Past perfect | **X** | Past continuous /past perfect/ past perfect continuous |
| 4. Past perfect continuous | **X** | Past continuous/past perfect/past perfect continuous |

# Exercise

**<u>1. Choose the correct form of the tense given in the bracket:</u>**

1. Prasad — (*attended, has attended*) the function yesterday.
2. Mr. Singh is — (*reads/reading*) the newspaper now.
3. When I reached the office, the phone — (*was ringing/is ringing/rang*)
4. I am sure my friend — the IELTS this time. (*passes, will pass*)
5. The crowd — soon after the meeting. (*dispersed/has dispersed*)
6. The people — before the minister came. (*had gathered/gathered*)
7. The police — the terrorist after a search yesterday. (*arrested/had arrested*)
8. Bob — (*saw/ had seen*) this movie before.
9. We have already —(*submitted/submit*) our assignments.
10. When I reached home, my mother — (*is preparing /was preparing*) dinner.

**Answers**

1. <u>Choose the correct form of the tense given in the bracket:</u>
    1. Prasad **attended** the function yesterday.
    2. Mr. Singh is **reading** the newspaper now.
    3. When I reached the office, the phone **was ringing**.
    4. I am sure my friend **will pass** the IELTS this time.
    5. The crowd **dispersed** soon after the meeting.
    6. The people **had gathered** before the minister came.
    7. The police **arrested** the terrorist after a search yesterday.
    8. Bob **had seen** this movie before.
    9. We have already **submitted** our assignments.
    10. When I reached home, my mother **was preparing** dinner.

—xxx—

# 7. Subject-verb agreement

1. The subject alone and not the nearest noun controls the verb.

    **e.g.:** i) The **man** who stole the vehicles **was** caught. *(was is used even though the nearest noun is plural.)*

    ii) The **men** who stole the vehicles **were** caught.

2. The **verb always agrees with the subject** and not with the complement.

    **e.g.:** i) Our guide **was** the stars.

    ii) The stars **were** our guide.

    iii) India's great need today **is** communal harmony, social justice and an efficient government. *(subject is singular while the complement is plural.)*

3. When two separate nouns are combined by **'and',** it takes a plural verb.

    **e.g.:** i) Rani and Razia **are** studying in the same college.

    ii) India and China **are** making rapid progress in their economy.

But if two nouns refer to the same idea or concept, they take a singular verb. Such nouns are called **parcel subjects**.

    **e.g.:** i) Slow and steady **wins** the race.

    ii) Time and tide **waits** for none.

4. When two nouns refer to the same person or thing, the article **'a/an/the'** is used only once and the **verb** is **in the singular** but if they refer to separate persons or things, the article 'a/an/the' is repeated before each noun and the **verb** is **in the plural**.

    **e.g.:** i) **The** owner and manager of the shop **is** on leave today. *(one person)*

    ii) **The** owner and **the** manager of the shop **are** on leave today. *(two persons)*

5. The following indefinite pronouns will take a **singular verb** when they start a sentence.

| | | | |
|---|---|---|---|
| **each** | **every** | **everyone** | **everybody** |
| **everything** | **anybody** | **anyone** | **anything** |
| **nobody** | **nothing** | **somcbody** | **someone** |
| **something** | **either** | **neither** | **one** |
| **no one,** etc. | | | |

| | | |
|---|---|---|
| Each + singular noun | : | Each student.....*is/was/has/verb+s......* |
| Each **of the** + plural noun | : | Each of the students....*is/was/has/verb+s.* |
| Every + singular noun | : | Every student.....*is/was/has/verb+s......* |
| Every one **of the** + plural noun | : | Everyone of the students...*is/was/has/verb+s* |

Subject-verb agreement

> After the use '**of the**' the noun is **plural.**

One student......        one **of the** students, any student ...any **of the** students
Every student...         everyone **of the** students

Every facilities **(X)**    :    Every facility/ every one of the facilities. (✓)
Each students **(X)**       :    Each student/each of the students. (✓)

> Do not use **every/each/one** with <u>always plural nouns</u>

Every staff **(X)**        :    Everyone of the staff (✓)
Every people **(X)**       :    Every person/everyone of the people. (✓)
Every children **(X)**     :    Every child/everyone of the children. (✓)
One staff **(X)**          :    One of the staff/ a member of the staff (✓)
One criteria **(X)**       :    One criterion /one of the criteria. (✓)

> Do not use **every/ each** with **<u>uncountable nouns</u>**

Every news **(X)**        :    A piece of news/ all the news (✓)
Each jewellery **(X)**    :    Each item of jewellery (✓)

eg.:    i) **Everyone** in this company *is* well paid.
       ii) **Nobody** *wants* to die early in life.
       iii) **Nothing** *has* been done to improve the quality of education in our state.

6. When we use terms such as '**either...or, neither...nor, or, not only... but also**', the verb
   is controlled by the second noun. Secondly, when there is a singular noun and a plural
   noun in a sentence, the plural noun should be placed last.
   **e.g.:**  i) **Neither** the boy **nor** his <u>parents</u> *have* come.
           ii) The management **or** the teachers *are* responsible for the low result.

7. When  we use terms such as '**as well as, with, together with, along with, besides,
   except,** etc., the verb is controlled by the  first noun.
   **e.g.:**  i) The **teacher** as well as the students **has** gone for a study-tour.
           ii) The **minister** along with his security men **has** been prevented from going
               ahead.

8. Two nouns qualified by *each* or *every*, even though connected by **and**, require a **singular**
   verb. The expression '**each and every**' also takes a singular verb.
   **e.g.:**  i) **Each man** and **each woman** present at the conference *was* given a gift.
           ii) **Every star** and **every planet** *is* a handiwork of God.
           iii) **Each** and **every participant** has performed well in this competition.

9. Collective nouns such as *family, team, committee, class, army, club, crowd, government, jury, public, mob,* etc. generally take **singular verbs.** Collective terms such as *a flock of, a herd of, a pack of, a shoal of, a bunch of, a piece of, a bar of, a loaf of, a set of,* etc. also take **singular verbs.**

> **e.g.:** i) My family **resides** in Guwahati, in Assam.
>
> ii) <u>A bunch of flowers</u> **costs** fifty rupees.
>
>     *collective term*

However, when we use plural determiners such as *some, most, a lot of,* etc. with a collective noun, the verb will be plural.

> **e.g.:** i) The audience **is** quite large.
>
> ii) Some of the audience **are** shouting.

**Special note:** <u>A group of people **are**....</u>

> **e.g.:** i) A group of people **are** standing over there.

10. The terms **mass media, press, government,** etc. are collective terms. They may take **singular/plural verbs.**

> **The** mass media **is/are**... **The** press **is/are**... The government **is/are**...Data **is/are**..

|  | mass medias**(X)** |  |
|---|---|---|
| **singular** | **plural** | **plural** |
| medium | mediums | media |

When we use the term **'mass media** or **press'** to mean the newspapers, magazines, television, etc. **'the'** has to be used and the verb can be singular or plural. When we use the term *'media'* to mean *'ways or means'*, **'the'** is not used unless it is specified.

> **e.g.:** i) **The** mass media in India **is/are** very influential.
>
> ii) Today **several mediums/media** are available for communication.

11. The noun following **'one of'** should be in **plural** but the verb is in **singular**.

| **one of the** + plural noun + singular verb |
|---|

**one of the** best students...*is/was/has/verb+s*

**e.g.:** i) **One of the** stars in the sky *is* shining brightly.

| **one of the** + **uncountable nouns (X)** |
|---|

**e.g.:** i) One of the news. **(X)**      : **a piece/ tip/bit of news**
ii) One of the scenery.**(X)**      : **a piece/ an item of scenery**

12. Nouns referring to **distance, heights, weights, time, money, measurement, etc.** are normally considered as a whole or as a single unit. Therefore they take singular verbs.

> **e.g.:** i) Ten kilometres **is** not a big distance.
>
> ii) Eight hundred rupees for this shirt **is** too much.

13. When we use relative pronouns such as, *that, which, who, what, where, whom,* etc. in between two clauses, they connect the second clause with the first clause. The subject noun that lies closest to the relative pronoun controls the verb of the second clause.

> **e.g.:** i) Give me the <u>book</u> which **is** over there.
> sub. noun
>
> ii) Give me the <u>books</u> which **are** over there.
> sub. noun
>
> iii) This is <u>a piece of scenery</u> which **is** really mesmerizing.
> sub. noun
>
> iv) These are the <u>books</u> of Prasanth which **have** been bought recently.
> sub. noun

14. If the term **'one of the'** is followed by relative pronouns such as **who, which, that, what**, etc., then **singular/plural verbs** can be used.

> **e.g.:** i) She is **one of the** women who **have/has** successfully completed her masters in psychology.
>
> ii) This is one of those books that **are/is** read by everybody.

15. When we use common determiners such as '*half, one-third, two-thirds or any fraction, majority, minority, percent, percentage, some, most, more, a lot of, lots of, all,* etc. with an uncountable noun, the verb is singular. If we use these terms with a plural noun, the verb is plural. (*with none the verb can be ..is/are: None of the children is/are* late.)

> **e.g.:** i) **Half** the **students** of this class **are** absent today.
>
> ii) **Half** the **information** you gave **is** wrong.
>
> iii) **Three-fourth** of the Indian **population lives** in rural areas.
>
> iv) **Three-fourth** of the **houses** of this town **have** been destroyed by fire.
>
> v) **A lot of** news **is** provided by various mass media.
>
> vi) **A lot of** people **have** come for the function.

**Special note: <u>Use of 'None'</u>**

| | |
|---|---|
| **None** + plural noun | : is/are, has/have... |
| **None** + uncountable noun | : is/was/has... |

> **e.g.:** i ) **None** of the children of this class **is/are** late.
>
> ii) **None** of the information you gave me **is** true.

16. If an uncountable noun is the subject of a sentence, the verb will be singular.

> **e.g.:** i) Some of the **furniture** that you bought <u>**is**</u> not up to the mark.
>
> ii) Your **advice** <u>**has**</u> been quite useful.

17. <u>A number of /the number of</u> :

The term **a number of** is followed by a plural noun and a plural verb while **the number of** is followed by **plural noun** and a **singular verb.**

| | |
|---|---|
| **A number of** | + plural noun + plural verb |
| **The number of** | + plural noun + **singular verb** |
| **A few** | + plural noun + plural verb |
| **The few** | + plural noun + plural verb |
| **A couple of** | + plural noun + plural verb |

**e.g.:**  i) **A number of** houses **have been** destroyed by the earthquake.

ii) **The number of** days in a week **is** seven.

iii) **A few** people **have** come for the meeting.

iv) **The few** students who came late for class **were** sent back home.

v) **A couple of** friends **have** come to see me today.

18. When the pronoun **'it'** is used at the beginning of a sentence, the verb is **singular**.

**e.g.:**  i) It <u>was</u> **they** who did the mischief.

ii) It <u>was</u> **these books** that I wanted.

19. When an infinitive, a gerund, a clause or phrase is the subject, the verb is in **singular**.

**e.g.:**  i) **Walking** *is* a good exercise for the body. (***gerund:*** *verb+ ING used as a noun.*)

ii) **To** err *is* human. (***infinitive***: *to + verb*)

iii) **<u>Success at any cost</u>** *is* Sham's sole aim in life. (***phrase***)

iv) **That you are an honest man** is known to all. (***clause***)

20. Sentences beginning with the introductory subject **'there'**, the number (*singular/plural*) depends on the noun that immediately follows the verb. But if *'there'* is followed by several singular nouns or a singular and a plural noun, the verb will be plural.

| |
|---|
| **There is/has** + singular noun |
| **There are/have** + plural noun |

**e.g.:**  i) There **is** a **man** who wants to speak to you.

ii) There **were** too many **candidates** for the vacant post.

iii) There **is** a lot of enchanting **scenery** here.

21. The ***titles of books, names of countries, names of buildings*** or ***hotels,*** etc. are followed by **singular verbs.**

**e.g.:**  i) The <u>United States</u> **<u>is</u>** one of the most developed countries in the world.

ii) The <u>'Tale of Two Cities'</u> written by Charles Dickens **<u>is</u>** an interesting book.

iii) <u>'Brown and Brown'</u> **<u>is</u>** one of the most expensive hotels in the town.

22. When terms such as **much, more, more than, less, little,** etc. stand as subjects, they are followed by a **singular verb.**

    **e.g.:**  i)**Much of** what he said *was* not clear.

          ii) **More than** a year *has* passed since I met my friend.

          iii) **Much of** the countryside *was* under water.

23. Adjectives such as ***good, bad, rich, poor, young, dead, healthy, sick, well-to-do, powerful,*** etc. are used with the article **'the'** to make them generic nouns (*class nouns*) standing for their whole class. The verbs after such nouns should be in **plural.**

    **e.g.:**  i) **The rich** *are* often unconcerned about the poor.

          ii) **The well-to-do** *live* in style.

24. When collective terms such as ***a pair of scissors/spectacles/trousers/shoes/gloves,*** etc. are used, it takes a **singular verb** and if **'a pair of'** is not used, the verb is **plural.**

    **e.g.:**  i) **A pair of** scissors *is* found missing from my table.

          ii) My **scissors are** missing.

25. The term **'more than one'** is followed by a singular noun and a **singular verb.**

    **e.g.:**  i) **More than one** student ***has*** scored 90% of marks.

          ii) **More than one** case ***has*** been reported.

26. The term **'a great many'** is followed by a plural noun and the verb also is in plural.

    **e.g.:**  i)    **A great many** students ***have*** committed the same mistake.

          ii)    **A great many** examples ***have*** been cited to prove the point.

27. When terms such as **'kind of /sort of/ type of'** is followed by a singular/non-count noun, the verb is singular. When these terms are followed by a plural noun, the verb is plural.

    **e.g.:**  i) This/that kind of **climate** ***does*** not suit me.

          ii) These types of **birds** ***are*** rarely seen here.

28. Numerals joined by **and /plus** show a single arithmetic unit. Hence they take a singular verb. But when numerals are treated as mere numerals, not as arithmetical expressions, they take a plural verb.

    **e.g.:**  i) Two and two **makes** four.

          ii) Five **plus** five **is** ten.

          iii) Three and thirteen **are** considered to be unlucky numbers. (*here 'three' and 'thirteen' are considered as mere numbers.*)

29. When **'all'** means **'everything'** it takes a singular verb; but when it refers to a plural noun, it takes a plural verb.

    **e.g.:**  i) **All** that glitters **is** not gold. (*here **'all'** is used in a sense of 'everything'.*)

          ii) **All** the ten students **have been** promoted. (*here 'all' is used in a plural sense.*)

30. When **'any of '** is followed by a plural subject, the verb can be singular/plural. If it is followed by an uncountable noun, it will take a singular verb.

      **e.g.:**  i) If **any of** your friends **is/are** interested, let me know.

            ii) If **any of** the **equipment is** not functioning well, please inform the hospital administrator.

31. **When a series of singular subjects is used:**

i) When a series of singular items end with **etc./so on.**, the verb is singular.

      **e.g.:**  i) Low agricultural output, rural poverty, lack of employment  opportunities, *etc.* **is** the main reason for the migration of rural people to cities.

ii) When a series of singular subjects ends with **'and',** it will take a plural verb.

      **e.g.:**  i) Low agricultural output, rural poverty *and* lack of employment opportunities **are** the main reasons for the migration of rural people to cities.

iii) When a **singular subject** ends with a series of singular items, the verb will be singular.

      **e.g.:**  i) The **cultivation** of rubber, tea, coffee, cotton, etc. **is** the major agricultural occupation of the people of India. (**subject is:** *cultivation*)

iv) When a **plural subject** ends with a series of singular items, the verb is plural.

      **e.g.:**  i) The various **elements** of nature such as temperature, rainfall, moisture, etc. greatly **affect** the cultivation of crops. (**subject is plural:** *elements; hence the verb is also plural: affect*)

# Exercise

Choose the correct verb from the bracket:

1. Tea as well as coffee (*is/are*) a refreshing drink.
2. Many a man *(has/have )been* ruined by bad friends.
3. None of the furniture *(is/are )* lost.
4. Some of the scenery (*is/are*) really mesmerizing.
5. Neither Ram nor his friends *(was/were)* present.
6. Every boy and girl *(was/were)* dressed for the occasion.
7. The mob *(has/have)* disappeared after the gathering.
8. The news *(is/are)* true.
9. Each of the winners *(was/were)* given a prize.
10. The manager and the owner of the shop *(was/were)* away.
11. Either he or you *(is/are)* wrong.
12. The captain, as well as the crew, *(was/were)* lost at sea.
13. This is one of the movies which *(have/has)* been selected for the award.
14. Two and two *(makes/make)* four.
15. The poor always *(suffers/suffer)* at the hands of the rich.
16. Some of your advice *(has/have)* been useful.
17. A lot of news *(is/are)* provided by the mass media.

18. Cycling *(is/are)* considered to be a good exercise.
19. To live without working *(is/are)* indeed shameful.
20.  A group of people (is/are) standing over there.
21. My spectacles *(is/are)* broken.
22. The United Arab Emirates *(has/have)* been making great progress in her economy.
23. The pair of gloves which I lost *(is/are)* found.
24. Mathews together with his friend *(has/have)* been arrested.
25. All except Mary *(has/have)* been promoted.

**Answers:**

| | | | | |
|---|---|---|---|---|
| 1.  is | 2.  has | 3.  is | 4.  is | 5.  were |
| 6.  was | 7.  has | 8.  is | 9.  was | 10. were |
| 11.  are | 12.  was | 13.  have | 14.  makes | 15.  suffer |
| 16.  has | 17.  is | 18.  is | 19.  is | 20.  is |
| 21.  are | 22.  has | 23.  is | 24.  has | 25.  have |

—xxx—-

## 4. English words without vowels ( A, E, I, O, U)

| | | | |
|---|---|---|---|
| cry | dry | fly | fry |
| gym | shy | sky | sty |
| sly | ply | spy | try |
| why | hymn | lymph | myrrh |
| myth | crypt | gypsy | lynch |
| nymph | pygmy | rhythm | tryst |

## 5. English words with all the vowels

| | | |
|---|---|---|
| education | automobile | evacuation |
| remuneration | equation | dialogue |
| regulation | authorize | misbehaviour |
| precarious | authentication | consequential |

# 7. Pronoun

**Pronoun:** A word that is used in the place of a noun so as to avoid its repetition is known as a pronoun.

<u>Kinds of pronoun:</u>

1. **Personal pronoun**

<table>
<tr><td>1<sup>st</sup> person</td><td>: **I**</td><td>-</td><td>**We**</td></tr>
<tr><td>2<sup>nd</sup> person</td><td>: **You**</td><td>-</td><td>**You**</td></tr>
<tr><td>3<sup>rd</sup> person</td><td>: **He, she, it**</td><td>-</td><td>**They**</td></tr>
</table>

2. **Possessive pronouns**

   mine, ours, yours, his, hers, its, theirs

3. **Reciprocal pronouns**

   each other, one another

4. **Demonstrative pronouns**

   This - that

   These - those

5. **Reflexive pronouns**

   Myself, ourselves, yourself, yourselves, himself, herself, themselves, etc.

6. **Emphatic pronouns (reflexive** *pronouns used for emphasis)*

   Myself, ourselves, yourself, yourselves, himself, herself, themselves, etc.

7. **Relative pronouns**

   Who, whom, which, where, what, that, etc.

8. **Interrogative pronouns:**

   Who, whom, whose, which, where, what, how much, how many, etc.

9. **Indefinite pronouns**

> Each, every, all,
> much, many, more, most
> little, less, least, few, fewer, fewest
> several, enough, one
> someone, somebody, something
> anyone, anybody, anything
> no, no one, nobody, none, nothing
> either, neither, etc.

Pronoun

## Important rules

1. When a sentence has 1st person, 2nd person and 3rd person together, the order of the persons should be the following in normal situations:

| **2nd person - 3rd person - 1st person** |
| --- |

### Position of different pronouns

| | |
| --- | --- |
| **2nd** person - **3rd** person | : **You** and **he, You** and **Sam** |
| **2nd** person - **1st** person | : **You** and **I, You** and **we** |
| **3rd** person - **1st** person | :**He** and **I, They** and **we** |

**e.g.:**  i) **You, he** and **I** are good friends.

ii) **You** and **Tom** have studied  in the same college.

The position of different pronouns changes in a sentence when one confesses guilt or expresses  remorse:

| **1st person - 2nd person - 3rd person** |
| --- |

**e.g.:**  i) **We, you** and **they** are to be blamed for this mischief.

ii) **I, you** and **Hari** are responsible for this great blunder.

## Different forms of personal pronoun

| Person | number | nominative | possessive | | objective | reflexive |
| --- | --- | --- | --- | --- | --- | --- |
| | | | adjective | pronoun | | |
| 1st person | singular | I | my | mine | me | myself |
| | plural | we | our | ours | us | ourselves |
| 2nd person | singular | you | your | yours | you | yourself |
| | plural | you | your | yours | you | yourselves |
| 3rd person | singular | he/she/it | her, his | hers, his | him/her/it | himself/herself |
| | | | its | its | | itself |
| | plural | they | their | theirs | them | themselves |

2. The nominative form of the pronoun (*I, we, you, he, she, they,* etc.) must be used when the pronoun acts as the **subject of a sentence**.

    **e.g.:**  i) **You** and **he** must do this job. (not *him*)

        ii) It was **they** (not *them*) who did the mischief.

        iii) It was **he** (*not him*) who struck me.

3. The objective form *(me, us, you, him/her/it)* of the pronoun should be used when the pronoun is **in the place of object** or **complement.**

    **e.g.:** i) The waiter told **us** to wait in the parlour.

        ii) The mad dog bit **him** on the leg.

        iii) They asked **me** to go in.

4. After **than** or **as,** the pronoun should be in the objective or accusative case (*me, us, you, her, him, etc.*) But if you want to use the nominative form (I, *we, you, they, etc.*), then supply the necessary verbs.

    **e.g.:** i) Sham is more intelligent **than me.**

        Sham is as intelligent **as me.**

        Sham  is more intelligent **than I am** (not *I*)

        ii) Mr. Dev speaks French better **than I do.**

5. The objective form of the pronoun is generally used after prepositions.

    **e.g.:** i) The policeman was searching **for** <u>him.</u>

        ii) Raj will speak **after** <u>*me.*</u>

        iii) The job was completed **by** <u>*us.*</u>

6. **'Between'** is a preposition and any pronoun that follows it must be in the objective form.

        between **him** and **me**

        between Sam and **them**

        between **you** and **him**

    **e.g.:** i) This prize is to be shared <u>between</u> **you** and **him.**

        ii) You can sit <u>between</u> **him** and **me.**

7. After **except** and **but** we should use the objective form of the pronoun when these terms are used as prepositions.

    **e.g.:** i) Nobody was present in the class but **me** *(not I)*

        ii) None <u>but</u> **him** saved the drowning boy.

        iii) All <u>except</u> **me** went for the show.

8. It is a serious error to use a pronoun in the same sentence when there is already a subject noun in the sentence.

    **e.g.:** i) My father, <u>he</u> is a businessman who lives in Mumbai.**(X)**

        My father is a businessman who lives in Mumbai.(✓)

9. The indefinite pronoun **'one'** should be used throughout if it is used in the beginning of a sentence.

    **e.g. :** i) **One** must know **one's** rights and duties.

        ii) **One** has to be hard-working if **one** wants to succeed in life.

10. In current English the objective form of the pronoun is used after the verb forms of 'Be' *(am/is/are/was/were,* etc.*)*

    **e.g.:**  i) Who is there? It's **me.**

          ii) Who has done this mischief? It's **us,** sir.

11. The objective form of the pronoun is used when pronouns stand alone.

    **e.g.**  i) 'Who came first?' "**Me**".

          ii) Who spoke first in the meeting? "**Him**".

12. **Reflexive pronouns** and **emphatic pronouns** have the same form: *myself, ourselves, yourself, yourselves, himself, herself, themselves,* etc. They are **reflexive pronouns** when the doer is both the subject and the object of the action expressed by the verb. It is used when the action is done to oneself.

    **e.g.:**  i) I made it **myself**.

          ii) Look at **yourself** in the mirror.

These become **emphatic pronouns** when these are used with nouns or pronouns for the sake of emphasis. Generally, these follow immediately after the noun or pronoun.

    **e.g.:**  i) I **myself** saw the thief. *(it is more emphatic than **I saw the thief**)*

          ii) He **himself** did the mischief. *(it is more emphatic than **He did the mischief**)*

13. **Emphatic pronouns** can never stand alone as subjects.

    **e.g.:**  i) He and myself went for our friend's party. **(X)**

          He and **I myself** went for our friend's party.(✓)

          ii) Myself is going to London next week. **(X)**

          **I am going** to London next week or **I myself** am going to London next week.(✓)

14. After indefinite pronouns such as **each, every, everyone, no one, neither,** etc. the **plural** form is more used nowadays, though the masculine form is often preferred.

    **e.g.:**  i) Everyone must do **their** work within the allotted time.

          ii) Each of them completed **their** project work as per the instructions of their teacher.

15. We should use a pronoun in possessive case before a gerund *(verb + ing)*

    **e.g.:** i) Mr. Williams disliked **me** asking so many questions to him. **(X)**

          Mr. Williams disliked **my** asking so many questions to him.(✓)

16. **Each other/one another:** *(known as reciprocal pronouns)*

    **Each other** is used when we speak of two persons or things only.

    **One another** is used when we speak of more than two persons or things.

    **e.g.:**  i) The two boys fought with **one another. (X)**

          The two boys fought with **each other.**(✓)

          ii) We should love **each other. (X)**

          We should love **one another.**(✓)

17. **Either/neither/anyone**

**Either** is used for choices between two items or persons.

**Neither** means *none of the two*.

**Anyone** is used  when the reference is to more than two persons.

**e.g.:**  i) **Either** of the two girls will get the prize.

ii) **Neither** of the candidates was selected for the post.

iii) Linda is more intelligent than **anyone** else in her class.

18. Use of **another/other:**

**Another, another one,  other, others,** etc. *are non-specific and can be used in a general way.*

**The other, the other one, the others, the other ones** *are specific and can be used only in situations where the item is clearly pin-pointed.*

**e.g.:**  i) Can you give me **another** book? *(any other book other than this)*

ii) This book is not at all good. Please give me **another one**.

iii) Can you give me **the other** book? *(specific)*

iv) I don't like this paper. Kindly show me **the other one**. *(specific)*

v) I don't want these books. Please give me **the other ones**. *(specific)*

vi) Some students are playing. Where are **the others?** *(specific)*

# Exercise

**1.Choose the correct form of the pronoun from the bracket:**

1. Most religious teachers advise us to love *(each other /one another)*.

2. Rani is more outgoing than *(I/ I am)*.

3.  The boy was asked to sit between Satish and *(I/me)*.

4. It was *(me/I)* who cleaned this room.

5. Talk to *(her/she)* when you have some time.

6. Isn't *(he/him)* a nice person to deal with?

7. Miss Rani is as pretty as *(I/me)*.

8. Shankar is richer than (he/he is).

9. The dog ran after *(they/them)*.

10. Mathews and *(I /me)* come from the same place.

11. All the students except *(he/him)* recited the poem.

12. There was a quarrel between Mohandas and *(they/them)*

13. The two ladies were quarrelling with *(each other/one another)*

14. Would you be kind enough to give me *(the other/other)* book?

15. *(I myself/Myself)* advised him not to drink any more.

**2. Correct the  mistakes in the  use of pronouns:**

1. Yours loving son.
2. Your's obediently.
3. I and you are expected to play the match.
4. He and you seem to be close friends.
5. I, you and he come from the same district.
6. None of the two girls have done well in the test.
7. Tom and John love one another.
8. It is I who is to be blamed for this accident.
9. Either of them will be sufficient for the time-being.
10. All men should love each other.
11. Abdul is taller than I.
12. You and me shall go there.
13. My dad took my sister and I to the movies yesterday.
14. He is certainly more cleverer than I.
15. I, you and Ram went for a movie last night.

**Answers**

**1. Choose the correct answers**

| | | | | |
|---|---|---|---|---|
| 1. one another | 2. I am | 3. me | 4. I | 5. her |
| 6. he | 7. me | 8. he is | 9. them | 10. I |
| 11. him | 12. them | 13. each other | 14. the other | 15. I myself |

**2. Correct the mistakes in the following sentences:**

1. **Your** loving son.
2. **Yours** obediently.
3. **You** and **I** are expected to play the match.
4. **You** and **he** seem to be close friends.
5. **You, he** and **I** come from the same district.
6. **Neither** of the two girls has done well in the test.
7. Tom and John love **each other**.
8. It is I who **am** to be blamed for this accident.
9. **Any of** them will be sufficient for the time-being.
10. All men should **love one another.**
11. Abdul is taller than **me** (or **I am)**
12. **You** and **I** shall go there.
13. My dad took my sister and **me** to the movies yesterday.
14. He is certainly cleverer than **I am.**
15. **You, Ram** and **I** went for a movie last night.

—xxx—-

# 8. Verb

**Verb:** A word that shows the action of the subject is known as verb.

    **e.g.:** The old man **walks** along the road.

**Main kinds of verbs:**

    i) Principal verbs *(verb which can stand by itself: eat, go, play, etc.)*

    ii) Auxiliary verbs (helping *verbs such as, must, can, may, etc.)*

## Important rules regarding the proper use of verbs

1. <u>The indirect object should be placed before the direct object.</u>

    **e.g.:**  i) The stranger asked a question to me.**(X)**

        The stranger asked **me** *(indirect)* a question. *(direct)* (✓)

        ii) The teacher told a story to her.**(X)**

        The teacher told **her** *(indirect)* a story. *(direct)* (✓)

2. Verbs of prevention such as **abstain, debar, desist, disqualify, hinder, prevent, prohibit, refrain, deviate, etc.** are always followed by **from** and are used with the gerund.

    **e.g. :** i) Praveen **abstained from** eating meat.

        ii) We **prevented** him **from coming** inside.

3. The verbs **discuss, describe, order, request, etc.** should not be used with prepositions.

    **e.g. :** i) We **discussed about** the matter in detail.**(X)**

        We *discussed* the matter in detail.(✓)

        ii) Angeline **requested for** my help.**(X)**

        Angeline *requested* my help.(✓)

<u>Correct the following sentences:</u>

    1. The stranger ordered for a cup of tea. *(ordered a cup of tea)*

    2. The teacher was describing about the incident. *(describing the incident)*

    3. The team requested for a change of the coach. *(requested a change)*

    4. The magistrate ordered for an inquiry into the incident. (ordered *an inquiry*)

    5. The committee discussed about the change of venue in detail. *(discussed the change of )*

4. The forms **built, burnt, dreamt, dwelt, knelt, learnt, leapt, smelt, spilt, etc.** are more used nowadays than their **-ed** forms *(builded, burned, dreamed, dwelled, learned, leaped, smelled, spilled, etc.)*

    **e.g.** i) The child **burnt** its finger.

        ii) The maid **spilt** the milk.

5. When one verb follows another in the same sentence the second verb should be either in **ING** form or **infinitive** *(to+ verb)*.

    **e.g.:**  i) John **denied stealing** the jewels from the house.

          ii) Bobby **decided to meet** his friend in the evening.

6. The use of inappropriate verbs is a common error. It lowers the quality of one's English.

    **e.g.:**  i) Try to hear the advice of your elders and teachers.**(X)**

          Try to **listen** to the advice of your elders and teachers.(✓)

          ii) Kindly find this word in the dictionary.**(X)**

          Kindly **look up** this word in the dictionary.(✓)

          iii) I sleep at 10. 30 p.m. **(X)**

           I **go to bed** at 10.30 p.m.(✓)

          iv) We spoke about the weather.**(X)**

           We **talked** about the weather.(✓)

          v) Our college team made two goals. **(X)**

           Our college team **scored** two goals.(✓)

7. The following verbs are generally followed by the **infinitive** *(to)*

| | | | |
|---|---|---|---|
| learn *to* | expect *to* | hope *to* | decide *to* |
| demand *to* | desire *to* | attempt *to* | fail *to* |
| forget *to* | hesitate *to* | claim *to* | intend *to* |
| agree *to* | need *to* | offer *to* | plan *to* |
| prepare *to* | pretend *to* | refuse *to* | seem *to* |
| strive *to* | tend *to* | want *to* | wish *to,* etc. |

<u>Examples:</u>

1. Learned **to** : Mary **learned to** swim when she was quite young.
2. *Expect* **to** : We **expect to** get a high band score in the IELTS test held last week.
3. *Hope* **to** : I **hope to** succeed in my first attempt.
4. *Agreed* **to** : We have **agreed to** meet at 5.00 p.m. this evening.
5. *Attempted* **to** : My friend **attempted to** take the OET without any preparation.
6. *Claim* **to** : The stranger **claims to** speak several foreign languages.
7. *Demanded* **to** : The dismissed employee **demanded to** know the reason for his dismissal.
8. *Decided* **to** : The committee has **decided to** postpone the match.
9. *Desire* **to** : The young man **desired to** speak to the director of the company.
10. *Fail* **to** : The candidate **failed to** meet the basic requirements of the post advertised.

8. The following verbs must be followed by the **<u>gerund</u>**. (*ING form*)

| admit | enjoy | avoid | can't help | consider |
|---|---|---|---|---|
| delay | interested | appreciate | finish | mind |
| postpone | practise | quit | recall | miss |
| report | resent | resist | resume | forgive |
| dislike | give up | put off | escape | excuse |
| risk | involve | fancy | mention | suggest |
| feel like | understand | imagine | detest | can't stand, etc. |

<u>Examples:</u>

1. *Admitted*    : The beggar <u>**admitted stealing**</u> the jewellery from my house.
2. *Enjoyed*    : We <u>**enjoyed seeing**</u> them again after so many years.
3. *Delay*    : The <u>**delay in executing**</u> the project has cost the company dearly.
4. *Avoid*    : Try to **<u>avoid standing</u>** in long queues.
5. *Denied*    : The man <u>**denied having**</u> entered the office forcefully.
6. *Mind*    : Would you <u>**mind not smoking**</u> here?
7. *Missed*    : The player **missed** hitting the ball.
8. *Recalled*    : I <u>**recalled seeing**</u> my friend after a long time.

9. After the following verbs either the **ING** form or the **infinitive** form can be used.

| start | hate | begin | continue | advise |
|---|---|---|---|---|
| forbid | hear | prefer | see | go on |
| love | remember | allow | forget | intend |
| propose | stop  go | like | regret, etc. | |

**Examples:**

1. Start    : Elizabeth **started to read** the lesson aloud *OR* Elizabeth **started reading** the lesson aloud.
2. Hate    : Tim **hates to walk** to school *OR* Tim **hates walking** to school.
3. Begin    : Joan **begins to study** for the weekly test *OR* Joan **begins studying** for the weekly test.

# Exercise

**Correct the mistakes in the following sentences:**

1. My friend, Mr. Anand, talks good English.
2. Mr. Sam tells that he will go away from India soon.
3. Please try to hear the advise of your elders.
4. Would you mind seeing my certificates?

5. I said to my friend about this matter.

6. Can you open this knot?

7. I would love to see you.

8. I am feeling tired this morning.

9. My father lay himself down in bed.

10. Tired and weary Andrews laid down on the bed.

11. Who hanged the bell here?

12. The murderer was hung by the court.

13. The bird has fled away.

14. Will you take a cigarette?

15. I hope it will take a week.

16. Miss Linda sung a patriotic song.

17. Mrs Panikar, our newly elected M.L.A, gave a speech.

18. The injured person was describing about the accident.

19. The police officer asked a question to the bystander.

20. I expect to succeed in the test in the first attempt itself.

**Answers:**

1. My friend, Mr. Anand, **speaks** good English.

2. Mr. Sam **says** that he will go away from India soon.

3. Please try **to listen** to the advice of your elders.

4. Would you mind **looking** at my certificates?

5. I **spoke** to my friend about this matter.

6. Can you **untie** this knot?

7. I would **like** to see you.

8. I **feel** tired this morning.

9. My father **laid** himself down in bed.

10. Tired and weary Andrews **lay** down on the bed.

11. Who **hung** the bell here?

12. The murderer was **hanged** by the court.

13. The bird has **flown** away.

14. Will you **have** a cigarette?

15. I **expect** it will take a week.

16. Miss Linda **sang** a patriotic song. *(or Miss Linda has sung a patriotic song)*

17. Mrs Panikar, our newly elected M.L.A, **made/delivered** a speech.

18. The injured person was describing the accident.

19. The police officer asked **the bystander** a question.

20. I **hope** to succeed in the test in the first attempt itself.

—xxx——

# 9. Preposition

**Preposition:** Preposition is a word placed before a noun or a pronoun to show time, place, cause, purpose, etc.

    **e.g.:** The students are taking the test **in** the hall.

<u>Kinds of prepositions</u>

## 1. Simple prepositions

> at, by, for, from, in, of, off, on, out, through, till, to, up, with, since, over, under, down, after, against, before, etc.

**2. Compound prepositions:** Prepositions which are formed by prefixing a preposition to a noun, adjective or an adverb are known as compound prepositions.

> about, above, across, along, amidst, among, amongst, around, behind, below, beneath, beside, between, beyond, inside, outside, underneath, within, without, up to, until, into, etc.

3. **Participial prepositions:** Present participles of verbs used as prepositions are known as participial prepositions:

| | | |
|---|---|---|
| Notwithstanding | considering | concerning |
| barring | pending | regarding |
| following | including | excluding |
| touching | during | respecting |
| permitting, etc. | | |

i) **Notwithstanding** (means *in spite of*)

    <u>Notwithstanding</u> your criticism I have decided to continue with my work.

ii) **Considering** (means *taking into account*)

    <u>Considering</u> your low economic condition, we shall give you fee concession for this year.

iii) **Concerning** (means *about*)

    <u>Concerning</u> your request for leave, I must say that the matter is still under consideration.

iv) **Barring** (means *except*)

    <u>Barring</u> a few stray incidents of violence, the hartal, on the whole, was peaceful.

**v) Pending** (means *until something happens*)

Sham was released on bail <u>pending</u> further inquiries.

**vi) Regarding** (means *about*)

<u>Regarding</u> the issue of reservation, the government has not made up its mind.

**vii) Following** (means *on the basis of*)

<u>Following</u> your orders, I have completed the job.

**viii) Including**

<u>Including</u> the irrelevant points in the report would be unnecessary.

**ix) Excluding**

<u>Excluding</u> Tom, everyone was given a prize each.

**x) Touching** *(means **with regard**)*

Touching the issue of dowry, the speaker spoke extensively on the harmful effects of dowry.

**xi) During**

<u>During</u> the Onam festival in Kerala, there is a marked increase in the flow of foreign tourists to the state.

**xii) Respecting***(means **on the basis of, giving due respect**)*

<u>Respecting</u> your view, we have agreed to adopt a new resolution in the conference.

**xiii) Permitting***(means **allowing**)*

Weather <u>permitting,</u> we shall go for an outing today.

## **Use of certain important prepositions**

1. **At, in, on**

<u>with regard to place</u>

<u>At</u> is used with *villages and small towns.*

<u>In</u> is used with big *towns, districts, states and countries.*

<u>On</u> is used with the *surface of an object.*

**e.g.:**   i) I was born **at** Coimbatore in Tamil Nadu.

ii) My elder brother lives **in** Mumbai. (*not at Mumbai*)

iii) The new books which I bought yesterday are lying **on** the table.

<u>with regard to time</u>

<u>At</u> indicates a *definite point of time or clock time.*

<u>In</u> is used with *months, weeks and years.*

<u>On</u> is used with *days and dates.*

**e.g.:**   i) The much-awaited match began **at** 5.00 p.m.

ii) Our school begins **at** 8.00 a.m.

iii) I was born **in** March1962.

iv) My friend goes to temple **on** Tuesdays.

## 2. By, with

**By** is used with the agent or doer of an action.

**With** is used with the instrument used to perform an action.

**e.g.:**  i) The boy was beaten **by** the teacher.

ii) The boy was beaten **with** a stick.

## 3. Between, among

**Between** is used with regard to two persons or things.

**Among** is used when there are more than two persons or things.

**e.g.:**  i) The property was divided **between** the two brothers.

ii) The sweets were distributed **among** the children.

## 4. Beside, besides

**Beside** means *'by the side of'*

**Besides** means' *in addition to'*

**e.g.:**  i) The beggar was sitting **beside** the road.

ii) We need clean environment besides air, food, and water.

## 5. In, within

<u>With regard to time</u>

**In** is used for the end of a period.

**Within** means before the end of the specified period.

**e.g.:**  i) I shall return **in** a month. *(after a month)*

ii) I shall return **within** a month. *(before the end of  a month)*

## 6. Since, for

**Since** stands for a particular point of time and shows the starting point of a period.

**For** is used with a general period of time.

**e.g.:**  i) I have been ill **since** Monday. *(specific time)*

ii) I have been ill **for** three days.

## 7. Till, by

<u>With regard to time</u>

**Till** means up to that time or not earlier than.

**By** means not later than.

**e.g.:**  i) I shall stay here **till** Sunday.

ii) I shall leave this place **by** Monday.

## 8. On, upon

**On** is used for things at rest.

**Upon** is used for things in motion.

**e.g.:**  i) The shepherd was sitting on a rock.

ii) The cat pounced upon the rat.

## 9. In, into

**In** indicates a condition of being inside something.

**Into** is used to show a movement to the interior of something.

**e.g.:** i) The milk is **in** the jug.

ii) The little boy fell **into** the well while playing.

## 10. About

**About** is used in the following situations:

i) 'in connection with'

**e.g.:** The teacher was speaking **about** the basic rules of English grammar.

ii) to speak about the approximate time, etc.

**e.g.:** You are requested to be here at **about** 10.00 a.m. tomorrow.

## 11. Above, over

**Above** is used in the following situations:

i) a position higher than something.

**e.g.:** My clothes are hanging above my bed.

ii) higher in rank, position etc.

**e.g.:** A major is above a captain.

iii) greater in weight or value.

**e.g.:** The temperature is above $45^0$ C today.

iv) beyond the reach of something.

**e.g.:** Maria is above such petty thinking.

**Over** is used in the following situations:

i) higher than and not in contact with the surface.

**e.g.:** The fan over the bed is not functioning well.

ii) more than

**e.g.:** This building is over 100 years old.

iii) period of time.

**e.g.:** Let us talk about the issue over a cup of tea.

## 12. Under

**Under** is used in the following situations:

i) below something.

**e.g.:** The poor beggar was sitting under a tree.

ii) below in rank or position.

**e.g.:** A captain is below a major in rank.

iii) to speak of lower age.

**e.g.:** Driving licence is not given to people below the age of eighteen years.

iv) state or condition.

**e.g.:** My car is under repair.

## 13. But, but for

**But** when used as a preposition means *'except'*

**e.g.:** None **but** me passed the test this time.

**But** indicating contrast is a conjunction.

**e.g.:** Mahesh is quite intelligent **but** lazy.

**But for** means '*without or except*'

  **e.g.:** But for your tips, I would have failed the test.

  *(if you had not given the tips, I would have failed the test)*

14. **Speaking of time**

  Use **'by'** to speak about time to someone.

  What is the time **by** your watch?(Not **on** *your watch*)

  It is ten o'clock **by** my match.

15. **On the right/ in the right**

  **On the right** means on the right-hand side of something.

   **e.g.:** Kindly sit **on the right** of Jayan.

  **In the right** means correct.

   **e.g.:** I was **in the right** in opposing your decision to join politics.

16. **In demand/on demand**

  **In demand** means in quest, highly demanded by people.

   **e.g.:** Gold is always **in demand**.

  **On demand** means as and when one demands it.

   **e.g.:** I shall give back your money **on demand**.

17. **On the north/in the north/to the north:**

  **On the north** refers to being on the border.

   **e.g.:** The Himalayas lies **on the north** of India.

  **In the north** means inside the country, within.

   **e.g.:** Uttar Pradesh lies **in the north** of India.

  **To the north** means being outside.

   **e.g.:** Tibet is **to the north** of India.

18. **At play/in play**

  **At play** means in the act of playing.

   **e.g.:** The students are **at play** now.

  **In play** means not seriously or jokingly.

   **c.g.:** I said it **in play**; do not take it seriously.

19. **In a week/within a week**

  **In a week** means at the end of a week.

   **e.g.:** Mahesh will return to the hostel **in a week**.

  **Within a week** means before the end of a week.

   **e.g.:** Jim will complete the assignment **within a week**.

20. **By foot/on foot**

  The correct term that is to be used is 'on foot'.

   **e.g.:** I came to the railway station **on foot**.

21. **On the street/in the street**

> **On the street** means located somewhere along the length of a street, usually on either side of it.
>
> **e.g.:** My uncle has a computer hardware shop **on Nehru Street** in the town.
>
> **In the street** means located between the edges of the street or the area that constitutes the road.
>
> **e.g.:** I found a lot of children playing **in the street**.
>
> When exact address of a person or a building is given, use the preposition **'at'** .
>
> **e.g.:** One of my sisters lives **at** Gandhi Street in Guwahati.

22. **Prefer to**

> The term **prefer** or **preferable** always takes the preposition **'to'**
>
> **e.g.:**  i) I prefer coffee **to** tea.
>
> ii) Death is **preferable to** cowardice.

## Some important rules regarding the use of prepositions

1. Sentences normally should **not begin with prepositions**. But a sentence may begin with a linking term or a modifier which has a preposition. There should be a comma after such words or terms.

> **e.g.:**  i) **To** meet a doctor I went to the town. **(X)**
>
> I went to the town to meet a doctor.(✓ )
>
> ii) **In my view**, India is witnessing great social changes due to globalization.
>
> *Linking term*

2. Verbs immediately after prepositions should be in the **ING** form except in the case of **but** and **except.**

> **e.g.:**  i) The crowd prevented the police **from moving** ahead.
>
> ii) Mohan does nothing **but/except** watch movies on TV.

3. The words **'discuss, order, request, describe, enter, marry, lack, resemble, approach'**, etc. are not normally followed by prepositions but by direct objects.

> **e.g.:**  i) We discussed about the plan in detail.**(X)**
>
> We **discussed** the plans in detail.(✓ )
>
> ii) The stranger ordered for a cup of tea.**(X)**
>
> The stranger **ordered** a cup of tea. (✓ )

4. Prepositions are not used before a number of expressions of time such as *'next, last, this, but, one, every, each, some, all'* etc.

> **e.g.:**  i) You can contact me on next week.**(X)**
>
> You can contact me **next** week.(✓ )
>
> ii) We have a special programme on every Sunday.**(X)**
>
> We have a special programme **every** Sunday.(✓ )

5. Generally, a preposition is not placed before a question word in an interrogative sentence. It is usually placed at the end of such sentences.

    **e.g.:**  i) For whom are you looking? **(X)**

          Whom are you looking **for**?(✓)

        ii) From where did you get it? **(X)**

          Where did you get it **from**?(✓)

6. A preposition is not generally placed before a relative pronoun. It is usually placed after the relative pronoun.

    **e.g.:**  i) The house <u>in</u> which my uncle lives is quite big.**(X)**

          The house where my uncle lives <u>**in**</u> is quite big.(✓)

        ii) The people <u>to</u> whom I am talking are total strangers. **(X)**

          The people I am talking <u>**to**</u> are total strangers.(✓)

7. When two or more words require the same preposition, only one is used and the rest are omitted. But when different prepositions are used, no preposition is omitted.

    **E.g.:**  i) Miss Jaya is desirous <u>of</u> and confident <u>of</u> success.**(X)**

          Miss Jaya is desirous and confident of success.(✓)

        ii) Good citizens prevent theft **of** and damage <u>**to**</u> national property.

8. Do not use **compare to/with, comparing to/with,** etc. Instead, use **compared to** or **compared with. 'Compared to'** highlights a similarity between two things. **'Compared with'** does the opposite: it contrasts them.

    **e.g.:**  i) India's economic power is often **compared with** that of China.

        ii) My character is **often compared to** that of my elder brother.

# Exercise

**1. <u>Choose the correct prepositions from the given choice:</u>**

1. Raju has a passion ——computer games.

    a) to               b) for

    c) in               d) with

2. Mr. Johnson deals —— textiles.

    a) in               b) with

    c) for             d) about

3. My father is devoted ——— religion.

    a) to               b) for

    c) with           d) in

4. Here is the book that you asked ——.

    a) to               b) for

    c) with           c) on

5. My father has retired —— business.
      a) from                        b) in
      c) to                          d) over

6. Sham killed two birds — one shot.
      a) with                       b) by
      c) over                     d) for

7. Man is liable ——err.
      a) with                       b) to
      c) against                d) at

8. Your conduct calls —— an explanation.
      a) for                        b) to
      c) in                        d) with

9. The clerk tampered—— the company records.
      a) in                        b) with
      c) against                d) over

10. I shall do it ——— pleasure.
      a) with                       b) in
      c) for                       d)  on

11. I shall soon tide ——— this difficulty.
      a) in                        b) by
      c) over                     d) with

12. Lucy sat——— the door of her cottage.
      a) at                        b) by
      c) in                        d) beside

13. In India most people prefer tea——coffee.
      a) with                       b) against
      c) to                        d) for

14. He stared ——— me in the face on hearing the news.
      a) in                        a) at
      c) to                        d) against

15. I fail to agree ——— you on this point.
      a) with                       b) for
      c) to                        d) from

**2. Correct the following sentences with proper prepositions:**

1. My friend insisted to leave us in the night itself.

2. I shall expect you at about 3.00 p.m. this evening

3. Mahesh caught Mohan in the neck.

4. It has been raining from Monday.

5. Shankar's face resembles to his father.

6. You are kindly requested to compare your answers to mine.

7. The stranger ordered for a cup of tea from the wayside teashop.

8. The Chennai Mail is running in full swing these days.

9. I am interested about the matter that you spoke about.

10. Can you give me a good pen to write?

**Answers**

**1. Choose the correct prepositions from the given choice:**

|  |  |  |  |  |
|---|---|---|---|---|
| 1. for | 2. in | 3. to | 4. for | 5. from |
| 6. with | 7. to | 8. for | 9. with | 10. with |
| 11. over | 12. by | 13. to | 14. at | 15. with |

**2. Correct the following sentences with proper prepositions:**

1. My friend insisted **on** leaving us in the night itself.

2. I shall expect you **about** 3.00 p.m. this evening.

3. Mahesh caught Mohan **by the** neck.

4. It has been raining **since** Monday.

5. Shankar's face **resembles** his father.

6. You are kindly requested to compare your answers **with** mine.

7. The stranger **ordered a cup of tea** from the wayside tea-shop.

8. The Chennai Mail is running **at** full swing these days.

9. I am interested **in** the matter that you spoke about.

10. Can you give me a good pen to write **with**?

—xxx—-

## **Useful data**

## **6. Phobias**(*extreme or irrational fear or dislike*)

| | | |
|---|---|---|
| 1. Acrophobia | : | fear of heights or high places |
| 2. Agoraphobia | : | fear of open or public places |
| 3. Claustrophobia | : | fear of confined or closed places |
| 4. Gynophobia | : | fear or deep dislike for women |
| 5. Necrophobia | : | fear of death or dead bodies |
| 6. Nyctophobia | : | fear of night or darkness |
| 7. Thalassophobia | : | fear of sea |
| 8. Triskaidekaphobia | : | fear regarding the number 13 |
| 9. Xenophobia | : | fear or dislike of strangers or foreigners |

# 10. Adjective

**Adjective:** An adjective is a word that is used to add something to the meaning of a noun or a pronoun.

> **e.g.** This flower is **beautiful.**

## Use of adjectives:

> i) Attributive use
> ii) Predicative use

i) **Attributive use:** Adjectives are used attributively when they are placed *before the noun* which they qualify.

> **e.g.:**  i) I was enchanted by the **mesmerizing** scenery of Munnar.
> ii) Amitabh Bachchan is an **incredible** actor

ii) **Predicative use:** Adjectives are used predicatively when they are placed *after the verb.*

> **e.g.:**  i) Maria's dance performance has been **wonderful.**
> ii) The new parliament building in New Delhi appears to be **charming.**

## Kinds of adjectives

1. Proper adjectives *(Indian, British, Vedic, Islamic, etc.)*
2. Adjective of quality *(beautiful, nice, good, etc.)*
3. Adjective of quantity *(little, enough, some, much, whole, etc.)*
4. Adjective of number *(first, second, few, all, etc.)*
5. Distributive adjective *(each, every, either, neither, etc.)*
6. Demonstrative adjective *(that, this, these, those, such, same, etc.)*
7. Interrogative adjective *(which, whose, what, etc.)*
8. Emphasizing adjectives *(own, very, etc.)*

## Comparison of adjectives

**i. Positive degree:** The positive degree shows an adjective in its simple form. It is used to denote the mere existence of some quality. It is *used when no comparison is made.*

> **e.g.:** The film 'Titanic' is a **mind-blowing movie.**

**ii. Comparative degree:** The comparative degree shows a higher degree of the quality than the positive, and is ***used when two things are compared.***

> **e.g.** The rose is **more** beautiful **than** the lotus flower.

**iii. Superlative degree:** The superlative degree of an adjective shows the highest degree of the quality and is used ***when more than two things are compared.***

> **e.g.:** New York is considered to be the **costliest** city in the world in 2023.

Adjective

<u>Rules for the formation of comparative and superlative degrees using **'er', 'est'/more, most:**</u>

    i) If an adjective has only **<u>one syllable</u>** (*A word or part of a word which consists of a vowel sound is known as a syllable*) **'er'** and **'est'** is used.

        **e.g.:** old, old**er**, old**est**

    ii) Adjectives of **<u>two</u> or <u>more syllables</u>** generally take **more** and **most.**

        **e.g.:** Important, more important, most important

    iii) An adjective with **<u>two syllables</u>** can take either **'er'/'est'** or **more/most.**

        **e.g.:** remote, remoter, remotest

            remote, more remote, most remote

    iv) Generally, adjectives that end in **'er', 'y',** or **'ly'** take **'er'** and **'est'** to form degrees of comparison.

        **e.g.:** clever, cleverer, cleverest

* In general, the structure with **more/ most** is becoming more common with two-syllable adjectives.

* Long adjectives generally take **more/most** to form degrees of comparison.

| **Positive** | **comparative** | **superlative** |
| --- | --- | --- |
| *kind* | more kind | most kind |
|  | less kind | least kind |
| *difficult* | more difficult | most difficult |
|  | less difficult | least difficult |
| *ordinary* | more ordinary | most ordinary |
|  | less ordinary | least ordinary |
| *beautiful* | more beautiful | most beautiful |
|  | less beautiful | least beautiful |
| *useful* | more useful | most useful |
|  | less useful | least useful |
| *cautious* | more cautious | most cautious |
|  | less cautious | least cautious |

## **Irregular comparisons** (*very important*)

| Positive | comparative | superlative |
|---|---|---|
| *Good* | better | best |
| *Well* | better | best |
| *Bad, evil, ill* | worse | worst |
| *Many* | more | most |
| *Much* | more | most |
| *Little* | less, lesser | least |
| few | fewer | fewest |
| *Far* | farther/further | farthest/furthest |
| *Late* | later, latter | latest, last |
| *Near* | nearer | nearest, next |
| *Old* | older, elder | oldest, eldest |

## **Some important rules**

1. The words **superior, inferior, senior, junior, prior, anterior** and **posterior** take **'to'** instead of *than* in comparative degree.

    **e.g. :** i. Prakash is **senior to** me in age and service.

        ii. The products of your company are much **inferior to** that of our company.

2. The following adjectives *expressing shape or time or the highest or lowest degree of some quality etc. cannot be compared.*

> **ideal, unique, empty, round, square, earthen, golden, daily, annual, perfect, extreme, eternal, chief, almighty, infinite, complete, supreme, unique, universal, dead, full, etc.**

    **e.g. :** i) This is the most unique monument I have ever seen in my life.**(X)**

        This is the **unique** monument I have ever seen in my life.(✓)

        ii) This room is more empty than the other room.**(X)**

        This room is **quite empty** in comparison to the other room.(✓)

3. Double comparatives and superlatives should be avoided.

    **e.g.:** i) Raj is the **most smartest** student I have ever seen.**(X)**

        Raj is the **smartest** student I have ever seen.(✓)

        ii) The skylark is supposed to be **more happier** than any other bird.**(X)**

        The skylark is supposed to be **happier than** any other bird.(✓)

4. The following nouns in English have lost their comparative meanings. Therefore, they cannot be used as comparatives. They are now used as  positive adjectives. These words *are neither followed by 'than' or 'to'.*

> **Former, latter, elder, hinder, upper, neither, outer, utter,  interior, exterior, ulterior, major, minor,** etc.

    **e.g.:**  i) I failed to understand my friend's **ulterior** motive in the project.

          ii) The Kashmir problem is a **major** irritant between India and Pakistan.

5. Whenever comparative terms/adjectives are used, the comparative sign **'than'** must be used.

    **E.g.:**  i) The figure in this graph is quite higher. **(X)**

          The figure in this graph is quite **higher than** those in the other graph.(✓)

          ii) The figure shows that there was **more** spending during this period. **(X)**

          The figure shows that there was **more** spending during this period **than** in the former period.(✓)

6. Do not use the comparative degree after the words **fairly** and **comparatively** which in themselves contain the idea of comparison.

    **e.g.:**  i)  I am *comparatively better* today.**(X)**

          I am comparatively **well** today.(✓)

          ii) The patient is *fairly better* today.**(X)**

          The patient is **better** today.(✓)

7. Illogical comparisons should be avoided. An illogical comparison is one in which two unlike entities have been compared. Make sure that what is compared is of the same type or category.

    **e.g.:**  i) The salary of a professor is higher than a lecturer.**(X)**

          (**because** *here the salary is compared to a lecturer*)

          The salary of a professor is <u>higher than</u> **that of** a lecturer.(✓)

          ii) The functioning of a mobile phone is better than a land phone. **(X)**

          The functioning of a mobile phone is <u>better than</u> **that of** a land phone.(✓)

8. It is possible to compare two items without using **'than'**. In this case, the expression **'of the two'** must be used.

    **e.g.:**  i) Sarita is the <u>taller</u> **of the two** girls.

          ii) **Of the two** books, the book with the red cover is <u>costlier.</u>

9. The term **'preferable'** should be used with **'to'** instead of **'than'**. Secondly, it should not be used with **'more'**.

    **e.g.:**  i) Gold is **more preferable** to silver. **(X)**

          Gold is **preferable** to silver.(✓)

10. Comparative degree is used when two persons or two groups of persons or things are compared. If we compare or choose from among more than two, the superlative must be used.

> **e.g.:** i) Raj is the **wisest** of the two boys.**(X)**
> Raj is the **wiser** of the two boys.(✓)
> ii) Miss Rani is the **fairest** among **those two** girls.**(X)**
> Miss Rani is the **fairest** among those girls.(✓)

11. Adjectives of different degrees cannot be joined by **'and'**.

> **e.g.** i) Mumbai is the <u>most developed</u> and a <u>fast-growing</u> city in India.**(X)**
> Mumbai is **the most developed** and **the fastest growing** city in India.(✓)
> ii) Nursing is <u>a noble</u> and the *most wanted* profession for most young girls in our country.**(X)**
> Nursing is **the noblest** and **the most wanted** profession for most young girls in our country.(✓)

12. Comparatives can be made **more emphatic** by using the following **intensifiers:**

> | **very, very much, by far, so much, even, still, yet, rather, somewhat, a little, a bit, a lot, a good deal of,** etc. |
> | --- |

> **e.g.:** i) London is **by far** the most expensive city in the world.
> ii) The patient is **much** better today.

13. When adjectives such as *'young, rich, poor, well-to-do, old, deaf, sick, healthy, etc.* are used with the article **'the'**, they become class nouns standing for the whole class. Such nouns are considered plural.

> **e.g.:** i) **The rich** hardly **care** for the poor.
> ii) **The sick** always **envy** the healthy.

14. Sometimes double comparatives can be used to emphasize a particular aspect or adjective.

**comparative clause+ comparative clause**

> **e.g.:** i) The **sooner** you take your medicines, the **better** you will feel.
> ii) The **higher** we climbed, the **cooler** we felt.
> iii) The **harder** you work, the **better** your result will be.
> iv) The **sooner** you leave, the **earlier** you will arrive at your destination.

> | **The more  clause+ the comparative clause** <br> **The more clause + the more clause** |
> | --- |

> **e.g.:** i) The **more** we went up, the **better** view we got.
> ii) The **more** we listened, the **more** we understood.
> iii) The **more** you waste your time, the **greater** your losses will be.
> iv) The **more** you earn, the **more** you spend.

15. When two qualities in the same person are compared, **more** is used instead of **'er'** to form comparatives.

      **e.g.:**  i) Linda is **more reserved** than outgoing.

            ii) Raj is **more silly** than wicked.

16. When a numerical noun is placed before another noun, it acts as an adjective. Such adjectives should be in singular.

      **e.g.:**  i) We took a <u>five-week tour</u> of the country.

                   **adj**     **noun**

            ii) This is a <u>twenty-dollar shirt</u> which I bought from the shopping mall.

                   **adj**     **noun**

17. The following order should be followed while using adjectives:

A. **Description before classification:** Words which describe should come before words which *classify.*

| description | classification | noun |
|---|---|---|
| long | water | bottle |
| red | playing | shoes |

      **e.g.:**  i) My friend bought a <u>**leather blue belt**</u> from the supermarket.**(X)**

            My friend bought **a blue leather belt** from the supermarket.(✓)

B. **Opinions before classification:** Words which express opinions, attitudes, views, etc. should be placed before description.

| opinion | description | noun |
|---|---|---|
| perfect | white | circle |
| enchanting | green | scenery |

      **e.g.:**  i) This is a <u>**set of beautiful furniture**</u>.**(X)**

            ii) This is a <u>beautiful set of furniture</u>. (✓)

C. **Order of descriptive words:** Words of description should be arranged in the following order: *size, age, shape, colour,* etc.

| size | age | shape | colour | noun |
|---|---|---|---|---|
| small | new | round | red | ball |
| big | old | square | blue-coloured | building |

**e.g.:** i) The **blue-shaped small diamond** is quite expensive.**(X)**

The **small-blue-shaped diamond** is quite expensive.(✓)

18. **Improper use of adjectives**:

Many times adjectives are improperly used in a sentence.

**e.g.:** i) My friend's handwriting is **poor.** ( *improper use of adjective*)

My friend's handwriting is **illegible/ not readable.**

ii) I could not come for duty because of bad weather.

I could not come for duty because of **inclement weather.**

## 19. Some important adjectives

| | |
|---|---|
| 1. Some, any | 11. All, whole |
| 2. Older, oldest, elder, eldest | 12. Fewer, less |
| 3. Few, a few, the few | 13. Later, latter, latest, last |
| 4. Little, a little, the little | 14. Either, neither |
| 5. Much, very | 15. Each, every |
| 6. Farther, further | 16. Few, little |
| 7. Former, latter | 17. Both |
| 8. First, foremost | 18. Preferable |
| 9. Much, many, many a | |
| 10. Near, nearest | |

1. **Some, any**

**Some** is used with affirmative words and can be used for both count nouns and non-count nouns.

> **Some + non-count nouns** is followed by a **singular verb.**

**e.g.:** i) **Some** of the tables in this classroom **are** broken.

ii) **Some** of his advice is not worth remembering.

**Any** is used in negative or interrogative sentence.

**e.g.:** i) Maria hasn't bought **any** new dress this month.

ii) Have you got **any** sweets with you?

**Any** is used in a **negative sense** when it is used with semi-negative terms such as *hardly, barely, scarcely, seldom*, etc.

**e.g.:** i) Mohan has **hardly any** good shirts.

ii) Hari **seldom** does **any** work properly.

**Any** is also used after *if* or *whether* and expressions of doubt.

**e.g.:** i) Call me if you need **any** help.

ii) I doubt **whether any** of you can do this task.

iii) I don't think that this will do **any** good to him. *(doubt)*

2. **Older, oldest, elder, eldest**

**Older and oldest** *may be said either of persons* or *of things.*

**Elder and eldest** *apply to persons only,* and are besides, strictly speaking, confined to members of the same family. The term **'elder/eldest'** is used to talk about order of birth than age while **'older than'** is generally used to indicate age.

      **e. g :** i)Where is your **eldest** son/ daughter? *( not oldest )*

           ii) John is **older** than Tom.

The terms **'elder than/ elder to'** should not be used. But we can use **older than**.

      **e.g.:** i) Paul is **elder than /elder to** his two brothers by five years.**(X)**

          Paul is the **elder of** the two brothers by five years.(✓ )

          *or* Paul is **older than** his brother by five years.

3. **Few, a few, the few,**

**Few** has a negative meaning - almost none, hardly any.

      **e.g.:** i) Christeena has **few** friends in her class.

          ii) The captain said that only few players played well this time.

**A few** means some.

      **e.g.** i) I have **a few** good books in my library.

          ii) Would you be kind enough to give me **a few** more biscuits?

**The few** means all that there are.

      **e.g.** i) **The few** friends I had in the town left for higher studies abroad last week.

          ii) **The few** students who failed in the examination discontinued their studies.

4. **Little, a little, the little**

**Little** has a negative meaning, meaning almost nothing, not much.

      **e.g.** i) There is <u>little</u> hope of his recovery.

          ii) I have only <u>little</u> time to spare. So, be quick and tell me what I should do.

**A little** means a small quantity, some though not much.

      **e.g.:** i) I am <u>a little</u> tired after the heavy work.

          ii) <u>A little</u> tact would have saved the unpleasant situation.

**The little** means whatever there is.

      **e.g.:** i) <u>The little</u> money I had in my pocket has been pick-pocketed.

5. **Very, much**

**Very** is generally followed by a positive adjective or adverb.

**Much** is generally used with a comparative.

      **e.g.:** i) The climate of Munnar in summer is **very** pleasant.

          ii) The patient feels **much** better today.

**6.Farther, further**

**Farther** is used to speak of distance.

**Further** means something additional. It can also be used to speak of distance.

e.g.: i) Mumbai is **farther** from Kochi than Chennai.

ii) Let us begin our class without **further** delay.

iii) My house is located a little **further** away from here.

**7. Former, latter**

**Former** refers to the *'first of the two people or things mentioned already'*.

**Latter** means *the second of the two people or things mentioned.*

e.g.: i) The city of Bangalore is developing faster than Chennai. The **former** is more of a planned city than the **latter**.

**8.First, foremost**

**First** refers to first in order.

**Foremost** means main, chief, the most notable, etc.

e.g.: i) Kottayam in Kerala is the **first** district in India to achieve cent percent literacy.

ii) India is one of the **foremost** developing nations in the world.

**9.Much, many, many a**

**Much** is used with regard to quantities particularly for non-count nouns.

**Many** is used with regard to number especially with count-nouns.

**Many a** means 'a person or a thing - many times'

e.g.: i) <u>**Many**</u> people came to see the accident site.

ii) The receptionist couldn't give us <u>**much**</u> information about the course.

iii) **Many a** man has been ruined by drinks.

**10. Nearest, next**

**Nearest** refers to nearness in space or distance.

**Next** refers to position or order.

e.g.: i) Where is the **nearest** police station situated?

ii) My room lies **next** to Mohan's.

**11. All, whole**

**All** refers to total of many things together. All is generally used before countable nouns and is followed by **'the'**.

**Whole** is generally followed by **'the'** and a noun.

e.g.: i) Maria wasted **the whole** day doing nothing.

ii) **All** the participants in the competition performed well.

**12. Fewer, less**

**Fewer** is used with countables and denotes number.

**Less** is used with non-count nouns and denotes quantity.

e.g.: i) **Fewer** students appeared for the National Medical Entrance Examination this year.

ii) There is **less water** in our well than in our neighbour's.

**Less** is sometimes used with countable nouns as well.

> **e.g.:**  i) **Less** number of candidates appeared for the test this month.
>
> ii) You may pay 150 rupees **less**.

13. **Latter, later, last, latest**

**Latter** means *'second in position* or *order'.*

**Later** means *'some time after'.*

**Last** means *'final in position* or *order'.*

**Latest** means *'most recent'.*

> **e.g.:**  i) Tom and John are rich. However, the **latter** is the richer of the two.
>
> ii) Manu came **later** than you.
>
> iii) Of the three games cricket, football and tennis, the **last** is my favourite.
>
> iv) Where is the **latest** issue of 'India Today'?

14. **Either, neither**

**Either** means *one of the two or both.*

**Neither** means *none of the two.*

> **e.g.:**  i) You may take **either** of the two shirts.
>
> ii) **Neither** of the two candidates could speak English.

15. **Each, every**

**Each** is used as one of the two things taken one by one.

**Every** is used to mean all of them taken individually.

> **e.g.:**  i) **Each** of them is to be blamed for the accident.
>
> ii) **Every** woman in India is given certain rights by the Constitution.

16. **Both**

**Both** is generally followed by **'the'** or a possessive person.

Both is generally not used in a *negative sentence.*

> **e.g.:**  i) **Both the** students failed to submit their assignments.
>
> ii) I met **both** of my friends in the town.
>
> iii) **Both** of them did **not** speak at the function.**(X)**
>
> **Neither** of them spoke at the function.(✓)

17. **Preferable**

**Preferable** has a comparative force and, therefore, does not require **more** before it. It is followed by **'to'.**

> **e.g.:**  i) Health is **preferable** (*not, more preferable*) **to** wealth.
>
> ii) Peace of mind is **preferable to** fame.

# Exercise

1. **Use correct adjectives in the following sentences:**

1. I read a *nice* book recently.

2. My new job is *quite hard.*

3. My sister is having *strong headache.*

4. Ramu's *older brother* is sick.

5. I was *much happy* to see my dad.

6. The new principal came *today morning.*

7. I am *much elder* than you.

8. This is my *dining time.*

9. Mohan is *cleverest* boy in his village.

10. My friend drives his car *most hopelessly.*

**2. Choose the correct adjective from the brackets:**

1. English is spoken— over the world. *(all/ whole/much)*

2. I am — older than you. *(little/much/a little)*

3. With — help from you I can do the job. *(a little/some/any)*

4. I cannot depend on — friends I have. *(the few/few/a few)*

5. Someone has picked —money I had in my pocket. *(little/a little/the little)*

6. Are there — oranges left in the basket? *(any/few/ lots of)*

7. — man has been ruined by drinks and bad friends. *(many a/ some/ many)*

8. — examples can be cited to prove this point. *(the number of /a number of/many a)*

9. There are only— boys left in the playground. *(some/few/many)*

10. I have — things to do this evening. *(many/lots of/few)*

11. The teacher has given us — advice. *(much/many/few)*

12. We shall stay here for  — while. *(a little/little/some)*

13. —wants happiness and love in this world. *(some/everyone/ many)*

14. — of the students has done their assignments. *(each/some/ many)*

15. There is — water left in this pond. *(little/a little/ the little)*

<u>**Answers:**</u>

<u>Use correct adjectives in the following sentences:</u>

    1. I read **an interesting** book recently.

    2. My new job is quite **tough.**

    3. My sister has a **severe headache.**

    4. Ram's **elder brother** is sick.

    5. I was **very happy** to see my dad.

    6. The new principal came **this morning.**

    7. I am **much older** than you.

    8. This is my **dinner time.**

    9. Mohan is **the cleverest** boy in his village.

    10. My friend drives his car most **carelessly.**

**2. Choose the correct adjective from the brackets:**

| | | | |
|---|---|---|---|
| 1. all | 2. much | 3. a little | 4. the few |
| 5. the little | 6. any | 7. many a | 8. a number of |
| 9. few | 10. lots of | 11. much | 12. a little |
| 13. everyone | 14. each | 15. little/ a little | |

# 11. Adverb

**Adverb:** An adverb is a word which generally modifies a verb, an adjective, or another adverb.

> **e.g.:** The chairman of the company read the report **<u>slowly.</u>**

<u>Kinds of adverb</u>

**i) Adverb of time:** It shows when a thing happens.

> **e.g.:** i) I have been living in this town **<u>since</u>**2000.

**ii) Adverb of place:** It shows where a thing happens.

> **e.g.:** The family searched for their lost puppy **<u>everywhere</u>** but they couldn't find it.

**iii) Adverb of manner:** It shows how a thing is done.

> **e.g.:** The minister acted **<u>wisely</u>** and solved the snowballing crisis.

**iv) Adverb of frequency or degree**: It shows how much or to what extent a thing happens.

> **e.g.:** The director **<u>rarely</u>** visits the factory but he is **<u>always</u>** on tour promoting his business.

**v) Adverb of cause and effect:** It shows why a thing is done and its effect.

> **e.g.:** It was raining heavily; **<u>therefore</u>**, the outdoor cultural programme was cancelled.

**vi) Adverb of order:** It shows the order in which a thing is done.

> **e.g.:** Rama came **<u>first</u>** in the race but was disqualified at the **<u>last</u>** minute.

**vii) Adverb of affirmation and negation:** It expresses affirmation or negation.

> **e.g.:** The recently released movie was **<u>certainly</u>** a great success.

## <u>Comparison of adverbs</u>

Adverbs are compared like adjectives with *er* and *est,* **more** and **most** or irregularly:

| Positive | comparative | superlative |
|---|---|---|
| **wisely** | more wisely | most wisely |
| **soon** | sooner | soonest |
| **fast** | faster | fastest |
| **rapidly** | more rapidly | most rapidly |
| **well** | better | best |
| **little** | less | least |
| **much** | more | most |
| **late** | later | latest, last |
| **badly, ill** | worse | worst |
| **far** | farther | farthest |

Adverb

## <u>Some important rules</u>

i) **Adverbs of manner** such as *slowly, carefully, kindly, well, badly, ill, aloud, wisely, quickly, highly, carefully, seriously, gently,* etc. should be <u>**placed after the object**</u> and not before it.

> **e.g.:** i) You must drive slowly the vehicle. **(X)**
>
> You must drive the <u>vehicle</u> *(object)* **slowly.**(✓)
>
> ii) Kick quickly the ball into the goal post.
>
> Kick the <u>ball</u> *(object)* **quickly** into the goal post.(✓)
>
> iii) Santhosh likes very much his bike. **(X)**
>
> Santhosh likes his <u>bike</u> *(object)* **very much.**(✓)
>
> iv) Miss Linda wrote carefully the application.**(X)**
>
> Miss Linda wrote the <u>application</u> *(object)* **very carefully.**(✓)

ii) **Adverbs of place and time** generally follow the verb or the object.

> **e.g.:** i) My brother purchased a new dictionary **yesterday**.
>
> ii) An accident took place **here**.

iii) If two or three adverbs occur together, they are placed in the following order: (**MPT order**)

manner - place - time

> **e.g.:** i) Raju performed <u>well in the interview</u> held <u>yesterday</u>.
>
>   *manner*    *place*                *time*
>
> ii)  We have to go **<u>there</u>** <u>tomorrow.</u>
>
>   *place*    *time*
>
> iii) The chairs were placed in a <u>disorderly manner in the hall.</u>
>
>   *manner*                *place*

iv) **Adverbs of frequency** or **degree** are generally placed before the principal verb or after the auxiliary verb if there is no principal verb.

> These words show how much or to what extent a thing happens:

### <u>Main words of frequency or degree:</u>

Almost, always, ever, never, often, seldom, sometimes, usually, rarely, scarcely, frequently, abundantly, perfectly, enough, half, hardly, very, much, too, less, least, little, rather, quite, once, twice, almost, very much, rather, more, most, etc.

> **e.g.:** i) Sometimes my brother comes to see me in the hostel.**(X)**
>
> My brother **sometimes** comes to see me in the hostel. (✓)

ii) I go home often on weekends.**(X)**
I **often** go home on weekends.(✓)
iii) Suraj is late always for school.**(X)**
Suraj is **always** late for school.(✓)

If there are two auxiliary verbs in a sentence, the adverbs of frequency and manner should be placed in between them.

**e.g.:** i) I will be coming with you also.**(X)**
I will **also** be coming with you.(✓)

v) Adverbs such as **today, perhaps, nowadays, generally, sometimes**, etc. can be placed before the subject as they influence the meaning of the whole sentence.

**e.g.:** i) **Today** India is considered to be a leader among developing countries.

vi) An adverb qualifying an adverb or an adjective *generally precedes it.*

**e.g.:** i) Never run **so** fast.

ii) The weather is **very** pleasant.

iii) My friend is **quite** sick.

vii) The adverb **'only'** can be placed in different parts of a sentence depending on the stress one wants to give. It is generally placed before the word it intends to modify or qualify.

**e.g.:** i) **Only** Sham promised me to write a letter. (*'only'* qualifies the noun *'Sham'*. No one else promised; only Sham did.)

ii) Mr. Sham **only** promised me to write a letter. (here *'only'* qualifies the verb *'promised'*. Sham only promised and did nothing else.)

iii) Mr. Sham promised me **only** to write a letter (here *'only'* qualifies *'writing'*. Sham promised only about writing a letter and nothing else.)

iv) Mr. Sham promised **only** to me to write a letter (*'only'* qualifies the pronoun *'me'*. It means Sham did not give promise to anyone else but only 'me'.)

v) Mr. Sham promised me to write **only** a letter. (*'only'* qualifies the term *'a letter'*. Sham did not promise to write many letters but only a letter.)

viii) The adverb **'quite'** is used in two senses.

When **quite** is used with gradable adjectives (such as *good, perfect, tired, exhausted,* etc. which can mean *more or less*), **'quite'** means *'fairly* or *rather'.*

**e.g.:** i) The show was **quite** good. (*The show was fairly good*)

When **quite** is used with non-gradable adjective words such as *impossible, finished, round, supreme,* etc. it means *completely.*

**e.g.:** i) Have you **quite** finished the work? (*Have you completely finished the work?*)

# Exercise

**1. Correct the mistakes in the following sentences**:

1. It is too hot today.
2. The injured person was lying senselessly.
3. It is bitter cold today.
4. The load was too much heavy for the old porter.
5. Mani only rests when he feels tired.
6. I shall be very obliged to you for your kind favour.
7. I do not know to drive a car.
8. Satish was very annoyed with you.
9. I am coming directly from New Delhi.
10. She comes seldom to see me.
11. It is nothing else than a folly.
12. I shall try as best as I can.
13. My friend is comparatively better today.
14. Mr. Hari was elected as chairman.
15. I considered him as my brother.

**Answers**

1. It is **very** hot today.
2. The injured person was lying **senseless.**
3. It is **bitterly** cold today.
4. The load was **much** too heavy for the old porter.
5. Mani rests **only** when he feels tired.
6. I shall be **much** obliged to you for your kind favour.
7. I do not know **how to** drive a car.
8. Satish was **much** annoyed with you.
9. I am coming **directly** from New Delhi.
10. She **seldom** comes to see me.
11. It is nothing **but** a folly.
12. I shall try **as best** I can.
13. My friend is **comparatively well** today.
14. Mr. Hari was elected **chairman.**
15. I considered him **my brother.**

—xxx—

# 12. Conjunctions

**Conjunction:** A conjunction is a word which is used to connect words, clauses and sentences.

**Kinds of conjunction:**

**<u>1. Coordinating conjunction:</u>** A conjunction which joins clauses of equal rank is known as a **<u>coordinating conjunction.</u>**

> **e.g.:** i) India is a fast-developing country **as well as** a major non-aligned nation.

**Main coordinating conjunctions**

| | | | |
|---|---|---|---|
| and | but | still | only |
| yet | for | so | as well as |
| or | while | also | provided |
| nevertheless | otherwise | whereas | therefore |
| hence | consequently | either...or | not only...but also |
| though...yet | although...yet | whether... or, etc. | |

Coordinating conjunctions are used *<u>to form compound sentences.</u>*

**<u>Examples:</u>**

1. **And** : The team came to the field **<u>and</u>** began to practise for the next day's match.
2. **But** : They found the lost boy, **<u>but</u>** he was very weak.
3. **Still** : Maria did well in the interview; **still** she was not selected for the post.
4. **Only** : Sham appeared to be all right; **only** he looked tired and exhausted.
5. **Yet** : Our team played well; **<u>yet</u>** it did not win the match.
6. **For** : I can't meet you tomorrow **<u>for</u>** I have an important appointment.
7. **So** : It is raining heavily; **<u>so</u>** I am unable to come for the function.
8. **As well as** : India **<u>as well as</u>** China is likely to dominate the international economy in the days to come.
9. **Provided** : I will give you the amount you asked for **<u>provided</u>** you return it within a month.
10. **Nevertheless** : Mahesh is quite sick; **<u>nevertheless,</u>** he wants to sit the test.
11. **While** : The students kept talking **<u>while</u>** the teacher was taking class.
12. **Whereas** : Harish was selected for the post **<u>whereas</u>** Manish, his friend, was not selected.
13. **Or** : The doctor must come soon **<u>or</u>** the patient might die.
14. **Also** : My son is good at mathematics; he is **<u>also</u>** good at science.
15. **Otherwise** : Speak slowly and clearly; **<u>otherwise</u>** people will not understand what you are saying.

16. **Therefore**          : Sarita did not do well in the interview; **therefore,** she was not selected for the post.

17. **Hence**          : It was raining heavily; **hence,** the match was  put off.

21. **Consequently** : Maran prepared well for the entrance examination; **consequently** he found it quite easy.

22. **Either... or**   : You can talk to me **either** in English **or** in French.

23. **Neither...nor**   : My uncle can speak **neither** English **nor** Hindi.

24. **Not only... but also**  : Linda can **not only** dance **but also** sing well.

25. **Both... and**    : Miss Helen is **both** beautiful **and** smart-looking.

26. **Though.. yet**   : **Though** our team played well, **yet** they lost the match.

27. **Although...yet** : **Although** India is making rapid progress in many sectors **yet** many negative forces are preventing her all-round development.

27. **Whether...or not:** I am not sure **whether** I will be able to come for the function **or** not.

**2. Subordinate conjunctions**: A conjunction which connects a subordinate clause to a principal clause (*main clause which is independent and fully meaningful*) is known as a **subordinate conjunction.**

### Main subordinate conjunctions

| | | | |
|---|---|---|---|
| that | who | what | which |
| where | whose | when | whom |
| though | although | even though | till |
| as | after | before | because |
| whether | if | since | than |
| unless | lest | as though | as if |
| in case | so that | so... that | such ....that |
| as....as | so... as | as... so | no sooner... than |
| hardly...when | scarcely...when | on condition that | whoever |
| provided that | whatever | wherever | however, etc. |

Subordinate conjunctions are used *to form complex sentences.*

**Examples:**

1. **That**          : The newspaper article stated **that** the government was planning to introduce a new reservation policy.

2. **Who**          : This is the man **who** lost his luggage in the train.

3. **What**          : Most youngsters spend **what** they earn.

4. **Which**          : This is the book **which** I was looking for.

5. **Where**          : This is the exact spot **where** we were robbed.

6. **Whose**          : This is the lady **whose** handbag was stolen in the bus.

| | |
|---|---|
| 7. **When** | : The children were happy **when** the movie started. |
| 8. **Whom** | : The man **whom** the police was searching for was finally caught. |
| 9. **Though** | : **Though** Sam prepared well for the Civil Service examination, he didn't get through it. |
| 10. **Although** | : **Although** Priya is very rich, she does not behave like one. |
| 11. **Even though** | : **Even though** I know you, I cannot allow you in. |
| 12. **Till** | : Kindly wait here **till** I finish my meeting with the officer. |
| 13. **As** | : **As** Sam was down with fever, he couldn't attend the marriage function of his friend. |
| 14. **After** | : The leaders gathered for a meeting **after** the crowd had left the venue. |
| 15. **Before** | : The teacher introduced herself **before** she commenced her class. |
| 16. **Because** | : Rani began to cry **because** she had lost her gold chain. |
| 17. **Whether** | : The foreign tourist asked me **whether** I had visited Europe. |
| 18. **If** | : **If** you work hard, you can definitely pass the IELTS test with a good score. |
| 19. **Since** | : **Since** the chief guest arrived late, the function was delayed. |
| 20. **Than** | : Robert speaks French better **than** his brother does. |
| 21. **As soon as** | : The crowd rushed out of the stadium **as soon as** the match ended. |
| 22. **As though** | : Mr. Raj speaks **as though** he were a great genius. |
| 23. **As if** | : The young man talked **as if** he were a scholar. |
| 24. **Unless** | : India will not become a permanent member in the UN Security Council **unless** the USA supports her. |
| 25. **Lest** | : Prepare well for the test **lest** you fail. |
| 26. **So that** | : Spend money carefully **so that** you don't have to beg from others. |
| 27. **So... that** | : Miss Angel is **so** fat **that** she cannot run. |
| 28. **Such ... that** | : Bob is **such** a fool **that** we cannot rely on him. |
| 29. **As... as** | : The city of Chennai is not **as** extensive **as** Mumbai. |
| 30. **As... so** | : **As** you sow, **so** shall you reap. |
| 31. **So... as** | : Come home early from the office **so as** to be present at the evening get-together. |
| 32. **No sooner ... than** | : **No sooner** had the minister arrived **than** the function started. |
| 33. **Hardly... when** | : **Hardly** had the speaker got up to speak **when** the lights went off. |
| 34. **Scarcely... when** | : **Scarcely** had Tom recovered from an attack of malaria **when** he fell sick with a bout of meningitis. |
| 35. **On condition that** | : I will give you my mobile number **on condition that** you do not give it to anyone else. |
| 36. **Provided that** | : You can use my car for the trip **provided that** you bear the fuel cost. |

| | | |
|---|---|---|
| 37. **In case** | : | Take some extra cash with you **in case** you need it on the way. |
| 38. **However** | : | **However** strong Dave may be, he cannot lift this weight. |
| 39. **Wherever** | : | I will follow you **wherever** you go. |
| 39. **Whoever** | : | **Whoever** you may be, I cannot allow you in now. |
| 40. **Whatever** | : | **Whatever** you may say, I do not believe your words. |

# Exercise

**1. Fill the blanks in the following sentences with proper conjunctions:**

1. Prasad remained at home— he was ill.

2. Man proposes — God disposes.

3. Would you be kind enough to wait — I come.

4. — you speak well of others, they too will speak well about you.

5. Catch my hand — you should fall.

6. My neighbour is very rich; — he is not happy.

7. —you tell me the details, I cannot give you my opinion on the matter.

8. My friend always talks about cricket — there is no other game in the world except cricket.

9. I will join the trip — my father allows.

10. The article stated — India is on the verge of becoming a major economic superpower within a decade.

11. Mahesh is - intelligent — he hardly reads the textbook twice.

12. Birds cannot fly — they have wings.

13. You can remain the captain of the team - it continues to win under your leadership.

14. — you may be, I must check your identity.

15. You can join our evening party — you  contribute your share for it.

**<u>Answers</u>**

| | | | | |
|---|---|---|---|---|
| 1. as/since | 2. but | 3. till | 4. if | 5. lest |
| 6. yet | 7. Unless | 8. as if/as though | 9. if | 10. that |
| 11. so...that | 12. unless | 13. so long as | 14. whoever | 15. provided that |

—xxx—

# 13. Active and passive voices

<u>Active voice</u>: A verb is said to be in the active voice when the person or the thing denoted by it acts.

**e.g.: Robertson wrote this novel.**

**Active voice is used** when we want to *stress the subject or make the subject prominent.*

<u>Passive voice</u>: When the subject of the verb is acted upon, i.e., something is done to the subject, the verb is said to be in the passive voice.

**e.g.: This novel was written by Robertson.**

**Passive voice is used** when we *want to stress the action.*

## <u>Important rules regarding active and passive voices</u>

1. The basic order of words in passive and active forms are:

| Passive form<br>**Object-verb-subject** | Active form<br>**subject-verb-object** |
| --- | --- |

    **e.g.:** The <u>assignment</u> was <u>completed</u> by <u>Mahesh</u> in time.
       *object*        *verb*     *subject*
    <u>Mahesh</u> <u>completed</u> the <u>assignment</u> in time.
    *sub*    *verb*     *object*

2. In all forms of passive voice, the verb is always in the **past participle** form ($V_3$ form).

    **e.g.** i) A letter is being <u>**written**</u> by Andrews.

3. Only sentences with transitive verbs can be converted into passive, i.e., only sentences with objects can be transformed into passive form.

    **e.g.:** i) Ravi <u>**broke**</u> the window (*active*)
        The window was <u>**broken**</u> by Ravi. (*passive*)
       ii) The baby is <u>**sleeping.**</u> (*It cannot be converted because it has an intransitive verb with no object*)

4. We can easily distinguish passive and active sentences by the following differences:

| | |
| --- | --- |
| **a m**<br>**is**<br>**was**<br>**are**<br>**were**<br>**been** | + verb in **ING form** shows **active voice**<br>+ verb in **past participle** shows **passive voice** |

    **e.g.:** Raj <u>**is playing**</u> cricket.         Cricket <u>**is being played**</u> by Raj.
         *active*                                    *passive*

5. When active sentences are converted into passive form, the tense does not change. **Never mix up the tenses** whether active or passive.

  **e.g.:** i) The maid **is preparing** dinner. (***active** present continuous tense*)

     The dinner **is being prepared** by the maid. (***passive** present continuous tense*)

6. We can interchange active and passive forms keeping the same tense but different forms.

  **e.g.:** Globalization **brings** about a lot of changes in developing countries. A lot of

      **active** present simple

  changes **have already been brought about** by globalization in developed countries.

  **passive** present perfect

## 7. <u>Active and passive forms of 12 forms of tenses</u>

| **Tense** | **Active** | **Passive** |
|---|---|---|
| i. Present indefinite | He **reads** a book. | A book **is read** by him. |
| ii. Present continuous | He **is reading** a book. | A book **is being read** by him. |
| iii. Present perfect | He **has read** a book. | A book **has been read by him.** |
| iv. Present perfect continuous | He **has been reading** a book. | *(same as the previous)* |
| v. Past indefinite | He **read** a book. | A book **was read** by him. |
| vi. Past continuous | He **was reading** a book. | A book **was being read** by him |
| vii. Past perfect | He **had read** a book. | A book **had been** read by him. |
| viii. Past perfect continuous | He **had been reading** a book. | *(same as the previous)* |
| ix. Future indefinite | He **will read** a book. | A book **will be read** by him. |
| x. Future continuous | He **will be reading** a book. | *(same as the previous)* |
| xi. Future perfect | He **will have read** a book. | A book **will have been read** by him |
| xii. Future perfect continuous | He **will have been reading** a book. | *(same as the previous)* |

## 8. Imperative sentences

***Rule:*** Generally, active imperative sentences (**command or order sentences**) are changed into passive sentences by using **Let** or **requested** or **advised** etc.

<u>Examples:</u>

| **Active** | **Passive** |
|---|---|
| 1. Do it at once. | **Let** it be done at once. |
| 2. Sit down. | You are **requested** to sit down. |
| 3. Never tell a lie. | Never **let** a lie be told. |
| 4. Post this letter. | **Let** this letter be posted. |

**9. Infinitive sentences** (*verb with 'to'* )

Generally, active infinitive sentences are changed into passive sentences by using **to be + past participle.**

<u>Examples:</u>

| **<u>Active</u>** | **<u>Passive</u>** |
|---|---|
| 1. We are **to do** this job. | This job is **<u>to be done</u>** by us. |
| 2. I expected you **to do** it. | It was expected **<u>to be done</u>** by you. |
| 3. There is no time to lose. | There is no time **<u>to be lost.</u>** |

**10. Sentences with auxiliary verbs**

When an active sentence has only one auxiliary, the method of forming its passive voice is as follows:

> Auxiliary verb + **be** + verb in past participle

When an active sentence has more than one auxiliary verb, the method for the formation of its passive form is as follows:

> Auxiliary verb + **have been** + verb in past participle

| **<u>Active</u>** | **<u>Passive</u>** |
|---|---|
| 1. He **may** sing a song. | A song **<u>may be sung</u>** by him. |
| 2. We **should** do our work. | Our work **<u>should be done</u>** by us. |
| 3. Maria might have missed the bus. | The bus might have been missed by Maria. |
| 4. The maid **must have** broken the cup. | The cup **<u>must have been broken</u>** by the maid. |

11. The passive voice of verbs with two objects is formed by changing either of the two objects into subject and retaining the other as the object.

| **<u>Active</u>** | **<u>Passive</u>** |
|---|---|
| I gave **<u>my friend</u>** a **<u>gift</u>** | **<u>My friend</u>** was given a <u>gift</u> by me. |
| (*two objects: my friend & gift*) | (*<u>gift</u>: retained object*) |
| | **or** |
| | **<u>A gift</u>** was given to <u>my friend</u> by me. |
| | (*<u>my friend</u>: retained object*) |

12. In changing the voice of complex sentences the voices of both the principal and subordinate clauses should be changed. The introductory **It** may also sometimes be used.

    **e.g.:** *Active* : I know that he completed the assigned work.

          *Passive* : It **is known** to me that the assigned work **was completed** by him.

13. Some active sentences sometimes may not have clear-cut subjects. Sometimes the passive form may not have definite objects as well. The commonly used subjects in such situations are **'it'** or **'they'** or **'we'**.

    i) *Active*        : They say might is right.

     *Passive*     : **It is said** that might is right.

    ii) *Active*      : People believe that God is one.

     *Passive*     : **It is believed** that God is one.

    iii) *Passive*   : You are given five minutes to prepare for the speech.

     *Active*      : **They** give you five minutes to prepare for the speech.

    iv) *Passive*   : He is expected soon.

     *Active*      : **We** expect him soon.

## **Situations where passive voice should be used**

1. *When it is not necessary to say who performed the action.*

    **e.g.:** Some of these items **are made** in India.

2. *When it is preferable not to mention the performer or doer.*

    **e.g.:** Satish **was told** that his behaviour was not up to the mark.

3. *When we want to give importance to the receiver rather than the doer.*

    **e.g.:** The old man **was killed** by a speeding vehicle.

4. *In situations of social and historical importance.*

    **e.g.:** America **was discovered** by Columbus.

5. *In invitations, requests and announcements.*

    **e.g.:** Passengers **are requested** to take care of their belongings.

6. *To describe mechanical processes and in giving scientific descriptions.*

    **e.g.:** Evaporation is a process by which water in the sea **gets evaporated** due to the heat of the sun and goes up in the form of steam.

### **Read through the following sentences:**

1. *Active*    : Sam <u>was driving</u> a new black car in the morning.

  *Passive*   : A new black car **<u>was being driven</u>** by Sam in the morning.

2. *Active*    : Kindly <u>grant me</u> a week's leave.

  *Passive*   : You are **requested** to kindly grant me a week's leave.

3. *Active*    : <u>People believe</u> that dreams come true.

  *Passive*   : **It is believed** that dreams come true.

4. *Active*    : Someone <u>has stolen</u> my newly bought coat.

  *Passive*   : My newly bought coat **has been stolen** by someone.

5. *Active*     : The committee <u>is discussing</u> the issue.

   *Passive*   : The issue **is being discussed** by the committee.

6. *Passive*  : The crop <u>had not been sown</u> by the farmer in time.

   *Active*    : The farmer **had not sown** the crop in time.

7. *Passive*  : The train was missed by our guests.

   *Active*    : Our guests missed the train.

8. *Passive*  : My master <u>was pleased</u> with me for my service.

   *Active*    : I **pleased** my master with my service.

## Some difficult active voice sentences and their passive forms

1. He was elected president.

   **Ans:** They elected him President.

2. I was requested to dance.

   **Ans:** They requested me to dance.

3. The promise was broken.

   **Ans:** They broke the promise.

4. Let him do the work.

   **Ans:** Let the work be done by him.

5. We know a man by his deeds.

   **Ans:** A man is known by his deeds.

6. Rome was not built in a day.

   **Ans:** The Romans did not build Rome in a day.

7. English is spoken in England.

   **Ans:** The people of England speak English.

8. What is done cannot be undone.

   **Ans:** People cannot undo what is done.

9. The politician was honoured.

   **Ans:** The people honoured the politician.

10. Motor cars are parked here.

   **Ans:** People park motor cars here.

11. The Chief Minister was given a warm welcome

   **Ans:** People gave the Chief Minister a warm welcome.

12. He is known to me.

   **Ans:** I know him.

13. People grow tea in Assam.

   **Ans:** Tea is grown in Assam.

14. Courage is always admired.

   **Ans:** People always admire courage.

15. A prize was declared.
>    **Ans:** They declared a prize.
16. None but God can save him.
>    **Ans:** He can be saved by none but God.
17. One should respect one's elders.
>    **Ans:** Elders should be respected.
18. It is time to take tea.
>    **Ans:** It is time for the tea to be taken.
19. Sugar tastes sweet.
>    **Ans:** Sugar is sweet when it is tasted.
20. He is expected soon.
>    **Ans:** We expect him soon.

# Interrogative sentences

### A. Present Indefinite

21. Does he carry a bag?
>    **Ans:** Is a bag carried by him?
22. What do you do?
>    **Ans:** What is done by you?

### B. Present continuous

23. Are you drawing a picture?
>    **Ans:** Is a picture being drawn by you?
24. Why are you making noise?
>    **Ans:** Why is noise being made by you?

### C. Present Perfect

25. Have you read this story?
>    **Ans:** Has this story been read by you?
26. Who won the gold medal?
>    **Ans:** By whom has the gold medal been won?
27. What have you done?
>    **Ans:** What has been done by you?

### D. Past indefinite

28. Did you waste money?
>    **Ans:** Was money wasted by you?
29. Who taught you science?
>    **Ans:** By whom were you taught science?

### E. Past Continuous

30. Were they playing chess?
> **Ans:** Was chess being played by them?
31. Who was laughing at you?
> **Ans:** By whom were you being laughed at?

### F. Past Perfect

32. Had you kept your promise?
> **Ans:** Had your promise been kept by you?
33. Who had sung a sweet song?
> **Ans:** By whom had a sweet song been sung ?

### G. Future indefinite

34. Will she draw a picture?
> **Ans:** Will a picture be drawn by her?
35. Who will pay your fine?
> **Ans:** By whom will your fine be paid?

### H. Future Perfect

36. Who will have done this job?
> **Ans:** By whom will this job have been done?
37. Why will he have missed the train?
> **Ans:** Why will the train have been missed by him?

# Exercise

A. **Change the following active sentences into passive sentences:**

1. May you live long.
2. I am preparing dinner.
3. Don't waste time.
4. I missed the train.
5. We shall discuss this matter tomorrow.

B. **Change the following passive sentences into their active forms:**

1. Our tickets have been booked by us.
2. This beautiful picture was painted by Hari Das.
3. The boy was asked several questions by the teacher.
4. Let me kindly be allowed to leave.
5. One's promise should be kept.

**C. Change the voice of the following sentences:** (*into the opposite voice*)

1. The food had already been cooked by Sangeeta.
2. Take medicines on time.
3. The patient is being examined by the doctor.
4. A novel was being written by Mr. Jones.
5. The children will watch a movie at night.

**Answers:**

A. **Change the following active sentences into passive sentences:**

**1.** May you be granted a long life.
2. Dinner is being prepared by me.
3. Never let your time be wasted.
4. The train was missed by me.
5. This matter shall be discussed by us tomorrow.

B. **Change the following passive sentences into their active forms:**

1. We have booked our tickets.
2. Hari Das painted this beautiful picture.
3. The teacher asked several questions to the boy.
4. Allow me to leave, please.
5. One should keep one's promise.

C. **Change the voice of the following sentences:**

1. Sangeeta had already cooked the food.
2. Let medicines be taken on time.
3. The doctor is examining the patient.
4. Mr. Jones was writing a novel.
5. A movie will be watched by the children at night.

—xxx—-

## Useful data

### 7. **Palindromes** (*words that are read the same way in both directions*)

| 1. madam | 2. noon | 3. radar | 4. mom |
| 5. dad | 6. civic | 7. eye | 8. pop |
| 9. peep | 10. did | 11. refer | 12. toot |

# 14. Direct and Indirect Speech

**Direct speech:** When we give the exact words of the speaker by way of quotation, it is known as direct speech.

**E.g.:** Jane said, "My father speaks French."

In the above sentence the verb 'said' reports the speech of the person. Hence it is known as 'reporting verb'.

What is said by the person 'My father speaks French' is known as 'Reported Speech'.

**Features of direct speech:**

1. The reported speech is enclosed within double inverted commas ("   ").
2. The reported speech is separated from the reporting verb by a comma.
3. The first word of the reported speech begins with a capital letter.
4. The last full stop is placed before the second inverted comma.

**Indirect speech:** When we give the substance of the actual words of the speaker, it is known as indirect speech.

**e.g.:** Jane said that her father spoke French.

The above sentence is not the exact words of the speaker. Its substance has been reported in the words of the reporter. Since the speech is given indirectly, it is known as indirect speech.

## Method of changing from direct speech to indirect speech

1. If the reporting verb is in the present tense - No change in the indirect speech.

    **e.g.:** Jaya says, "I **am taking** medicine on time."

    Jaya says that **she is taking** medicine on time.

2. Present indefinite-past indefinite.

    **e.g.:** Jaya said, "I **take** medicine on time."

    Jaya said that she **took** medicine on time.

3. Present continuous - past continuous.

    **e.g.:** Jaya said, "I **am taking** medicine on time."

    Jaya said that she **was taking** medicine on time.

4. Present perfect - past perfect.

    **e.g.:** Jaya said, "I **have taken** medicine on time."

    Jaya said that she **had taken** medicine on time.

5. Present perfect continuous - past perfect continuous.

    **e.g.:** Jaya said, "I **have been taking** medicine on time."

    Jaya said that she **had been taking** medicine on time.

6. Past indefinite - past perfect.

> **e.g.:** Jaya said, "I **took** medicine on time."
> Jaya said that she **had taken** medicine on time.

7. Past continuous - past perfect continuous.

> **e.g.:** Jaya said, "I **was taking** medicine on time."
> Jaya said that she **had been taking** medicine on time.

**8.** Past perfect - past perfect.

> **e.g.:** Jaya said, "I **had taken** medicine on time."
> Jaya said that she **had taken** medicine on time.

**9.** Past perfect continuous - past perfect continuous.

> **e.g.:** Jaya said, "I **had been taking** medicine on time."
> Jaya said that she **had been taking** medicine on time.

10. Will, shall - would/should

> **e.g.:** Jaya said, "I **will take** medicine on time."
> Jaya said that she **would take** medicine on time.

**11.** If the interrogative sentence in the direct speech is formed by question words, such as, *what, which, who*, etc. then the same question words are to be used in the indirect speech.

> *Question words - use the same question words.*

> **e.g.:** Jaya asked the receptionist, "Who is the chief paediatrician at this hospital?
> Jaya asked the receptionist **who** the chief paediatrician at that hospital was.

**12.** If the interrogative sentence in the direct speech is formed by auxiliary verbs such as, *are, will, can, is,* etc., then **if** or **whether** is to be used in the indirect speech.

> *Interrogative sentences with auxiliary verbs - use **if** or **whether.***

> **e.g.:** Jaya asked the doctor, "**Can** I give solid food to the patient?"
> Jaya asked the doctor **whether** she could give solid food to the patient.

**13.** Imperative sentence (*command or order sentences*) of the direct speech is changed into indirect speech by changing the reporting verb into ***request, order, command, advise***, etc. and by putting the sentence in the infinitive (*to + verb*).

> *Imperative sentence - add '**to**'*

> **e.g.:** The nurse said to the patient, "Lie down on the bed."
> The nurse ordered the patient to lie down on the bed.

**14.** Exclamatory words of the direct speech are changed into indirect speech by using suitable words which express exclamation, wish or prayer and by making the sentence into an <u>assertive sentence</u>. (*a sentence that makes a statement.*)

> *Oh, well, hurrah, alas, bravo - Use words which express their idea.*

      **e.g.:** Bill said, "Goodbye, my friends."

        Bill **bade** his friends goodbye.

**15.** Universal/general truths of direct speech remain the same in the indirect speech.

      **e.g.:** The teacher said, "Honesty is the best policy."

        The teacher said that honesty is the best policy.

**16:** Words expressing nearness are changed into words showing distance.

| direct | indirect | direct | indirect |
|---|---|---|---|
| ago | before | come | go |
| here | there | can | could |
| hereby | thereby | hence | thence |
| these | those | today | that day |
| tomorrow | the next day | last night | previous night the following day |
| this | that | last week | the previous week |
| yesterday | the previous day | next day | the following day |
| tonight | that night | next month | the following month |

### **Rules in Short Form**

| <u>Direct speech</u> | <u>Indirect speech</u> |
|---|---|
| **Rule:1:** If reporting verb is in present tense | No change |
| **Rule:2:** Present indefinite | Past indefinite |
| **Rule:3:** Present continuous | Past continuous |
| **Rule:4:** Present perfect | Past perfect |
| **Rule:5:** Present perfect continuous | Past perfect continuous |
| **Rule:6:** Past indefinite | Past perfect |
| **Rule:7:** Past continuous | Past perfect continuous |
| **Rule:8:** Past perfect | *No change* |
| **Rule:9:** Past perfect continuous | *No change* |
| **Rule:10.** Future tense-will, shall | would/should |

| | |
|---|---|
| **Rule:11:** Interrogative with question words | Use the same question words |
| **Rule:12:** Interrogative with auxiliary verb | Use **if** or **whether** |
| **Rule:13:** Imperative sentence | Use 'to' |
| **Rule:14:** Exclamatory and optative | Use words which express similar ideas |
| **Rule:15:** Universal/general truths | *No change* |
| **Rule:16:** Words showing nearness | Words showing distance |

## Common errors in Direct and Indirect speech

Using **direct speech words** such as **today, tomorrow, yesterday, tonight, can, etc**. in indirect speech is wrong in English. However, these words can be used in simple sentences.

**e.g.:**   **i)** Our class teacher said that she would come late **tomorrow.(X)**

Our class teacher said that she would come late <u>the following day.</u>(✓)

The New Year celebrations will commence at 10.30 a.m. **tomorrow.**(✓)*(simple           sentence)*

  **ii)** The soldier told the captain that he had done his patrol duty as per the schedule **yesterday.(X)**

The soldier told his captain that he had done his patrol duty as per the schedule <u>**the previous day.**</u>(✓)

My uncle met with a serious accident **yesterday.**(✓)*(simple sentence)*

# Exercise

**A. Change the following direct speech into indirect speech:**

1. She asked me, "Why are you crying?"
2. Santhosh said," I won a prize."
3. Leela said, " I am very busy and do not disturb me."
4. My father said, "A friend in need is a friend indeed."
5. The teacher remarked, "The stars are far from us."

**B. Change the following indirect speech into direct speech:**

1. My father told me to listen to the BBC regularly.
2. The man said that history repeats itself.
3. The servant said that he would do it the next day.
4. The minister told the students that the country needed them.
5. Sarita said that she did not want to go home.

**C. Change the narration of the following sentences:**
   (Change the *narration means give the opposite speech.*)
1. The boy asked me if I knew him.
2. "I have some money," Anil said.
3. He said, "I did it."
4. He asked him, "Is not your name Tom?"
5. I replied that I was not.

**Answers**

A. **Change the following direct speech into indirect speech:**
1. She asked me why I was crying.
2. Santhosh said that he had won a prize.
3. Leela said that she was very busy and not to disturb her.
4. My father said that a friend in need is a friend indeed. (*general truth*)
5. The teacher remarked that the stars are far from us. (*general truth*)

B. **Change the following indirect speech into direct speech:**
1. My father said to me, "Listen to the BBC regularly."
2. The man said, "History repeats itself."
3. The servant said, "I will do it tomorrow."
4. "The country needs you," the minister told the students.
5. Sarita said, "I do not want to go home."

C. **Change the narration of the following sentences:**
1. The boy said to me, "Do you know me?"
2. Anil said that he had some money.
3.He said that he had done it.
4. He enquired whether his name was not Tom.
5. I said, "I am not."

—xxx—-

## <u>Useful data</u>

**8. Pangram**(*a sentence that contains all the letters of the alphabet*)

1. The quick brown fox jumps over a lazy dog.
2. Pack my box with five dozen liquor jugs.
3. Six of the women quietly gave back prizes to the judge.
4. All questions asked by five watch experts amazed the judge.

# 15. Formation of compound sentence

**Compound sentence:** A sentence which contains two or more co-coordinating clauses is known as a compound sentence.

    **E.g.:** India is a fast-developing country **as well as** a leader in space technology.

We can form compound sentences by using the following <u>**co-coordinating conjunctions**</u>.

| | | | |
|---|---|---|---|
| and | but | still | only |
| yet | for | so | as well as |
| or | while | also | provided |
| nevertheless | otherwise | whereas | therefore |
| hence | consequently | either...or | not only...but also |
| though...yet | although...yet | whether... or, etc. | |

**Points to remember:**

1. When the following coordinating conjunctions are used to form compound sentences, they must be **preceded by a semi-colon:**

> *still, only, so, nevertheless, otherwise, therefore, hence, consequently,* etc.

2. In order to form a compound sentence, two or more clauses are required.

    **e.g.:** Maria is very clever and smart. (This is a **simple sentence** because there are no clauses.)

        Maria is very clever and she is smart. (This is a **compound sentence** because there are two clauses.)

3. Using a co-ordinate conjunction does not make a compound sentence. Certain co-ordinate conjunctions are preceded by a **semi-colon.**

    **e.g.:** It is raining. Nevertheless, I am going out. (*two simple sentences.*)

        It is raining**; nevertheless,** I am going out. (*compound sentence*)

<u>**Examples**</u>(more examples are given in the section on <u>conjunction</u>)

1. **and**

Today China is considered to be the fastest growing economy in the world **<u>and</u>** she is reckoned to be the most advanced in technological development as well. (*pronoun 'she' is used because countries are generally considered feminine*)

2. **but**

India has made rapid strides in the industrial sector **<u>but</u>** her social development has been rather slow.

3. **still**

I don't agree with your point; **<u>still</u>** I will support you for the sake of peace.

**4. only**

You can come into the auditorium; **only** do not make any noise.

**5. yet**

Sam is very intelligent; **yet** he spends a great deal of time studying.

**6. for**

I will have to stop the class now, **for** I have an important appointment with my lawyer.

**7. so**

You have performed well in the music competition; **so** you are likely to get the first prize.

**8. as well as**

John is quite proficient in playing violin **as well as** he is good at singing.

**9. provided**

I will come with you to your house **provided** you come to my house next weekend.

**10. nevertheless**

Manu is bed-ridden with paralysis; **nevertheless** he wants to become a doctor.

**11. while**

The students were talking **while** the teacher was taking class.

**12. whereas**

Arjun is hard-working **where as** his younger brother is quite lazy.

**13. or**

You can ring me up **or** send a mail regarding the matter that I spoke about earlier.

**14. also**

India has made tremendous progress in the field of literacy and she has **also** achieved remarkable success in community healthcare.

**15. otherwise**

Take a flight to Bangalore; **otherwise** you may not reach there in time for the conference.

**16. therefore**

The IT sector offers abundant job opportunities; **therefore,** children should be encouraged to opt for IT-related studies.

**17. hence**

My father is a diabetic; **hence** he avoids ice-creams and cool drinks.

**18. consequently**

Maria has been sick for a month; **consequently** she couldn't attend  her friend's marriage.

**19. either...or**

Our college team will play a cricket match **either** against the near-by college team **or** the local cricket team.

**20. neither... nor**

Mr. Dev has **neither** written the medical entrance examination **nor** plans to take up medical studies.

**21. not only...but also**

Sam is **not only** intelligent **but also** highly talented.

**22. both... and**

Miss Maya is **both** beautiful **and** smart-looking.

**23. though... yet**

**Though** India has made tremendous progress in the industrial sector, **yet** her agricultural sector has not made much headway.

**24. although...yet**

**Although** Sheila did well in the singing competition, **yet** she did not get a prize.

**25. whether..or**

I cannot allow you to go out now **whether** you like it **or not.**

Read through the following sentences and see how simple sentences are combined to form **compound sentences** with the help of co-ordinate conjunctions:

1. *Simple*   : The night is dark. I am far from home

   *Comp*      : The night is dark **and** I am far from home.

2. *Simple*   : Mahajan is poor. He behaves like a rich man.

   *Comp*      : Mahajan is poor **but** behaves like a rich man.

   *OR* **Although** Mahajan is poor, **yet** he behaves like a rich man.

3. *Simple*   : It was late in the night. Nazar went home.

   *Comp*      : **Though** it was late in the night, **yet** Nazar went home.

   *OR* It was late in the night; **still** Nazar went home.

5. *Simple*   : Anil did not do the test well. He passed it.

   *Comp*      : Anil did not do the test well; **yet** he passed it.

   *Or* **Though** Anil did not do the test well, **yet** he passed it.

   *OR* Anil did not do the test well; **nevertheless** he passed it.

6. *simple*   : Raj will complete his graduation this year. His brother will also do so this year.

   *comp*      : **Both** Raj and his brother will complete their graduation this year.

   *OR* Raj **as well as** his brother will complete their graduation this year.

7. *simple*   : Ravi was sleeping in the class. The teacher was taking the class.

   *Comp*      : Ravi was sleeping in the class **while** the teacher was taking the class.

8. *simple*   : The rich lady must weep. She will die.

   comp        : The rich lady must weep **or** she will die.

   *OR* The rich lady must weep; **otherwise** she will die.

# Exercise

**1. Combine the following simple sentences into compound sentences:**

1. I cannot help you with financial assistance. I am quite poor.
2. Mr. Singh is planning to visit Europe this summer. He is also planning to visit the US.
3. Make haste. You will be late for the programme.
4. It was a stormy night. Manu went out.
5. Santhosh is quite lazy. He is also quite dishonest.
6. There was an accident on the road. No one was injured.
7. I am right. You are right.
8. Prepare well for the test. You may fail.
9. Shankar is quite rich.  He is very generous to the poor.
10. Bob did not come to the party. Jill also did not come to the party.

## Answers

1. I cannot help you with financial assistance **_for_** I am quite poor.
2. Mr. Singh is planning to visit **_both_** Europe and the US during this summer. (also: *as well as)*
3. Make haste **_or_** you will be late for the programme. (also: *otherwise*)
4. **_Though_** it was a stormy night, **_yet_** Manu went out.
5. Santhosh is **_not only_** quite lazy **_but also_** dishonest.
6. There was an accident on the road, **_yet_** no one was injured.
7. **_Both_** you and I are right.
8. Prepare well for the test, **_otherwise_** you may fail. (also: *or)*
9. Shankar is quite rich; **_nevertheless_** he is generous to the poor.
10. **_Neithe_**r Bob **_nor_** Jill came to the party.

—xxx—

## Useful data

### 9. Manias (*Deep desire or an abnormal desire for something*)

| | | |
|---|---|---|
| 1. Alcohol | : | Dipsomania |
| 2. Books | : | Bibliomania |
| 3. Eating | : | Phagomania/Sitomania |
| 4. Stealing | : | Kleptomania |
| 5. Work | : | Ergomania |
| 6. Sex | : | Erotomania/Nymphomania |
| 7. Pleasure | : | Hedonomania |
| 8. Personal cleanliness | : | Ablutomania |

# 16. Formation of complex sentence

**Complex sentence:** A sentence which is made up of one main or principal clause and one or more subordinate clauses is known as a complex sentence.

    **e.g.:** India is a country which is making rapid progress in every sector of the economy.

    The <u>principal clause is</u>: *India is a country.*

    The <u>subordinate clause is</u>: *which is making rapid progress in every sector of the economy.*

## <u>Methods of combining simple sentences into complex:</u>

We can combine simple sentences into complex by using the  following **subordinate conjunctions.**

| | | | |
|---|---|---|---|
| that | who | what | which |
| where | whose | when | whom |
| though | although | Even though | till |
| as | after | before | because |
| whether | if | since | than |
| unless | lest (*if not*) | as though | as if |
| in case | so that | so... that | such ....that |
| as....as | so... as | as... so | no sooner... than |
| hardly...when | scarcely...when | on condition that | provided that |
| whatever | wherever | whoever | however, etc. |

<u>**Examples**</u> (*More examples are given in the section on **conjunction***)
1. **that:**

    I know **that** you are doing well in your business.
2. **who**

    I know the gentleman **who** was the chief guest at the function.
3. **what**

    Maria spent **what** she earned.
4. **which**

    The mangoes **which** I bought yesterday were fresh.
5. **where**

    This is the place **where** the accident took place recently.
6. **whose**

    I know the boy **whose** father died last week.

**7. when**

It was raining heavily **when** we went out.

**8. whom**

I have met the officer **whom** the minister had slapped.

**9. though**

**Though** Sathyan is from a rich family, he doesn't behave like a rich boy.

**10. Even though**

**Even though** the doctor tried his best, he couldn't save the patient.

**11. although**

**Although** the doctor had advised Sam not to take alcohol, he continued to take drinks without any control.

**12. till**

You can stay  with us **till** you complete your course in this town.

**13. as**

**As** it was raining heavily, I couldn't go to the town.

**14. after**

**After** Sham had taken the medicine, he felt much better.

**15. before**

**Before** the minister arrived at the venue, the people had dispersed.

**16. because**

I couldn't attend the seminar **because** I was sick.

**17. whether**

I am not sure **whether** you like your present job.

**18. if**

**If** you put in your best efforts, you can definitely get a high band score in IELTS.

**19. since**

**Since** it was  raining, the match was put off.

**20. than**

My sister cooks better **than** my mother does.

**21. unless**

Unless India  gets the support of the USA, she won't get a permanent seat in the UN Security Council.

**22. lest** *(lest is always accompanied by the modal verb 'should')*

Hold on to the wall for support **lest** you should fall.

**23. as though**

Mithun speaks about cricket **as though** he knows all about it.

**24. as if**

The asst. manager behaves **as if** he were the director of the company.

**25. in case**

You needn't come to class **in case** it rains.

**26. as soon as**

**As soon as** the minister reached the venue of the meeting, there was a sudden explosion.

**27. so that**

Do exercise everyday **so that** you may have good health.

**28. such ....that**

'The God of Small Things' is **such** an interesting book **that** you won't stop reading it until you finish it.

**29. so... that**

India is developing **so** fast **that** within a few years she might become an economic superpower.

**30. as....as**

The city of Bangalore is not **as** planned **as** that of  Chandigarh.

**31.  no sooner... than** *(do not use: no sooner ... when)*

**No sooner** had the match started **than** the crowd began shouting.

**32. hardly...when**

**Hardly** had Tom completed his engineering course **when** he was offered a high post in one of the IT companies in Bangalore.

**33. scarcely...when** *(do not use: scarcely....than)*

**Scarcely** had the patient got up to stand **when** he felt dizzy and fell to the floor.

**34. as long as**

You can stay with us **as long as** you work in this town.

**35. on condition that**

I shall  give you the amount you asked for **on condition that** you pay it back within a month.

**36. provided that**

You can take my vehicle **provided that** you get a good driver to drive it.

**37. whatever**

**Whatever** you may say, India is on the verge of becoming an economic superpower.

**38. wherever**

Some individuals shine out **wherever** they go.

**39. whoever**

**Whoever** you may be, you must stand in the queue like everyone else.

**40. however**

**However** hard you try, you are not going to solve this puzzle.

Formation of complex sentence

## Important rules regarding complex sentences

1. A complex sentence consists of **one main** or **principal clause** and **one** or **more subordinate clauses**. Make sure that:

If the principal clause is in the **past tense**, the subordinate clause should also be in **the past tense**.

e.g. <u>The watchman asked me</u> what <u>I wanted.</u>
past tense    past tense

2. Placing which clause first or second *(principal or subordinate clause)* depends on what one plans to emphasize. Generally, the most important information or the point one wants to emphasize is given last. That can be principal clause or subordinate clause.

 **e.g.:** i) When I was playing basketball, **<u>I slipped and fractured</u>** my leg. (The emphasis is **on what happened**)

   ii) I slipped and fractured my leg when I **<u>was playing basketball.</u>** (The emphasis is on ***when the event happened)***

3. When we start a complex sentence with a subordinate clause, a comma should be placed after the subordinate clause.

 **e.g.:** After I completed my assignment**,** I watched a movie.

## From simple to complex
(More than one simple sentence combined to form complex)

1. <u>Read the following and see how simple sentences are combined to form complex sentences.</u>
*(you can combine the sentences in more than one way)*

1. *Simple* : The old woman is weak. She is unable to walk.
 *Complex* : The old woman is **<u>so</u>** weak **<u>that</u>** she is unable to walk. (also :*as/ since/ because,*etc.)

2. *Simple* : He completed his work. He went home.
 *Complex* : **<u>As soon as</u>** he completed his work, he went home. (also: *when/before/ after,* etc.)

3. *Simple* : I saw a beggar. He was carrying a lantern.
 *Complex* : I saw a beggar **<u>who</u>** was carrying a lantern.

4. *Simple* : My brother failed. This news disappointed me.
 *Complex* : The news **<u>that</u>** my brother had failed disappointed me.

5. *Simple* : The old woman fell down. She hurt herself.
 *Complex* : **<u>As</u>** the old woman fell down she hurt herself. (also: *since/because,* etc.)

6. *Simple* : He passed the test. It was fortunate.
 *Complex* : It was fortunate **<u>that</u>** he had passed the test.

122

7. Simple    : He worked hard. His health broke down.
   Complex  : He worked **so** hard **that** his health broke down.( also : *as/since/because,* etc.)
9. *Simple*     : Don't eat too much. You will become ill.
   *Complex*  : **If** you eat too much you will become ill.
10. *Simple*   : You have made a mistake. I think so.
   *Complex*  : I think **that** you have made a mistake.

**(From a single simple sentence to complex)**

2. <u>Read the following sentences:</u>
1. *Simple*    : This is a beautiful flower.
  *Complex*  : This is a flower **which** is beautiful.
2. *Simple*    : He was too dull to understand.
  Complex  : He was **so** dull **that** he could not understand.
3. *Simple*    : His silence proves his guilt.
  *Complex*  : The fact **that** he is silent proves his guilt.
4. *Simple*    : Tell the truth.
  *Complex*  : Tell **what** is true.
5. *Simple*    : We eat to live.
  *Complex*  : We eat **that** we may live.
6. *Simple*    : He is too lazy to succeed.
  *Complex*  : He is **so** lazy **that** he cannot succeed.
7. *Simple*    : Tell me your age.
  *Complex*  : Tell me **what** your age is.
8. *Simple*    : It is too late to retreat.
  *Complex*  : It is **so** late **that** one cannot retreat.
9. *Simple*    : Come back at six o'clock.
  *Complex*  : Come back **when** it is six o'clock.
10. *Simple*   : Birds cannot fly without wings.
  *Complex*  : Birds cannot fly **unless** they have wings.

# Exercise

1.**<u>Combine the following simple sentences into complex sentences:</u>**
1. Tom will pass the test this time. There is no doubt about it.
2. Don't walk too fast. You will be tired.
3. My grandfather is too weak. He cannot walk without help.
4. Robin is my best friend. He is a journalist.
5. John wanted to go abroad. He studied IELTS.
6. I visited the village. I was born there.

7. The peon rang the bell. The students ran to their classrooms.

8. Hariharan was selected. He looked very smart.

9. The doctors did their best. They could not save the patient.

10. This is a scenery. It is very beautiful.

11. Linda went to the supermarket. Later she visited her friend in the hospital.

12. Mr. Jones met with an accident with his bike. He was driving very fast.

13. Raman missed the bus. He reached the school late.

14. The mangoes were ripe. I bought them yesterday.

15. You are ready. We shall go for a walk.

**Answers**

1. There is no doubt **that** Tom will pass the test this time.

2. You will be tired **if** you walk too fast.

3. **As** my grandfather is weak, he cannot walk without help. (also: *because, since, for*)

4. Robin, **who** is a journalist, is my best friend.

5. John studied IELTS because he wanted to go abroad. (also: *as, since, for*)

6. I visited the village **where** I was born.

7. The students ran to their classrooms **as soon as** the peon rang the bell. (also: *when*)
   *OR* **No sooner** did the peon ring the bell **than** the students ran to their classrooms.

8. Hariharan was selected **because** he looked smart (also: *as, since, for*)

9. **Although** the doctors did their best, they could not save the patient.

10. This is a scenery **which** is very beautiful.

11. **After** Linda went to the supermarket, she visited her friend in the hospital.

12. **As** Mr. Jones was driving his bike very fast, he met with an accident. (also: *because, since, for*)

13. **Since** Raman missed the bus, he reached the school late. (also : *as, because*)

14. The mangoes, **which** I bought yesterday, were ripe.

15. **If** you are ready, we shall go for a walk.

—xxx-—
**Useful data**

## 10. Binomials (*These are words that are joined either by 'and' or 'or'.*)

| | | |
|---|---|---|
| bag and baggage | body and soul | bread and butter |
| time and tide | ways and means | pros and cons |
| profit and loss | law and order | bloom and gloom |
| ups and downs | friend or foe | first and foremost |
| rank and file | glitter and litter | twists and turns |
| hustle and bustle | spic and span | wear and tear |
| flora and fauna | safe and sound | give and take |
| heat and dust | hit and run | boon or bane |

# 17. Question Tag

<u>**Points to note**</u>

The question tag is also known as the *note of interrogation* (?).

The question tag is generally used at the end of an assertive sentence.

There is a comma after the statement.

The question tag begins with a small letter.

<u>**Use of question tag:**</u> The question tag is used when the speaker makes a statement but is not completely certain of the truth and wants to verify the statement.

## Important rules

**1.** If the given sentence is affirmative, the question tag is negative.

> **auxiliary verb + n't + subject pronoun**

**e.g.:**   1. This is a beautiful scenery.

This is a beautiful scenery, **isn't it**?

2. Mr. Andrews has done well in the test.

Mr. Andrews has done well in the test, **hasn't he**?

3. I am well.

I am well, **<u>aren't I</u>**? (*Not amn't I*)

2.If the given sentence is negative, the question tag is positive.

> **auxiliary verb + subject pronoun**

**e.g.:**   1. This is not a beautiful scenery.

This is not a beautiful scenery, **is it**?

2. Mr. Andrews has not done well in the test.

Mr. Andrews has not done well in the test, **has he**?

3. I am not well.

I am not well, **am I?**

<u>**A special note:**</u>

1. Whenever the auxiliary verb is not given, the understood auxiliary verbs for present tense are:

**does** (*for singular nouns*)

**do** (*for plural nouns*)

For past tense, the understood auxiliary verb is: **did**

**e.g.:**   i) My sister sings well.

My sister sings well, **doesn't she?**

        ii) Australians speak English.

          Australians speak English, **don't they**?

        iii) Anand wrote an excellent article for the magazine.

          Anand wrote an excellent article for the magazine, **didn't he?**

2. If there are two auxiliaries in a sentence, only the first is used in the formation of the question tag.

    **e.g.:**  i) You <u>should</u> have done this job.

          You should have done this job, **shouldn't you**?

3. In sentences beginning with **'Let us'** the question tag is *shall we?*

    **e.g.:**  i) **Let us** go for a picnic.

          Let us go for a picnic, **shall we**?

4. In sentences starting with *'There'*, use **'there'** in the question tag as well.

    **e.g.:**  i) **There** are many questions to be answered.

          There are many questions  to be answered, **aren't there**?

5. After imperative sentences, the question tag usually is: **will you**?

    **e.g.:**  i) Shut the door.

          Shut the door, **will you**?

6. When semi-negative terms such as *few, little, hardly, rarely, scarcely, barely, seldom*, etc. are used, the question tag is positive.

    **e.g.:**  i) Mr. Singh **hardly** speaks English.

          Mr. Singh hardly speaks English, **does he**?

7. **A few** and **a little** convey a positive idea. Hence the question tag is negative.

    **e.g.:**  i) A few students were waiting for me.

          A few students were waiting for me, **weren't they**?

8. The adverb **'only'** has a negative touch and so the question tag is positive.

    **e.g.:**  i) Only two students took the test this time.

          Only two students took the test this time, **did they?**

9. For **everyone** and **everybody** the question tag generally is plural when these terms have a collective rather than a distributive sense.

    **e.g.:**  i) Everybody can't be clever.

          Everybody can't be clever, **can they**?

10. The question tag for **'everything'** is generally *'it'*.

    **e.g.:**  i) Everything looks really charming here.

          Everything looks really charming here, **doesn't it?**

11. The negative forms in question tags are usually contracted to **n't**. If they are not contracted the following order should be followed.

**auxiliary verb + subject pronoun + not**

**e.g.:**  i) You have done well.
You have done well, **have you not**?

Special cases of 'n't'

am + not  = **aren't**
do + not  = **don't**
will + not = **won't**
can + not = **can't**

# Exercise

1. **Fill the gaps with suitable question tags:**
1. It is very hot today,—?
2. I am quite all right,—?
3. Mohan does not take milk,—?
4. Your father is a doctor,—?
5. You are doing well, ___?
6. It isn't ready yet, —?
7. I needn't get up early tomorrow, —.
8. I can hardly understand your language,—?
9. I will come later, —?
10. You like him,—?

**Answers**

1 **Fill the gaps with suitable question tags:**

| | |
|---|---|
| 1. isn't it? | 2. aren't I? |
| 3. does he? | 4. isn't he? |
| 5. aren't you? | 6. is it? |
| 7. need I? | 8. can I? |
| 9. won't I? | 10. don't you? |

—xxx—-

# 18. Modal auxiliaries

**Modal auxiliaries:** The auxiliary verbs which are mainly used to form tenses, question tags, to indicate certainty, obligation, possibility, necessity, permission, ability, etc. are known as modal auxiliaries. Modal auxiliaries, unlike primary auxiliaries *(be, has, does)*, cannot be used alone in a sentence. These can be used only with main verbs.

**Main features**:

    i) Modal verbs have only one form.

    ii) They have **no -ing** or **ed forms.**

    iii) They do not add **'s'** to the 3rd person singular.

### Main modal auxiliaries

| | |
|---|---|
| 1. Will | 8. Would |
| 2. Shall | 9. Should |
| 3. Can | 10. Could |
| 4. May | 11. Might |
| 5. Must | 12. Ought |
| 6. Dare | 13. Need |
| 7. Used to | |

### 1. Will

1) <u>**Will** in the first person</u> is used to denote determination, promise, threat, wish, willingness, etc.

    **e.g.:**  i) I **will** do it the way I like. *(determination)*

          ii) We **will** help you in your difficulty. *(promise)*

          iii) I **will** fine you if you do not complete the work in time. *(threat)*

          iv) We **will** visit Goa soon. *(wish)*

          v) I **will** give you my wholehearted support. *(willingness)*

2) <u>**Will** in the second and third persons</u> indicates simple future.

    **e.g.:**  i) The train **will** arrive at 7.30 p.m.

3) To express a characteristic habit.

    **e.g.:**  i) Maya **will** never keep quiet.

4) To express an assumption or probability.

    **e.g.:**  i) That **will** be a letter for me.

5) To express an invitation or a request.

    **e.g.:**  i) **Will** you come with me to the market?

6) **Will you + please** is used to express a request or an invitation.

    **e.g.:**  i) **Will** you please open the window?

          ii) **Will** you have a cup of coffee, please?

7) **Will you** without **please** is usually used to express command.

    **e.g.:**  i) **Will you** open the window?

Special Note:  **Will** is never used in the first person to ask a question.

    **e.g.:**  i) **Will** I go? **(X)**

        **Shall** I go? (✓)

        ii) I **will** not be able to go to the office today. **(X)** *(because **will** expresses a determination on the part of the speaker)*

        I **shall** not be able to go to the office today.

        iii) I **will** be only happy to do so. **(X)**

        I **shall** be only happy to do so. (✓)

        iv) I **will** have much pleasure in accepting your invitation. **(X)**

        I **shall** have much pleasure in accepting your invitation. (✓)

**2. Would** (*past form of* **will**)

<u>**Would** is used:</u>

1. **Would** is the past form of **'will'**. It does the same function in the indirect speech as **will** in the direct speech.

    **e.g.:**  Mr Williams said that he **would** visit England in the coming month.

2. **Would** expresses the idea of **'probability'** and does not stand for any commitment.

    **e.g.:** My friend **would** come tonight. *(probably)*

3) To express a past habit.

    **e.g.:** My father **would** read the newspaper in the evening.

4. To express a wish or desire.

    **e.g.: Would** that I were a minister?

5. To express a determination.

    **e.g.:** He **would** not give up his efforts.

6. To express a polite request.

    **e.g.: Would** you please lend me your bike?

7. 'Would' used with *'prefer'* to express preferences.

    **e.g.:** I **would** prefer death to dishonour.

8. **Would** is used with *'like'* to express a wish.

    **e.g.:** We **would like** to meet the director now.

9. **Would** is used in conditional sentences to express unreal conditions.

    **e.g.:**  i) If you studied well, you **would** pass the test.

        ii) If I were a bird, I **would** fly.

10. To express extreme politeness.

    **e.g.: Would** you mind if I open the window?

## 3. Shall

<u>**Shall** is used</u>:

1) <u>In the first person</u> to denote simple future.

    **e.g.:** i) I **shall** meet you later today.

2) <u>Shall is used in the **second and third persons**</u> to denote *a promise, threat, Command, determination, certainty,* etc.

    **e.g.:** i) The watchman **shall** be dismissed. *(threat)*

        ii) You **shall** complete it before I go. *(command)*

        iii) They **shall** do it now. *(determination)*

        iv) If you do not have any goals in life, you **shall** not reach anywhere. *(certainty)*

3) To express offer or request.

    **e.g.:** i) **Shall** we begin our class now?

4) **Shall** is used for seeking further instructions.

    **e.g.:** i) Where **shall** we go now?

<u>Special note</u>:

i) **Shall** is normally used with 1$^{st}$ person (**I-we**)

    **e.g.:** I **shall** go home tonight.

ii) **Shall** and not **will** is normally used in legal terms.

    **e.g.** The criminal **shall be** punished.

iii) **Shall,** not **will,** is used to express universal truth.

    **e.g.:** We **shall** all die one day.

## 4. Should *(past form of shall)*

<u>**Should is used in the following situations**</u>:

1) **Should** is the past form of shall. It does the same function in indirect speech as **shall** in direct speech.

    **e.g.:** The police officer said that the culprit **should** be severely punished.

2) **Should** is used to express duty, purpose, determination, probability, moral obligation, etc.

    **e.g.:** i) We **should** obey our parents. *(duty)*

        ii) Work hard lest you **should** fail. *(purpose)*

        iii) We **should** meet tomorrow. *(determination)*

        iv) Rakesh **should** be playing now. *(probability)*

        v) We **should** help the poor and the needy. *(moral obligation)*

3) **Should** is used in **if** clauses to express a supposition or probability.

    **e.g.:**  i) If it **should** rain, the meeting would be postponed.

          ii) **Should** I be given a chance to work in your esteemed organization, I shall be grateful.

4) **'Should have'** is used to refer to duty not done in the past.

    **e.g.:**  You **should** have behaved well in the meeting.

5) **Shouldn't have** is used to express the idea that something wrong was done in the past.

    **e.g.:**  He **shouldn't** have gone there.

6) **'Should'** is used with **'lest'** to express a negative purpose.

    (*The term **'lest'** is always accompanied by **'should'**.*)

    **e.g.:**  You must study well **lest** you **should** fail in the test.

7) **Should** is used with **'like to'** to make a polite request.

    **e.g.:**  I **should like** to congratulate you on your success.

# 5. Can

<u>**Can**</u> is used :

1) To show power or ability.

    **e.g.:**  i) Mr. Sanders **can** speak German quite fluently.

2) To express permission.

    **e.g.:**  i) You **can** go home after you complete your work.

3) To express possibility or an impossibility.

    **e.g.:**  i) It **cannot** be done.

          ii) The answer **can** be easily found out.

4) To ask questions.

    **e.g.:**  i) **Can** I go now?

5) With verbs of perception such as *'see, hear, smell, taste'* etc. as a substitute for continuous tense.

    **e.g.:**  i) I **can** see a boy climbing the wall.

          ii) We **can** hear the music coming from the room.

6) **Cannot** or **can't** is one word and is used in the sense of prohibition.

    **e.g.:**  You **can't** enter this room.

7) **'Can't help'** is used in the sense of *'cannot avoid'*.

    **e.g.:**  I **can't help** laughing at his witty remark.

<u>Special note</u> :

i) *For permission it is better to use **'may'** instead of **'can'**.*

    **e.g.:**  **Can** I come in? ***(not-so-correct)***

          **May** I come in?

ii) *Do not use* **can** *for permission from someone above you.* Use instead *'may'* or *'could'.*

      **e.g.:**   **Can** I speak to you for a moment, sir?

              **May** I speak to you for a moment, sir?

              **Could** I speak to you for a moment, sir?

## 6. Could *(past form of 'can')*

i) **'Could'** is the past form of **'can'** and is used to indicate an ability that existed in the past.

      **e.g.:**   I **could** swim for long hours when I was young.

ii) **Could** is used as the past form of **'can'** in indirect speech.

      **e.g.:**   The foreign tourist said that she **could** understand Malayalam quite well.

<u>**Could** is used</u>:

1) To express ability, request, possibility, permission, etc.

      **e.g.:**   i) Anish **could** run very fast. *(ability of the past)*

              ii) **Could** you lend me a few rupees?*(request)*

              iii) We **could** win the match  if we played harder. *(possibility)*

              iv) **Could** I speak to your director? *(permission)*

2) **Could** is used to express a feeling of impatience.

      **e.g.:**   i) How **could** it happen?

              ii) How **could** you do it alone?

3) **'Could have'** is used in **if clauses.**

      **e.g.:**   If Elizabeth had danced well, she **could have** got the first prize in the dance  competition.

4) **'Couldn't help'** is used in the sense of *'could not avoid'.*

      **e.g.:**   I **couldn't help** scolding him as he continued to make the same mistake again and again.

<u>Special note</u>:

**Polite requests** are generally introduced by *'would, may, can,* etc. **'Could'** is considered <u>more polite</u> than the above terms.

      **e.g.:**   **Could** you spare some time for me?

## 7. May

<u>**May** is used</u>:

1) To express permission.

      **e.g.:**   **May** I come in? Yes, you may.

2) To express doubt, uncertainty, possibility, etc.

      **e.g.:**   It **may** rain tonight.

3) To express a purpose.

    **e.g.:**  We eat so that we **may** live.

4) To express wishes or prayers.

    **e.g.:**  i) **May** his soul rest in peace.

           ii) **May** God bless you.

5) To ask a question.

    **e.g.:**  **May** I trouble you a minute to ask a doubt?

## 8. Might (*past form of 'may'*)

1) **'Might'** is the past form of *'may'* and is used in indirect speech.

    **e.g.:**  I asked Arjun if he **might** accompany me to the market.

2) **'Might'** is used to express doubtful possibility.

    **e.g.:**  i) I think you better study hard. The questions **might** be tough.

           ii) Rani could not attend the marriage function. She **might** be sick.

3) To express a purpose.

    **e.g.:**  The team played well so that they **might** get the trophy this time.

4) To express a future condition.

    **e.g.:**  If Maria works harder, she **might** be able to come top in the class.

5) To express good wishes in the past.

    **e.g.:**  We wished that India **might** win the match.

6) **'Might'** is used (*not **may***) when one wants to be very polite.

    **e.g.:**  You **might** make a little less noise.

7) To express a suggestion.

    **e.g.:**  You **might** go home now.

8) **'might'** is used when we want to be extremely polite.

    **e.g.:**  **Might** we go now?

9) **'might'** is used to express more doubtful possibility than **'may'**.

    **e.g.**  I may pass the test.

           I **might** pass the test. (*shows more doubtful possibility*)

## 9. Must

<u>**Must** is used:</u>

1) To express compulsion.

    **e.g.:**  You **must** do this work before you go home.

2) To express certainty.

    **e.g.:**  I **must** go through today's paper.

3) To express duty.

    **e.g.:**  Everyone **must** do their duty.

4) To express determination.

> **e.g.:** I **must** not get wet.

5) To express inevitability.

> **e.g.:** What cannot be cured **must be** endured.

6) To express strong likelihood or possibility.

> **e.g. :** My grandfather **must** be over eighty years old.

7) To express an inevitable result.

> **e.g.:** We **must** all die one day.

8) To express prohibitions.

> **e.g.:** You **must** not smoke here.

9) To ask a question.

> **e.g.:** **Must** I wait for him?

<u>Special note</u>:

**'Must'** is much stronger than '**should**' as regards obligation.

> Past equivalent of *must*       :      **had to**
> Future equivalent of *must*     :      **will have to**

## 10. Ought

**<u>Ought</u> is used:**

1) To express duty or obligation in the present tense.

> **e.g.:** You **ought** to have done this job before.

2) To express desirability.

> **e.g.:** You **ought** to have seen the match.

3) To express a strong probability.

> **e.g.:** Sam is hard-working. He **ought** to get a high score in the examination.

4) To express an advice.

> **e.g.:** You **ought** to consult a doctor.

5) **'Ought to have'** with a past participle is used to indicate a past obligation that was not fulfilled.

> **e.g.:** i) You **ought** to have helped the poor beggar who asked you for some help.
>
> ii) You **ought** to have studied well if you wanted a good result.

6) **'Ought not to have'** is used to indicate disapproval of something that was done in the past.

> **e.g.:** You **ought not to have** gone there.

## 11. Dare

**Dare** means *'brave enough to challenge'*. It is generally used in negative and interrogative sentences.

    1) Dare is used in the present tense.

        **e.g.:**  i) Mr. Dave **dares** to face his opponent.

               ii) He doesn't **dare to** ring her up again.

    2) '**Dares not**' means *'not to have courage'*.

        **e.g.:**  i) Hari **dares not** take such a foolish step.

               ii) He **dares not** punish his only child.

    3) **Dare** is used in negative past tense.

        **e.g.:**  i) He **dared** not say it again.

               ii) They **dared** not go out in the night.

    4) **Dare** is used in interrogative sentences.

        **e.g.:**  i) How **dare** you take my book?

               ii) How **dare** you say such words to me?

## 12. Need

**Need** is used as a main verb.

        **e.g.:** I **need** some good books to read.

**Need** as a modal verb is used in negative and interrogative sentences. In such sentences, **need** is used to express *weakness, necessity* or *obligation*.

    1) To express absence or obligation.

        **e.g.:**  Mohan **need** not go now.

    2) To show an unnecessary action which was anyway done.

        **e.g.:**  I **needn't** have gone there.

    3) Used in questions.

        **e.g.:**  i) **Need** she apologize to him?

               ii) **Need** I return you the book within a few days?

## 13. Used to

**'Used to'** is used

i) To express a **past habit** which no longer exists.

    When *'used to'* is used in this meaning, the subject is used without an auxiliary verb.

Sub + used to + verb in simple form

        **e.g.:**  i) I <u>**used to**</u> smoke in my younger days.

               ii) Sham **used to** come here.

2. To express an *'accustomed habit in the present or past'*.

When **'used to'** is used in this meaning, the subject is used along with some auxiliary verb and the accompanying verb is in *ing* **form**.

> Sub + Aux. verb + **used to** + verb in **ING** form

> **e.g.:**   I am <u>used to </u>taking tea in the morning. *(an accustomed habit in the present)*
>
> I was <u>used to</u> taking tea in the morning. (*a habit that began in the past which may or may not be going on now.)*

# Modals + perfective *(have + past participle)*

### 1. <u>May have/could have/might have</u>

*May have/could have/might have....* indicates a **past possibility**. It may also mean a possibility in the present.

> **e.g.:**   i) The train <u>**may have**</u> already reached the station.
>
> ii) The cause of the child's death <u>**could have been**</u> malaria.
>
> iii) Mr. Roy <u>**might have**</u> joined the new post last month.

### 2. <u>Should have</u>

*Should have ....* is used to indicate an **obligation** that was supposed to occur in the past but for some reasons did not.

> **e.g.:**   i) Tom <u>**should have**</u> studied this morning. (*Tom did not study in the morning)*
>
> ii) The engineer <u>**should have**</u> come to inspect the site.
>
>    (*The engineer did not come to inspect the site.*)
>
> iii) Sarita **shouldn't have** gone out with him. (*Sarita did go with him.*)

### 3. <u>Must have</u>

*'Must have'....* is used to indicate a **logical conclusion**.

*'Must have'* should not be used to show a past obligation.

> **e.g.:**   i) It is raining. My brother <u>**must have**</u> got wet.
>
> ii) Roy had prepared well for the test. He <u>**must have**</u> passed it.
>
> iii) The lights in Tom's room are no longer on. He <u>**must have**</u> gone to bed.

* To speak of meeting someone whom you have met before, do not use **'** **must have'**. Use **'might have'**.

> **e.g.:**   I **must have seen** you before. **(X)**
>
> I **might have** seen you before.(✓)

### 4. <u>Supposed to</u> = **should have**

*Supposed to...* is used to indicate **a past obligation** which did not take place due to some reasons.

Modal auxiliaries

**e.g.:**   i) I was **<u>supposed to</u>** meet my friend yesterday. (*But I didn't meet him.*)

ii) The programme was **<u>supposed to</u>** begin at 6.30 p.m.

(*But it did not begin at 6.30 p.m.*)

iii) The meeting is **<u>supposed to</u>** begin now. (*The meeting hasn't begun yet.*)

# Exercise

## 2. <u>Fill the blanks with the correct modal auxiliaries:</u>

1. Prakash said that he — take the test soon.
2. None of you — leave the room now.
3. The grass is wet. It — rained last night.
4. Cling on to the wall lest you— fall.
5. If Marcia had worked hard, she ...... passed the test.
6. — we go for a movie tonight?
7. What cannot be cured — be endured.
8. Mohan ran fast that he — catch the train.
9. — you lend me your book, please?
10. — you please stop talking?
11. — you mind passing the cake?
12. Rani is absent. She — be sick.
13. — we start the function an hour later?
14. You — go home if you want.
15. I — smoke in my younger days.

### <u>Answers</u>

2. **Fill the blanks with correct modal auxiliaries:**

| | | | | |
|---|---|---|---|---|
| 1. would | 2. should | 3. must have | 4. should | 5. would have |
| 6. Shall | 7. must | 8. might | 9. Could | 10. Could |
| 11. Would | 12. must | 13. Shall | 14. may | 15. used to |

—xxx—

# 11. Proper terms for comparisons/simile

| | | |
|---|---|---|
| As beautiful as a rainbow | As bitter as gall | As black as coal |
| As blind as a bat | As blithe as a lark | As blue as the sky |
| As boundless as the ocean | As brave as a lion | As brief as a dream |
| As brittle as glass | As busy as a bee | As clear as crystal |
| As cold as ice | As cool as a cucumber | As cozy as a bird's nest |
| As countless as the stars | As cruel as death | As cunning as a fox |
| As deceptive as the mirage | As deep as the ocean | As desolate as a tomb |
| As devoted as a faithful dog | As dumb as a statue | As faithful as a dog |

# 19. Conditional sentences (*if clause*)

**If clause** is generally used in four tense forms:
1. If I **study** well......................(*present tense*)
2. If I **studied** well................ (*past simple*)
3. If I **had studied** well........ .(*past perfect*)
4. If I **were**......................... ( *hypothetical situation*)

A. **The real conditional sentence:** The real conditional **if clause** is used for actions that are likely to take place. There should be a possibility of action.

### i) If clause **present simple** - main clause **future tense**

> **If** clause + **simple present** - main clause **future tense/ present simple**

**e.g.:** i) If you **get** the first rank in the test, I **will give** you a prize.

ii) If you **go** to the town, kindly post this letter.

B. **Unreal conditional sentence:** Unreal conditional **if clause** is used for actions that may not happen or would not happen at all.

### ii) If clause **simple past** - main clause **conditional tense** (*would/could/might*)

> *would*
> **If** clause + **simple past** + main clause *could* + verb in simple form
> *might*

**e.g.:** i) If you **worked** hard, you **could get** a better result.

ii) If Jayan **didn't speak** so fast, we **could understand** him.

<u>Special note</u>
* **If** and **will** cannot be used together in the same clause as 'if' has a touch of future. Therefore, all the four future tense forms (*future simple, future continuous, future perfect and future perfect continuous*) cannot be used with 'if'.

### iii) If clause **past perfect/past perfect continuous** - main clause **conditional perfect** tense (*would have/could have/ might have*)

> *would have*
> If clause + **past perfect** + main clause - *could* have + verb in past participle
> *might have*

**e.g.:** i) If you **had worked** hard, you **could have** got a better result.

ii) If Maria **had been working** in the US, she **would have earned** a lot of money.

iii) <u>If clause in **'were' form** - main clause **conditional simple tense**</u>( *would/could/might*)

The 'were' form of 'if clause' is used for actions or situations which are purely hypothetical or imaginary or a mere wish.

                                                       **would**

If clause + were ...main clause **could**  + verb in the simple form

                                                       **might**

**e.g.:** i) If I were a bird, I would fly.

ii) If I were you, I wouldn't do it.

### **B.** <u>Use of ' **had**' in place of '**if**'</u>

The **'if clause'** of past perfect conditional sentence can be replaced with **'had clause'**.

                                                    **would have**

**Had** + sub + verb (*in past participle form*) +  **could have** + verb in past participle

                                                        **might have**

**e.g.:** i) **Had** I gone there, I *could have* met him.

ii) **Had** we complained in time, the matter *would have* been settled by now.

**It is incorrect to say:**

1. If you **are going** to the town, ...**(X)**

2.If you **have completed** your studies...**(X)**

3. If you **have been** working...**(X)**

4. If I **will pass** the examination **(X)***( if has a touch of future and so it cannot go with 'will'.)*

5. If I **will be** working in the US...**(X)**

6. If I **would have been** a rich man ...**(X)**

7. If I **would** win a lottery....**(X)**

**Exception:**

i) **If +  will** is allowed for an obstinate habit.

    **e.g.:  If you will** go on gambling, you will get into trouble.

ii) **If +  will** is allowed when the 'If clause' is the object of the sentence.

    **e.g.:**  I don't know **if I will** have time to visit you.

**Use of 'if' in hypothetical situations:**
> i) If I were there, this wouldn't happen the way it happened.(✔)
>
> **or** If I had been there, this wouldn't have happened the way it happened.(✔)
>
> ii) If I were you, I wouldn't do it. (✔)
>
> If I were you, I would slap him with my sandals. (✔)

# Exercise

1. **<u>Fill the blanks with suitable conditional terms from the given choice:</u>**

1. If it rains, the match ——— be postponed.
>   a) will                    b) could
>
>   c) should             d) would

2. If Mahesh had taken the test, he ——— passed it.
>   a) would            b) would have
>
>   c) could             d) will

3. If I were a millionaire, I ——— give half of my wealth to the poor.
>   a) could            b) would
>
>   c) will               d) should

4. Had I met him, I ——— told him about the accident.
>   a) could have       b) will
>
>   c) should           d) might have

5. Buy for me a set of sketch pens if you — to the town.
>   a) go                  b) went
>
>   c) had gone        d) could go

6. Maham ——— passed if he had tried a bit harder.
>   a) would have       b) will have
>
>   c) have             d) would

7. If I —— a doctor I would not charge any fees from poor patients.
>   a) was               b) were
>
>   c) will               d) was

8. She —— secure a first class if she works hard.
>   a) would           b) will
>
>   c) could           d) might

9. If I had strength, I ——carry my luggage.
>   a) could have       b) would
>
>   c) will              d) shall

10. If you —— time to spare, then do come and meet me.
>   a) will have        b) have
>
>   c) could have      d) would have

<u>**Answers**</u>

|   |   |   |   |
|---|---|---|---|
| 1. will | 2. would have | 3. would | 4. could have |
| 5. go | 6. would have | 7. were | 8. will |
| 9. would | 10. have | | |

—xxx—

## <u>Useful data</u>

# 12. Differences between American and British English spellings

| American spelling | | British spelling | American spelling | | British spelling |
|---|---|---|---|---|---|
| 1. aluminum | : | aluminium | 18. jewelry | : | jewellery |
| 2. analyze | : | analyse | 19. labor | : | labour |
| 3. center | : | centre | 20. neighbor | : | neighbour |
| 4. color | : | colour | 21. organize | : | organise/ organize |
| 5. defense | : | defence | 22. pajamas | : | pyjamas |
| 6. enroll | : | enrol | 23. paralyze | : | paralyse |
| 7. fulfill | : | fulfil | 24. program | : | programme |
| 8. honor | : | honour | 25. realize | : | realise |
| 9. elevator | : | lift | 26. sidewalk | : | pavement |
| 10. first floor | : | ground floor | 27. truck | : | van, lorry |
| 11. garbage, trash | : | rubbish | 28. two weeks | : | fortnight, two weeks |
| 12. hood | : | bonnet | 29. vacation | : | holidays |
| 13. intersection | : | crossroads | 30. closet | : | cupboard |
| 14. mad | : | angry | 31. parking lot | : | car park |
| 15. movie, film | : | film | 32. billboard | : | hoarding |
| 16. resume | : | CV (curriculum vitae) | 33. candy | : | sweets |
| 17. zip code | : | postal code | 34. filling station | : | petrol station, etc. |

# 20. Punctuation

<u>**Punctuation:**</u> Punctuation is the art of placing certain visual indicators in written or printed text in order to separate sentences or a part of a sentence from another.

<u>**Principal marks of punctuation:**</u>

|  |  |  |
|---|---|---|
| 1. | Full stop | (. ) |
| 2. | Comma | (, ) |
| 3. | Semi-colon | (; ) |
| 4. | Colon | (: ) |
| 5. | Question mark | (? ) |
| 6. | Exclamation mark | (! ) |
| 7. | Quotation marks | (" ") |
| 8. | Apostrophe | (' ) |
| 9. | Hyphen | (- ) |
| 10. | Dash | ( _ ) |
| 11. | Ellipsis | (...) |
| 12. | Parentheses | ( ) |
| 13. | Brackets | [ ] |
| 14. | Virgule: | ( / ) |

## 1. <u>Full stop</u> (. )

The full stop or the period shows the longest pause.

<u>**Full stop is used:**</u>

1) At the end of all sentences unless they are interrogative or exclamatory.

    **e.g.:**  i) The world is becoming a global village.

          ii) Kindly sit down here.

2) In abbreviations and initials.

    **e.g.:**  i) B.C. (Before Christ)

          ii) U.S.A. (United States of America)

          iii) R.C. Mohan

<u>**Special note**</u>

    1) The full stop is generally used in abbreviations. But they are often omitted in modern writing.

    **e.g.:**  i) M.A. **or** MA

          ii) U.N.O. **or** UNO

          iii) U.S. **or** US

2) The full stop is not used in modern writing after the abbreviations of
        i) Mr (Mister)        ii) Mrs (Missis)
        iii) Ms (Miss)        iv) Dr (Doctor), etc.
    **e.g.:**  I had an appointment with Dr Hariprasad.

3) A full stop is replaced by an exclamation mark when an imperative command is given in a very angry and harsh manner.
    **e.g.:**  Get out of this place at once!

4) A question mark is replaced by a full stop when an interrogative sentence expresses a very formal and polite request.
    **e.g.:**  May I have your attention, please.

5) An acronym is written without full stops (*an acronym is a word formed from the initial letters of two or three words*)
    **e.g.:**  i) Radar ***(Radio And Detection And Ranging)***
        ii) GST (***Goods and Services Tax***)

6) Abbreviations of weights and measures of various kinds are written without stops.
        i) kg (kilogram)  ii) ft (foot/feet)
        iii) C (Celsius)     iv) kph (kilometres per hour)

**Note:** *a.m./p.m. can be written with or without stops.*

## 2. Comma (, )

The comma gives the shortest pause and is the most frequently used punctuation mark.

**Comma is used**

1) When several words of the same class follow.
    **e.g.:**  i) I shall have some apples, grapes, bananas, and tea.
        ii) Mohan is clever, handsome, brave, and hard-working.

2) Before and after words in apposition (*noun that immediately follows another*)
    **e.g.:**  i) Mr. Roberts, our principal, is on leave today.
        ii) Gandhi, the father of the nation, spent every drop of his blood for our country.

3) To separate a participle phrase
    **e.g.:**  i) Seeing my friend walking along the road, I ran after him.

4) Before and after the nominative of address.
    **e.g.:**  i) My dear students, I wish you all success.
        ii) Sir, may I leave now?

**Note:** When a word of address is placed at the end, a comma is used.
    **e.g.:**  i) Sit down, children.
        ii) Come in, Sangeeta.

5) To mark off a direct quotation from the reporting verb.

    **e.g.:** i) The old man said, "Man is mortal."

        ii) "No," replied the witness.

**Note:** *The full stop must be placed before the end of the last inverted comma.*

    **e.g.:** Robinson says, "Money is what money does**.**"

6) To separate parenthetical word, phrase or clause

    **e.g.:** i) India, in my view, would become an economic superpower within a few years.

        ii) Akbar, it is said, loved his subjects irrespective of caste or creed.

7) After introductory phrases and clauses.

    **e.g.:** i) As far as I am concerned, I am against the reservation policy of the government.

        ii) This morning, I would like to welcome our honourable chief guest.

8) To separate each pair of words connected by **'and'**.

    **e.g.:** rich and poor, high and low, wise and foolish, etc.

9) Before and after words, phrases or clauses let into the body of a sentence.

    **e.g.:** i) The mind, after all, is the most sensitive part of our person.

        ii) He, nevertheless, came to see me the other day.

10) To separate the words **Yes** or **No** from the rest of the sentence when some answer is made.

    **e.g.:** i) Yes, he is my best friend.

        ii) No, I don't think so.

11) To mark off two or more adverbs or adverbial phrases coming together.

    **e.g.:** i) Then, at length, India won independence from foreign rule.

        ii) Slowly, steadily he walked along the road.

12) To indicate the omission of a verb when repetition is to be avoided.

    **e.g.:** i) Shankar was a pure Brahmin; she, a Sudra.

        ii) Tom received a watch; Mohan, a pen.

13) To separate short co-ordinate clauses of a compound sentence.

    **e.g.:** i) I came, I saw, I conquered.

        ii) The way was long, the climb sharp.

14) To separate the date from the year:

    **e.g.:** i) July 10, 2021.

        ii) 12th May, 2020.

15) To separate a word or a phrase emphatically repeated.

    **e.g.:** Work, work, work till you are tired.

16) When an adverbial clause is placed first in a complex sentence.

    **e.g.:** i) When I reached the school, the class had already started.

        ii) After I had gone to the supermarket, I visited my friend in the hospital.

**Note:** *A comma is not used before an adverb clause when it follows the main clause.*

   **e.g.:**   The class had started when I reached school. *(no comma is required)*

17) When we start a sentence with modifiers:

   **e.g.:**   From 1990 to 2000, the sale of digital computers went up dramatically.

18) When we start a sentence with a linking term:

   **e.g.:**   In my humble view, the present economic downtrend is going to last for some time.

19) After the word **'well'** when it is used as an interjection.

   **e.g.:**   i) Well, it was an excellent performance.

   ii) Well, I will think about it.

20) It is used to separate a name from a degree /title/designation, etc.

   **e.g.:** i) This is Dr Ashok Kumar, head of the orthopaedic dept.

   ii) Mr Hariparsad, M.A., B.Ed.

21) It is used before **'please'** when it is placed at the end of the sentence.

   **e.g.:** i) Give me a glass of water, please.

   ii) Walk slowly, please.

22) It is used before question tags.

   **e.g.:**   i) It is an enchanting piece of scenery, isn't it?

   ii) You have finished your assignment, haven't you?

23) It is used before and after the following parenthesis expressions when they occur in the middle of a sentence.

> *as far as I know, in my view, if I think right, I believe,*
> *I hope, I think, I suppose, I presume, it seems, you know,* etc.

   **e.g.:**   i) Your argument, *if I think right,* is off the main point.

   ii) Your scheme, *to tell you very frankly,* is too vague.

24) It is used after  the following words or expressions.

> *in fact, perhaps, namely, in short, of course, nevertheless, however,*
> *moreover, for example, for instance, fortunately, luckily,* etc.

   **e.g.:**   i) Maria is quite intelligent. **However**, she does not make use of her intelligence.

   ii) My grandmother is over eighty. **Nevertheless,** she works like a young woman.

25) It is used in sentence adverbs,  i.e., adverbs placed at the beginning of a sentence.

   **e.g.:**   i) Perhaps, you will agree with my view.

   ii) Fortunately, we had a miraculous escape from the burning bus.

26) It is used after salutation and after the complimentary close in letters.

    **e.g.:**  Sir,

           Dear Sir,

           Yours sincerely,

           Yours faithfully,

           Sincerely yours, etc.

### 3. Semi-colon  (;)

The semi-colon makes a greater pause than that indicated by a comma.

**<u>A semi-colon is used</u>**:

1) To separate clauses in compound sentences not joined by a conjunction such as **'and, but, or '** etc.

    **e.g.:**  i) The road is winding; you will find the going tough.

           ii) He was a humble, broad-minded man; he passed away at 40.

2) It is used between main clauses joined by sentence connectives such as the following:

        ***besides, however, moreover, therefore,*** etc.

    **e.g.:**  The house looks majestic; besides, it has beautiful surroundings.

3) To separate several co-ordinate clauses joined by conjunction.

    **e.g.:**  Mr. Das is intelligent and hard-working; he is well appreciated by his colleagues.

4) To separate co-ordinate clauses

    **e.g.:**  To err is human; to forgive divine.

5) To separate pairs of words joined by a comma.

    **e.g.:**  heal, heel; fair, fare, etc.

6) When we use the following co-ordinate conjunctions:

    ***still, only, so, nevertheless, otherwise, therefore, hence, consequently,*** etc.

7) It is used to separate parts of a sentence when they contain many commas. In this type of sentence semi-colon is necessary to give clarity to the sentence.

    **e.g.:**  Our principal, Mr. Roberts, inaugurated the conference with an introductory talk; Mr. Dharam Singh, the senior most teacher, was the main speaker at the conference; Mr. Jayan, the vice-principal, concluded the conference with a short talk.

## 4. Colon (: )

The colon is a longer pause than a semi-colon.

**Colon is used:**

1) Before enumerating facts or things.

> **e.g.:**   The main kinds of nouns are:

2) To introduce maxims or sayings.

> **e.g.:**   Shakespeare says: "Brevity is the soul of wit."

## 5. Question mark:  (?)

**Question mark is used:**

1) At the end of a direct question.

> **e.g.:**   What do you want from me?

**Note:**  *A question mark is not used at the end of an indirect question.*

> **e.g.:**   The man asked me what I wanted.

2) After question tags.

> **e.g.:**   Shankar has done it, hasn't he?

3) A full stop is preferred to a question mark if an interrogative form expresses a formal request.

> **e.g.:**   May I have your attention, please.

**Note:** *Do not put a full stop after a question mark.*

> **e.g.:**   Do you think it is correct?. (*X*)
>
> Do you think it is correct?(✓)

## 6. Exclamation mark (!)

**Exclamation mark is used**

1) At the end of an exclamation expressing *joy/sorrow/surprise/praise/contempt,* etc.

> **e.g.:**   i) What a surprise!
>
> ii) How wonderful she is!
>
> iii) Ah! It's really nice!

2) After words of interjections

> **e.g.:**   i) Hurrah!          ii) Oh!
>
> ii) Alas!            iii) Lo!
>
> iv) Ah!

## 7. Quotation mark: (" ")

Quotation mark is of two types:

      i) Single quotation mark: (' ')

      ii) Double quotation mark: (" ")

1) **Single quotation marks** are generally used in British English while **double quotation marks** are used in American English.

2) We can use single or double quotation marks for direct speech or quotations.

    **e.g.:** i) The old man said, "Honesty is the best policy."

        ii) Keats says, 'Beauty is truth, truth beauty.'

3) We use single quotation marks (*not double quotation marks*) for words used in special ways such as, when we talk about a particular subject or topic or proverb, when we use a title, when we want to emphasize a particular word, etc.

    **e.g.:** i) 'The Loss of Inheritance' which won the Booker Prize recently, is written by Kiran Desai.

        ii) The question of 'reservation' in professional educational institutions is a debatable topic.

4) When there is a quotation within a quotation, single quotation marks can be used outside while double quotation marks are used within or double quotation marks are used outside while single quotation marks are used within. Both the forms are allowed.

    **e.g.:** My teacher said, " 'Time and tide waits for none' is a popular saying."

            My teacher said, ' "Time and tide waits for none" is a popular saying.'

**Note:** *The full stop must be placed before the last quotation mark.*

## 8. Apostrophe (')

**Apostrophe is used:**

1) To indicate possession.

    **e.g.:** i) Raj's umbrella.

        ii) Priya's toys.

2) To make plurals of letters and figures.

    **e.g.:** MA's, t's , 5's etc.

3) To indicate contraction of a word.

    **e.g.:** i) Don't (*do not*)

        ii) I'm (*I am*)

        iii) It's (*It is/it has*)

        iv) Hon'ble (*honourable*)

## 9. Hyphen: (-)

Hyphen is a shorter line than dash.

**Hyphen is used:**

1) To join parts of a compound word.

       i)  touch-me-not        ii)  mother-in-law

      iii)  dining-room       iv) passers-by

2) In writing out compound numbers from 21 to 99.

    **e.g.:**  i) twenty-five (*not twenty five*)

           ii) sixty-six (*not sixty six*)

3) To show fraction.

    **e.g.:** i) one-third   ii) two-third   iii) three-fourth, etc.

4) It is used to form compound words using prefix and a noun.

    **e.g.:**  i) ex-principal        ii) ultra-violet

          iii) co-education      iv) vice-president

## 10. Dash ( _ )

**Dash is used:**

1) After the colon.

    **e.g.:**  i) The main types of sentences are: -

          ii) The main results of globalization are: -

2) To make a parenthesis in a sentence.

    **e.g.:**  Mr. Singh had two sons - Raj and Anand.

3) To sum up several things or facts.

    **e.g.:**  Health, wealth, peace - all were lost.

## 11. Ellipsis (...)

A break or interruption in speech indicated by **three dots** is known as **ellipsis.** Ellipses are used when the whole is not relevant to the context of the discussion or writing. Ellipses are also used with direct quotation to indicate that word or words have been omitted.

    **e.g.:**  The stranger came dragging a heavy box; he looked ...

### 12. **Parentheses  (  )**

Parentheses  or double dash are used to separate a phrase or clause from the main part. A parenthetical clause has no grammatical relationship with the rest of the sentence.

    **e.g.:**  i) Dave sang the song (none of his colleagues could do it) with great ease and skill.

### 13. **Brackets  [    ]**

1) Brackets are used to enclose a parenthetical matter within parentheses.

    **e.g.:**  Shakespeare's most difficult tragedy (Hamlet [about 1600]) has been performed numerous times.

### 14. **Virgule  ( / )**

1) A virgule is used between two words to indicate that the meaning of either word could apply.

    **e.g.:**  This gift is for Williams/his brother.

2) It is used as a dividing line between dates, fractions and abbreviations.

    **e.g.:**  i ) 12/2/06      ii)  C/o (care of ), etc.

# Capital letters

1) A capital letter is used at the beginning of every sentence.

    **e.g.:**  One of my friends met with an accident recently.

2) It is used at the beginning of quotations.

    **e.g.:**  Jesus says, "Love your enemies."

3) Proper nouns begin with a capital letter.

    **e.g.:**  India is on the threshold of becoming a major economic power in the world.

4) The first personal pronoun '**I**' is always written in capital letter.

    **e.g.:**  I am not sure of the answer to this question.

5) Before interjections.

    **e.g.:**  i) Oh!     ii) Alas!    iii) Ah!

6) Degrees, titles, official designation, etc. begin with a capital letter.

    **e.g.:**  B.Sc. Sir, Principal, Headmaster, etc.

7) It is used at the beginning of every line of a poem.

    **e.g.:**  She dwelt among the untrodden ways

          Beside the springs of Dover;

8) The first letter of the name of a day/month/religion/festival/special day or occasion should be in capital letter.

> **e.g.:** Monday, Saturday, Diwali, New Year's day, etc.

**Note:** *Names of seasons are written in small letter.*

> **e.g.:** This year the summer seems to be quite short.

9) The first letter of the words *'God/Almighty/Lord'* is written in capital letter. The pronouns referring to God are also capitalized.

> **e.g.:** God comes to the help of anyone who seeks Him.

10) Generally the name of a book, magazine, subject, chapter of a book, etc. is written in capital letter.

> **e.g.:** 'The Da Vinci Code' is written by Dan Brown.

11) Names of political parties, organizations, schools, colleges, universities, etc. are written in capital letters.

> **e.g.:** St. Stephen's College, situated in New Delhi, is one of the best colleges in India.

12) Capital letters are used for the names of roads, streets, colonies, etc.

> **e.g.:** i) Nehru Road, Krishna Nagar, Lal Marg, etc.

13) In titles of distinction or position.

> **e.g.:** Secretary of State, Prime Minister, President, etc.

14) For historical events and important events.

> **e.g.:** First World War, Industrial Revolution, Green Revolution, etc.

# Exercise

### 1. Punctuate the following sentences:

1) stand up maria
2) i have read the book named the city of joy
3) that is no business of mine the police chief answered good-bye I am busy.
4) do you pray to the almighty he asked me
5) babur it is said never lost heart
6) it is really my mistake sir forgive me said tom
7) he was brave large hearted man and we all honoured him
8) my dear child said the police inspector he is a thief
9) my sons said he a great treasure lies hidden in the estate
10) your scheme to tell you frankly is quite useless

### Answers

> 1) Stand up, Maria.
> 2) I have read the book named 'The City of Joy'.
> 3) "That is no business of mine," the police chief answered.
>    "Good-bye. I am busy."

4) "Do you pray to the Almighty?" he asked me.

5) Babur, it is said, never lost heart.

6) "It is really my mistake, Sir. Please forgive me," said Tom.

7) He was brave, large-hearted; and we all honoured him.

8) "My dear child," said the police inspector, "he is a thief."

9) "My sons," said he, "a great treasure lies hidden in the estate."

10) Your scheme, to tell you frankly, is quite useless.

—xxx—-

**<u>Useful data</u>**

# 13. Marriage anniversaries

| Years | Anniversary |
|---|---|
| 1st | Paper |
| 2nd | Cotton |
| 3rd | Leather |
| 4th | Silk |
| 5th | Wood |
| 6th | Iron |
| 7th | Wool |
| 8th | Bronze |
| 9th | Copper (or pottery) |
| 10th | Tin (or aluminum) |
| 11th | Steel |
| 12th | Linen |
| 13th | Lace |
| 14th | Ivory |
| 15th | Crystal |
| 20th | China (porcelain) |
| 25th | Silver jubilee |
| 30th | Pearl |
| 35th | Coral (or jade) |
| 40th | Ruby |
| 45th | Sapphire |
| 50th | Golden jubilee |
| 55th | Emerald |
| 60th | Diamond jubilee |
| 65th | Blue Sapphire |
| 70th | Platinum jubilee |
| 80th | Oak Jubilee |

# 21. Change of degree of comparison

**Change of degree of comparison:** An adjective can change form to show comparison. This is known as change of degree of comparison. There are three degrees of comparison.

    i) Positive degree

    ii) Comparative degree

    iii) Superlative degree

**i) Positive degree:** The positive degree shows the simple form of an adjective, when no comparison is made.

    **e.g.:** Christian Medical College, Vellore, is an <u>excellent</u> multi-specialty hospital.

**ii) Comparative degree:** Comparative degree shows comparison between two things or persons. It shows more or less degree of the same quality of an adjective.

    **e.g.:** The city of New York is **bigger than** the city of Mumbai.

**iii) Superlative degree:** Superlative degree shows comparison between more than two things or persons. It shows the highest or the lowest degree of the same quality of an adjective.

    **e.g.:** Maria is the <u>smartest</u> student of her batch.

## Important points to be kept in mind

1. Many sentences of positive degree start with **'very few'** or **'no other'** at the beginning of the sentence. When such sentences are changed into comparative degree, they should have **'any other'** or **'many other.'**

    **e.g.:** i) **Very few** metals are **as** precious **as** gold.

        Gold is more precious than **many other** metals.

       ii) **No other** king in India is **as** great **as** Asoka.

        Asoka is greater than **any other** king in India.

2. The comparative form generally has **'more... than'** or **'adjective + er... than'** and when it is changed into positive degree, it should be followed by **'not so..as'.**

    **e.g.:** i) Savita is **more beautiful than** Sonia.

        Sonia is **not so** beautiful **as** Savita.

3. When a superlative degree is changed into a positive degree, it should have **'very few...as ...as'**, **'no other... as...as'**.

    **e.g.:** i) The lion is the strongest animal.

        **Very few** animals are **as** strong **as** the lion.

4. When superlative degrees are changed into comparative degrees, they should have **'any other'**, **'all other'**, etc.

    **e.g.:** i) Jaya is the most beautiful among her friends.

            Jaya is more beautiful than **any other** of her friends.

5. The comparative form can be used only for a comparison between two items. If there are more than two items, the superlative degree should be used.

6. Generally the superlative degree is formed by adding **'st, est,** or **most'** to the adjective. The definite article **'the'** should be used before the superlative degree.

### A. From positive to comparative

**Positive**        : No other city in the world is as large as London.

**Comparative** : London is larger than any other city in the world.

**Positive**        : Few have written as much as he has written.

**Comparative** : He has written more than many others.

### B. From positive to superlative

**Positive**        : Very few regions in the world are as cold as the Arctic region.

**Superlative** : The Arctic region is one of the coldest regions of the world.

**Positive**        : No other place is as good as home.

**Superlative** : Home is the best place.

### C. From comparative to positive

**Comparative** : The lion is not stronger than the leopard.

**Positive**        : The lion is not so strong as the leopard.

**Comparative** : An aeroplane flies faster than birds.

**Positive**        : Birds cannot fly as fast as an aeroplane.

### D. From comparative to superlative

**Comparative** : Mumbai is larger than any other city in India.

**Superlative** : Mumbai is the largest city in India.

**Comparative** : Gold is costlier than any other metal.

**Superlative** : Gold is the costliest metal.

### E. From superlative to positive

| | |
|---|---|
| **Superlative** | : Asoka was the noblest king of ancient India. |
| **Positive** | : No other king in India was as noble as Asoka. |
| **Superlative** | : Priya is the brightest student in her class. |
| **Positive** | : No other student in her class is as bright as Priya. |

### F. From superlative to comparative

| | |
|---|---|
| **Superlative** | : Rice is the most popular food item in India. |
| **Comparative** | : Rice is more popular than all other food items in India. |
| **Superlative** | : The Pacific Ocean is the deepest ocean in the world. |
| **Comparative** | : The Pacific Ocean is deeper than all other oceans in the world. |

Use the same adjective in all the three degrees of comparison:

| | | |
|---|---|---|
| **1. Positive** | : | No other city in India is as **big** as Mumbai. |
| **2. Comparative** | : | Mumbai is **bigger than** any other city in India. |
| **3. Superlative** | : | Mumbai is the **biggest** city in India. |

# Exercise

**Change the following adjectives into the degrees mentioned in the bracket:**

| | | |
|---|---|---|
| 1. **Positive** | : | No other metal is as useful as iron. *(comparative)* |
| 2. **Positive** | : | Raju is as strong as his brother. *(comparative)* |
| 3. **Comparative** | : | Gold is more precious than many other metals. *(positive)* |
| 4. **Comparative** | : | Punjab is more fertile than many other states in India. *(positive)* |
| 5. **Positive** | : | No other king is as great as Akbar. *(comparative)* |
| 6. **Positive** | : | No other building in the world is as splendid as the Taj Mahal. *(superlative)* |
| 7. **Comparative** | : | No place is better than home. *(superlative)* |
| 8. **Positive** | : | Very few animals can run as fast as the kangaroo. *(superlative)* |
| 9. **Positive** | : | Very few languages in the world are as difficult as Chinese. *(superlative)* |
| 10. **Superlative** | : | Japan is the richest country in Asia. *(positive)* |

**<u>Answers</u>**
**Change the following  adjectives into the degrees given in the bracket:**
1. **Comparative**          : Iron is more useful than all other metals.
2. **Comparative**          : His brother is not stronger than Raju.
3.  **Positive**              : Very few metals are as precious as gold
4. **Positive**              : There are few states in India so fertile as Punjab.
5.**Comparative**          : Akbar is greater than all other kings.
6. **Superlative**          : The Taj Mahal is the most splendid building in the world.
7. **Superlative**          : Home is the best place.
8. **Superlative**          : The kangaroo is the fastest animal/ The kangaroo runs fastest.
9. **Superlative**          : Chinese is the most difficult language of the world.
10. **Positive**             : No other countries in Asia are as rich as Japan.

—xxx—

## <u>Useful data</u>

# 14. Anniversaries of events

| years | Anniversaries of events |
|---|---|
| 1 year | Annual |
| 2 years | biennial |
| 3 years | triennial |
| 4 years | quadrennial |
| 5 years | quinquennial |
| 6 years | sexennial |
| 7 years | septennial |
| 8 years | octennial |
| 9 years | novennial |
| 10 years | decennial |
| 20 years | vicennial |
| 50 years | semicentennial |
| 100 years | centennial/centenary |
| 200 years | bicentennial/bicentenary |
| 300 years | tercentenary/tricentennial |
| 400 years | quatercentenary/quadricentennial |
| 500 years | quincentenary |
| 1000 years | Millennial |

# 22. Interchange of noun, verb, adjective & adverb

## Formation of adjectives from nouns

| Nouns | Adjective | Nouns | Adjective |
|---|---|---|---|
| advice | advisable | air | airy |
| anger | angry | book | bookish |
| brother | brotherly | centre | central |
| child | childlike/childish | courage | courageous |
| fool | foolish | fruit | fruitful |
| glory | glorious | day | daily |
| ease | easy | expense | expensive |
| fate | fateful | fault | faulty |
| life | lifelike/lifeless | affection | affectionate |
| angel | angelic | blood | bloody |
| boy | boyish | cheer | cheerful |
| force | forceful | friend | friendly |
| fury | furious | coward | cowardly |
| danger | dangerous | fame | famous |
| favour | favourable | love | lovely |
| man | manly | gloom | gloomy |
| greed | greedy | haste | hasty |
| heaven | heavenly | home | homely |
| joy | joyful | mercy | merciful |
| milk | milky | mystery | mysterious |
| nation | national | play | playful |
| price | precious | profit | profitable |
| stone | stony | virtue | virtuous |
| woman | womanly | gold | golden |
| hero | heroic | pride | proud |

## Formation of verbs from nouns

| Nouns | Verbs | Nouns | Verbs |
|---|---|---|---|
| advice | advise | apology | apologize |
| bath | bathe | beauty | beautify |
| belief | believe | black | blacken |
| blood | bleed | breath | breathe |
| cloth | clothe | light | light |
| memory | memorize | sale | sell |

| | | | |
|---|---|---|---|
| sermon | sermonize | speech | speak |
| success | succeed | achievement | achieve |
| admiration | admire | approval | approve |
| amusement | amuse | behaviour | behave |
| bound | bind | blessing | bless |
| carriage | carry | conversion | convert |
| decision | decide | denial | deny |

Examples

1. **Noun**    : The **cost** of this pen is high.
   **verb**    : This pen **costs** high.
2. **Noun**    : He was stoned to **death** by the mob.
   **Verb**    : He **died** due to stoning by the mob.
3. **Noun**    : He showed **generosity** even to his enemies.
   **Adj.**    : He was **generous** even to his enemies.
4. **Noun**    : Morning walk provides **refreshment** to the mind.
   **Verb**    : Morning walk **refreshes** the mind.
5. **Adv.**    : He fought **bravely.**
   **Adj**    : He put up a **brave** fight.
6. **Verb**    : I was **sorry** to hear this sad news.
   **Adv.**    : I heard this sad news **sorrowfully.**
7. **Noun**    : Tom is a man of sense.
   **Adj.**    : Tom is a **sensible** man.
8. **Noun**    : Life sometimes appears to be full of gloom.
   **Adj.**    : Life sometimes appears to be **gloomy.**
9. **Adj.**    : It was fortunate that I met him.
   **Adv.**    : **Fortunately** I met him.
10. **Adj**    : She had a narrow escape from death.
   **Adv.**    : She **narrowly** escaped death.

## Special note:

**Try to use the same word in different parts of speech form as it shows better proficiency of the language.**

It is a fact that globalization has brought a lot of **<u>success</u>** to the Indian industrial sector. But it has not **<u>succeeded</u>** much in improving the status of the Indian farmer although several schemes have been initiated **successfully** in this regard. However, it must be said that globalization has been **<u>successful</u>** in changing the lifestyles of most Indians both in the urban and rural areas of the country.

# Exercise

Change the underlined word into the part of speech which is shown in the bracket.

1. **Noun** : The **cost** of this medicine is high. *(verb)*
2. **Verb** : John **succeeded** in getting the first rank in his class. *(adj)*.
3. **Noun** : There are many **critics** of politics nowadays. *(verb)*
4. **Adj.** : The merchant was **successful** in his business. *(noun)*
5. **Noun** : The manure gives **fertility** to the soil. *(adjective)*
6. **Noun** : He wasted his time in **idleness** at home. *(adverb)*
7. **Adv.** : Walk **carefully**. *(noun)*
8. **Noun** : The hospital staff welcomed the new director with great **joy.** *(adverb)*
9. **Adv.** : **Fortunately,** the doctor came into the ward at the right time. *(adjective)*
10. **Noun** : The **expense** involved in medical treatment these days is quite high. *(adj)*
11. **Noun** : We rushed home in haste. *(adverb)*
12. **Adv.** : Sam always acted **obediently.** *(noun)*
13. **Adj.** : My teacher was an **affectionate** person. *(noun)*
14. **Noun** : His **death** was caused by a snake bite. *(verb)*
15. **Verb** : This is the place where you have to **sit**. *(noun)*

**Answers**

**Change the underlined word into the part of speech which is shown in the bracket.**

1. **Verb** : This medicine **costs** high.
2. **Adj.** : John was **successful** in getting the first rank in his class.
3. **Verb** : There are many who **criticize politics** nowadays.
4. **Noun** : The merchant had great **success** in his business.
5. **Adj.** : When manure is added to the soil it becomes **fertile.**
6. **Adv.** : He wasted his time **idly** at home.
7. **Adj.** : Walk with **care.**
8. **Adv.** : The hospital staff welcomed the new director **joyfully.**
9. **Adj.** : It was **fortunate** that the doctor came into the ward at the right time.
10. **Adj.** : Medical treatment these days has become very **expensive**.
11. **Adv.** : We rushed home **hastily.**
12. **Noun** : Sam always acted in **obedience.**
13. **Noun** : My teacher was a person full of **affection.**
14. **Verb** : He **died** as a result of a snake bite.
15. **Noun** : This is your **seat.**

—xxx—

# 23. Parallel structure in sentence construction

**Parallel structure:** Making all items in a series or list in a sentence grammatically parallel or equal is known as parallel structure. For example, if the first component of a series is an adjective, the rest of the series should also be adjectives.

**e.g.:**    i) Bob is <u>clever,</u> <u>handsome</u> and <u>people like him.</u>**(X)**
          *adj*     *adj*          *clause*

       Bob is <u>clever, handsome</u> and <u>popular.</u> (✓)
         *adj*       *adj*        *adj*

      ii) Mahesh likes <u>to play,</u> <u>swim</u> and <u>cycling.</u>**(X)**
                *infinitive*   *infinitive*   *present participle*

       Mahesh likes <u>to play,</u> <u>swim</u> and <u>cycle.</u> (✓)
        *infinitive*   *infinitive*    *infinitive*

     iii) Children like <u>playing</u> in the water, <u>running</u> around and <u>shout aloud.</u>**(X)**
            *verb+ ing*          *verb+ ing*          *verbal phrase*

       Children like <u>playing</u> in water, <u>running</u> around and <u>shouting</u> aloud. (✓)
        *verb+ing*         *verb+ing*         *verb+ ing*

     iv) Nowadays youngsters are <u>taking</u> up any job, <u>following</u> their own life-
                  *present participle*        *present participle*

       styles, and <u>want to become rich at any cost.</u> **(X)**
                *clause*

       Nowadays youngsters <u>take</u> up any job, <u>follow</u> their own lifestyles
                  *verb*            *verb*

       and <u>want</u> to become rich at any cost. (✓)
          verb

      v) Lakshmi <u>got</u> up from her seat, <u>asked</u> a question to her teacher and
        *simple past*        *simple past*

    <u>has sat</u> down.**(X)**
     *present perfect*

       Lakshmi <u>got</u> up from her seat, <u>asked</u> a question to her teacher
        *simple past*        *simple past*

       and <u>sat</u> down. (✓)
        *simple past*

—xxx—-

160

# 24. Formal and Informal English

**i) Formal English :** By *'Formal English'* we mean the type of English that is generally used in official notices, business letters, interviews, conferences, polite conversations with strangers, professional examinations, etc.

**ii) Informal English:** By *'Informal English'* we mean the type of English that is used among friends, letters to one's family, in ordinary conversation, etc.

> Writing is considered to be formal while speech is more informal.

Some words and expressions are mainly used in formal situations while some words are used generally in informal situations.

**Examples**

| | | |
|---|---|---|
| i) *Informal* | : What's your name? |
| *Formal* | : Could I know your name, please? |
| 2) *Informal* | : Please tell me your name. |
| *Formal* | : Would you be kind enough to tell me your name? |
| 3) *Informal* | :What's up? |
| *Formal* | : How do you do? |
| 4) *Informal* | : The toilet is at the back of the building. |
| *Formal* | : The washroom/comfort room is at the rear of the building. |
| 5) *Informal* | : Thanks a lot/thank you. |
| *Formal* | : I am grateful to you/ I am indebted to you. |
| 6) *Informal* | : Get down/get off from the bus. |
| *Formal* | : Alight from the bus, please. |
| 7) *Informal* | : All right/OK |
| *Formal* | : I think that it is satisfactory. |
| 8) *Informal* | : Sit down, please. |
| *Formal* | : Take a seat, please. |
| 9) *Informal* | : What?/Pardon? Say it again. |
| *Formal* | : I beg your pardon. |
| 10) *Informal* | : Can you help me a bit? |
| *Formal* | : Would you like to help me for a few minutes? I wonder if you could help me for a few minutes. |
| 11) *Informal* | : I'm sorry to tell you that you failed in the test. |
| *Formal* | : I regret to inform you that you failed in the test. |
| 12) *Informal* | : See you next week. |
| *Formal* | : I look forward to meeting you next week. |

| | |
|---|---|
| 13) *Informal* | : Sorry, I can't come for the function. |
| *Formal* | : I am afraid that I shall not be able to attend the function. |
| 14. *Informal* | : She is older than me. |
| *Formal* | : She is older than I am /he is/you are. |
| 15. *Informal* | : Don't forget it. |
| *Formal* | : I would like to remind you about it. |
| 16. *Informal* | : Nice to meet you. |
| *Formal* | : It is a pleasure to meet you. |
| 17. *Informal* | : As soon as you can |
| *Formal* | : At your earliest convenience. |
| 18. *informal* | : I'm worried about you. |
| *Formal* | : I am concerned about you. |
| 19. *informal* | : Say hello to |
| *Formal* | : Give my regards to. |
| 20. *Informal* | : Thanks a lot |
| *Formal* | : I appreciate your assistance. |
| 21. *informal* | : Open the window |
| *Formal* | : Kindly/Please open the window. |
| 22. *informal* | : The patient got over his illness |
| *Formal* | : The patient recovered from his illness. |
| 23. *Informal* | : It will do you good. |
| *Formal* | : This will be of great benefit to you. |
| 24. *Informal* | : What's going on? |
| *Formal* | :  How are you doing? |
| 25. *informal* | : Write back soon. |
| *Formal* | : I hope to hear from you at your earliest convenience. |
| 26. *Informal* | : Say hello to your elder brother. |
| *Formal* | : Give my regards to your elder brother. |
| 27. *Informal* | : Sorry for the inconvenience caused. |
| *Formal* | : Please accept my apologies for the inconvenience caused. |
| 28. *informal* | : If you need any more info, you can contact us. |
| *Formal* | : Should you require any further information, please do not hesitate to contact us. |
| 29. *Informal* | : Congrats, it was a good show. |
| *Formal* | : Congratulations, it was a great performance. |
| 30. *Informal* | : You can go now. |
| *Formal* | : You may leave now. |

# Some informal words and their formal variants

**<u>Special note:</u>**
Use of **formal words** instead of **informal words** can definitely enhance the quality of your English.

| Informal | Formal | Informal | Formal |
|---|---|---|---|
| get | obtain | So | therefore |
| Dad | Father | Yummy | Excellent |
| Hopeless | Futile | Look at | Examine |
| Keep | Preserve | Empty | Vacant |
| Any way | Nevertheless | Find out | Ascertain |
| Put up | Tolerate | Lack | Deficiency |
| Childish | Immature | Help | Assist |
| At once | Immediately | Say sorry | Apologize |
| Think about | Consider | tough | Difficult |
| At first | Initially | Death | Demise |
| Need | Require | Live | Reside |
| Take out | Remove | Buy | Purchase |
| Go after | Pursue | Choose | Select |
| Danger | Peril | Say | Express |
| Job | Occupation | Go up | increase/enhance |
| Wage | Remuneration | Use | Utilize |
| Ask for | Request | Enough | Sufficient |
| Hungry | Famished | Lucky | Fortunate |
| But | However | Right | Correct |
| Wrong | Incorrect | Avoid | Evade |
| Show | Demonstrate | Talk about | Discuss |
| Give up | Quit | Throw away | Discard |
| Check | Verify | Call off | Cancel |
| Get | Receive | A bit | A little |
| Hurry | Haste | Think about | Consider |
| Break down | Collapse | In the end | Finally/in conclusion |
| Cheap | Inexpensive | Seem | Appear |
| Put off | Postpone | Stop | Cease |
| House | Residence | Try out | Test |
| Get off | Alight | Drop out | Discontinue |
| Begin | Commence | Again and again | Repeatedly |
| Worse | Inferior | Funny | Humorous/amusing |

—xxx—

# 25. Correct use of certain confusing terms

1.  <u>People/peoples:</u>

**People** means human beings in general or considered collectively.

> **e.g.:** Many **<u>people</u>** have come for the function held in memory of the late chief minister.

**Peoples** means the members of a particular nation, community, or ethnic group.

> **e.g.:** The **peoples** of India are quite different from the peoples of America.

2.  <u>Everyone/ every one</u>

**Everyone** means everybody and refers to every member of a group.

> **e.g.:** **<u>Everyone</u>** came for the function in time.

**Every one** is generally used to refer to things and not people.

> **e.g.:** I have a good number of books in my library. **Every one** of them has been bought recently.

3.  <u>Hope/wish:</u>

'**Hope**' is used to indicate something that *possibly happened or will possibly happen.* The verb hope can be followed by any tense.

> **e.g.:** i) We **<u>hope</u>** the team will do better this time. (*future*)

'**Wish**' is used to indicate something that definitely *did not happen or definitely will not happen.* The word 'wish' must not be followed by any present tense or present tense auxiliary.

> **e.g.:** i). We **<u>wish</u>** that they had done the test well.
>
> ii) I **<u>wish</u>** I were a minister.

4. <u>As if/ as though:</u>

When we use **as if/as though** in a hypothetical situation, the second clause must have the auxiliary verb in **'were'** form. In other situations the second clause should be in **past simple** or **past perfect.**

> **e.g.:** i) The old man <u>talks/talked</u> **as if/as though** he **were** a scholar. (*hypothetical situation*)
>
> ii) Miss Mary **<u>teaches</u>** as *if/as though* she **<u>knew</u>** the subject well. (*past simple*)
>
> iii) Miss Mary **<u>taught</u>** as if she **<u>had known</u>** the subject well. (*past perfect*)

5. <u>Altogether/ all together:</u>

**Altogether** means ' in total'.

> **e.g.:** i) We have invited twenty guests **<u>altogether</u>** to the party.
>
> ii) I am not **<u>altogether</u>** convinced of his argument.

**All together** means '*all in one place*' or '*all at once*'.

> **e.g.:** i) Can you put your books **all together** in this box?
>
> ii) We shall sing this song **all together.**

6. <u>Some time, sometime and sometimes</u>

**Some time** means *'quite a long time'*

  **e.g.:** I will take **<u>some time</u>** to complete this task.

**Sometime** refers to an indefinite time, usually in the future.

  **e.g.:** I will meet you **<u>sometime</u>** later.

**Sometimes** means occasionally, more than once.

  **e.g.:** Prasad **<u>sometimes</u>** goes home on weekends.

7. <u>All ready/already</u>

The term **'all ready'** means *'everything is in a position of readiness or everyone is ready to do something'*.

  **e.g.:** We are all **<u>ready</u>** for the examination.

The term **'already'** is an adverb and refers to an action that is completed. It is used to express surprise that something has happened so soon or too early.

  **e.g.:** Shankar has **<u>already</u>** left for the U.K.

8. <u>All right/alright</u>

The term **'all right'** means everything is in the correct position or order.

  **e.g.:** i) Are you getting along **all right** in your new job?

**'Alright'** is the commonly used term to mean that everything is OK or in correct order.

**'All right'** is the correct term to be used. Many grammarians consider **alright** incorrect.

  ii) You look **alright** now. (*incorrect*)

  You look **<u>all right</u>** now.

9. <u>It's / Its</u>

**It's** is the contracted form of *'It is /it has'*.

  **e.g.:** **<u>It's</u>** a beautiful house, isn't it?

**Its** is the possessive form of *'it'*.

  **e.g.:** I bought a new dog recently. **<u>Its</u>** tail is quite short.

10. <u>Though/although</u>

Both **though/ although** mean the same thing. Both the terms are used as conjunctions. The major difference between though and although is that **though** is more used in spoken English than in written English. The sentence containing though/although should have a contrast.

  **e.g.:** **<u>Though/although</u>** Rajan is very intelligent yet he spends a great deal of time studying.

11. <u>Cloth /clothes/clothing</u>

**Cloth** refers to the material made from wool, cotton, etc.

  **e.g.:** **Cotton <u>cloth</u>** is quite common in north India.

**Clothes** are things that we wear.

  **e.g.:** I must buy some new **<u>clothes</u>** for my children.

The term **'clothing'** refers to those clothes that are generally used to protect against heat, cold, water, machinery.

  **e.g.:** Winter **clothing** is quite expensive in our country.

12. <u>a lot of/lots of</u>

There is no much difference between **a lot of** and **lots of:**

'**a lot of** ' is more informal than '**lots of**' .

Both the terms are used with <u>non-count and plural nouns.</u>

  **e.g.:**  i) **A lot of** work remains uncompleted.

  ii) **Lots of** examples have been cited to prove this point.

13. <u>Anyone/ any one</u>

**Anyone** is generally singular and takes a singular verb. It is used for persons.

  **e.g.:**  **Anyone** can forward and claim this gift.

**Any one** is used to refer to things.

  **e.g.:**  **Any one** of these songs can be selected for the competition.

14. <u>Short/shortly/ in short</u>

**Short** means '*not long*'.

  **e.g.:**  This stick is quite **short**.

**Shortly** means '*soon, a little while before or after*'.

  **e.g.:**  I shall meet you **shortly**.

**In short** means '**briefly**'.

  **e.g.:**  Kindly state your arguments **in short**.

15. <u>Ago/before</u>

**Ago** refers to a period of time measured back from now.

  **e.g.:**  An earthquake occurred a few months **ago** in the state of Jammu and Kashmir.

**Before** refers to a specific time in the past.

  **e.g.:**  I have seen this movie **before**.

16. <u>Lastly/ at last</u>

**Lastly** is used to introduce the last in a list of things.

  **e.g.:**  **Lastly** I would thank this institute.

**At last** is used when something happens after a long time especially when there has been some difficulty or delay.

  **e.g.:**  **At last** we arrived at our destination after a long search.

17. <u>In front/ in the front of</u>

**In front** means outside, just ahead of something.

  **e.g.:**  I will meet you **in front of** your hotel.

**In the front of** means '*the most forward part of something*'.

  **e.g.:**  Kindly put the flowers **in the front of** the altar.

18. <u>Everyday/ Every day</u>

**Everyday** is used as an adjective and means *ordinary, usual, routine, etc.*

  **e.g.:**  In **everyday** life, most people hardly give any importance to health.

**Every day** means each day and the stress is on day.

  **e.g.:**  You must come to school **every day**..

19. <u>Very/ very much</u>

**Very** is used before adjectives and  adverbs.

  **e.g.:** i) It's **<u>very</u>** hot here.

    ii) It is a **<u>very</u>** interesting story.

**Very much** is used before comparatives, past participles, etc.

  **e.g.:** i) John is **<u>very much</u>** happier here.

    ii) She was **<u>very much</u>** loved by her husband.

20. <u>On time/ in time</u>

**On time** means the exact time,  at the planned time, the precise time, etc.

  **e.g.:** The train arrived **<u>on time</u>**. (*not earlier, not later*)

**In time** means not later, more or less at the correct time.

  **e.g.:** The professor started his lecture **<u>in time.</u>**

21. <u>At no time/ in no time</u>

**At no time** means never.

  **e.g.:** I will say such words **<u>at no time </u>**in my life.

**In no time** means very quickly or within a short time.

  **e.g.:** I will complete this task **<u>in no time</u>**.

22. <u>In the same time/at the same time</u>

**In the same time** means same amount of time taken.

  **e.g.:** We reached the venue of the show **<u>in the same time</u>**.

**At the same time** means all together.

  **e.g.:** We reached the venue of the show **<u>at the same time.</u>**

23. <u>Million/millions</u>

The singular form **'million'** is used to describe a particular number.

  **e.g.:** The first prize of the state lottery is **<u>one million</u>** rupees.

The term **'millions'** is used to describe a large number that is not exact or definite.

  **e.g.:** **<u>Millions of</u>** people watched the Football World Cup-2022.

24. <u>Program/programme</u>

Computer program is generally spelt **'program'** in both British and American English.

  **e.g.:** Most of the computer software **<u>program</u>** installed in my computer are quite old.

In British English, the term **'programme'** is used in all other situations.

  **e.g.:** The government has initiated a new welfare programme for the weaker sections of the society.

In American English, the term **'program'** is used in all situations.

25. <u>Fish/fishes</u>

The term **'fish'** can be used both as singular and plural.

    one **fish**

    two **fish** (*of the same type*)

    two **fishes** (*of different types*)

26. Right/true

   **'Right'** is usually used to say something is correct or to agree with something someone has said.

         **e.g.:**   Your answer seems to be **right**.

   The term **'true'** is usually used to say that something is based on facts.

         **e.g.:**   The news is true.

27. Say/tell

      Both **'say'** and **'tell'** are used with direct and indirect speech.

      However, **'say'** is more common than **'tell'** with direct speech.

         **e.g.:**   Anand <u>said</u>, " I am going to Chennai tonight."

   The term **'say'** is never followed directly by a person as an object.

         **e.g.:**   She **said** to me that she would be late for class.**(X)**

                She <u>said</u> that she would be late for class.(✓)

   The term **'tell'** is always followed by the person that the information or order is given to.

         **e.g.:**   The teacher <u>told</u> us not to repeat the same mistake.

   We do not usually use **tell** with greetings, exclamations, questions, etc.

         **e.g.:**   He told him, 'Good evening, sir'.**(X)**

                He **said,** 'Good evening, sir'.(✓)

                Paul **told**, 'what a nice idea'.**(X)**

                Paul **said**, 'what a nice idea'.(✓)

28. No one /none

   **No one**( *used as separate words)* is used to mean *'nobody'*. It cannot be followed by **'of'**.

         **e.g.:**   <u>No one</u> can solve this puzzle.

   **'None'** is used to express the idea of *' not a single one'*. It is generally used with the preposition **'of'**.

         **e.g.:**   <u>None of</u> the participants of the quiz competition performed well.

29. Speak/talk

      The term **'talk'** is used for informal situations.

         **e.g.:**   Can you <u>talk</u> to me in French?

      The term **'speak'** is used in formal situations.

         **e.g.:** The principal will <u>speak</u> to the student concerned.

  **Talk** is often used for the act of giving an informal lecture while **speak** is used for formal lecture, sermons etc.

30. Medium/media

   **'Medium'** means the method or way of expressing something. Its plurals are **media** and **mediums**.

         **e.g.:**   i) The art form of ' Kathakali' expresses stories through the <u>medium</u> of dance.

ii) Nowadays several **media** *are* available for communication.

'**The Media**' refers to newspapers, magazines, radio, television etc. It is used as a collective noun which is generally considered singular. However, it can take a **singular/plural** verb. But never say '**The medias**'.

      **e.g.:** The media **has/have** great influence on people.

31. Sound/noise

'**Sound**' refers to something that you hear or that can be heard.

      **e.g.:**  We heard the **sound** of a loud explosion in the distance.

'**Noise**' refers to a sound that is loud, unpleasant and unwanted.

      **e.g.:**  The teacher requested the students not to make **noise** in the class.

32. Purposely/purposefully

'**Purposely**' refers to doing something deliberately and not by accident or chance.

      **e.g.:** I  kept the windows open **purposely**. I wanted to get some fresh air.

'**Purposefully**' means doing something with a definite plan or useful purpose in mind and  has a strong desire to achieve it.

      **e.g.:**  He strode purposefully into the room.

33. Kindly/please

'**Kindly**' is generally used when we speak to elders, superiors or someone in position.

      **e.g.:**  Please be seated, sir. **(X)**

      **Kindly** be seated, sir.(✓)

'**Please**' is normally used when we speak to our peers or persons below our position.

      **e.g.:**  **Open** the window, please.

It is incorrect to use both the terms together in a single sentence.

      **e.g.:** Please kindly open the window. **(X)**

      **Please** open the window/**Kindly** open the window.(✓)

---xxx---

## Useful data

## **15. Names of different age groups above 40 years**

| | | |
|---|---|---|
| person aged 40 and above | : | Quadragenarian |
| person aged 50 and above | : | Quinquagenarian |
| person aged 60 and above | : | Sexagenarian |
| person aged 70 and above | : | Septuagenarian |
| person aged 80 and above | : | Octogenarian |
| person aged 90 and above | : | Nonagenarian |
| person aged 100 and above | : | Centenarian |

# 26. Correct the grammatical errors

1. Every children **(X)**
2. Every people **(X)**
3. Every staff **(X)**
4. Every friends **(X)**
5. One staff **(X)**
6. All the staffs **(X)**
7. One criteria **(X)**
8. Each facilities **(X)**
9. A lot of sceneries **(X)**
10. One of the news **(X)**
11. Any students **(X)**
12. One of my friend **(X)**
13. Some datas **(X)**
14. Many information **(X)**
15. Any other items **(X)**
16. Each of my friend **(X)**
17. A lot of pollutions **(X)**
18. Everyone of my friend **(X)**
19. Many data **(X)**
20. One data **(X)**
21. A lot of bacterias **(X)**
22. Several new equipments **(X)**
23. Expensive jewelleries **(X)**
24. Everybody have **(X)**
25. A lot of mass medias **(X)**
26. My family have **(X)**
27. Today morning **(X)**
28. Much people **(X)**
29. Repeat it again **(X)**
30. Return back **(X)**
31. More better **(X)**
32. I belongs to **(X)**
33. My teeth is.. **(X)**
34. A new poetry **(X)**
35. Yesterday night **(X)**
36. An year has been spent...**(X)**
37. Tomorrow at 6.00 pm **(X)**
38. He is senior than me **(X)**

1. Every child/everyone of the children (✓)
2. Every person/everyone of the people (✓)
3. Everyone of the staff (✓)
4. Every friend/everyone of the friends (✓)
5. One of the staff/ a staff member (✓)
6. All the staff (✓)
7. One criterion/one of the criteria (✓)
8. Each facility/each of the facilities (✓)
9. A lot of scenery (✓)
10. A piece of news/an item of news (✓)
11. Any student/any of the students (✓)
12. One of my friends (✓)
13. Some data (✓)
14. Some/lots of information (✓)
15. Any other item (✓)
16. Each of my friends (✓)
17. A lot of pollution (✓)
18. Everyone of my friends (✓)
19. Much data (✓)
20. A piece of data (✓)
21. A lot of bacteria (✓)
22. Much new equipment (✓)
23. Expensive jewellery(✓)
24. Everybody has (✓)
25. A lot of mass media (✓)
26. My family has...(✓)
27. This morning (✓)
28. Many people (✓)
29. Repeat it (✓)
30. Return (✓)
31. Much better (✓)
32. I belong to...(✓)
33. My tooth is...(✓)
34. A new poem..(✓)
35. Last night/previous night (✓)
36. A year has been spent...(✓)
37. at 6.00 pm tomorrow (✓)
38. He is **senior to** me. (✓)

# Correct the grammatical errors

39. You are elder than me. **(X)**

40. I will not come for class. **(X)**
41. I am wishing you success in...**(X)**
42. I, you and they study in the same class. **(X)**
43. If I will get time...**(X)**
44. I am having two years experience. **(X)**
45. Sometimes I go home on weekends.**(X)**
46. Myself/me is Mrs Rani Panicker. **(X)**
47. The teacher as well as the students are..**(X)**
48. The owner and the manager is...**(X)**
49. My pair of scissors are missing. **(X)**
50. I am an alumni of this college. **(X)**
51. I am used to work for long hours. **(X)**
52. Me cannot come now. **(X)**
53. I was absent due to illness.**(X)**
54. He is my cousin brother. **(X)**
55. Meet me in the evening at 4.30 pm. **(X)**
56. You came today an hour late. **(X)**
57. When is your date of birth? **(X)**
58. Sam hanged a picture on the wall. **(X)**
59. I am working here since...**(X)**
60. My father, he is a businessman. **(X)**
61. The stranger asked a question to me. **(X)**
62. Can you open this knot? **(X)**
63. I am feeling tired this morning. **(X)**
64. I expect to succeed in my examination. **(X)**
65. We have class on every Saturday. **(X)**
66. From where did you get it? **(X)**
67. The new machineries are not working.**(X)**
68. Always keep your words. **(X)**
69. I received my transfer order...**(X)**
70. For whom are you looking? **(X)**
71. Please excuse me for the troubles. **(X)**
72. I forgot to bring my scissor. **(X)**
73. The road is closed for repair. **(X)**
74. I will be coming with you also. **(X)**
75. I came to pay my respect to my teacher. **(X)**
76. She sings good. **(X)**
77. If I would win a lottery..**(X)**

39. You are **elder to** me/older than me (✓)

40. I **shall not be able** to come for class (✓)
41. I **wish** you...(✓)
42. **You, they and I** study ...(✓)
43. **If I get** time..(✓)
44. I **have** two years...(✓)
45. I **sometimes go** home...(✓)
46. **I am** Mrs Rani Panicker.(✓)
47. The teacher as well as ... **is**...(✓)
48. The owner and the... **are**..(✓)
49. My pair of scissors **is**..(✓)
50 I am an **alumnus/alumna**.(✓)
51. I am **used to working**...(✓)
52. **I cannot** come now. (✓)
53. I was absent **owing to** illness. (✓)
54. He is my **cousin.** (✓)
55. ..**at 4.30 pm** in the evening. (✓)
56. You came **an hour** late **today**. (✓)
57. ....date of **your birth?**(✓)
58. Sam **hung** a picture on the ...(✓)
59. I **have been** working ..since ..(✓)
60. **My father is** a businessman. (✓)
61. ...asked **me** a question. (✓)
62. Can you **untie** this knot? (✓)
63. I **feel tired** this morning. (✓)
64. I **hope to** succeed.. (✓)
65. ...class **every** Saturday. (✓)
66. Where did you get it **from?** (✓)
67. The new **machinery is** not..(✓)
68. Always keep **your word.** (✓)
69. .... my **transfer orders.** (✓)
70. Whom are you **looking for?** (✓)
71. ....excuse me for the **trouble.** (✓)
72. ..bring my **scissors.** (✓)
73. ..is closed for **repairs.** (✓)
74. I will **also** be coming... (✓)
75. ...to pay my **respects**...(✓)
76. She sings **well.** (✓)
77. If I **were to win/If I win**..(✓)

78. India won the match by an inning. **(X)**

79. I left smoking long ago. **(X)**

80. My brother had leave of ten days. **(X)**

81. My neck is paining. **(X)**

82. She does not care for her health. **(X)**

83. Yours affectionate daughter. **(X)**

84. Your watch is ten minutes behind. **(X)**

85. Maria is becoming smart. **(X)**

86. His tooth is paining. **(X)**

87. You have put in much efforts. **(X)**

88. Keep this duster on the table. **(X)**

89. My father keeps good health. **(X)**

90. Both his son-in-laws came to visit him. **(X)**

91. All the class was ready for the work. **(X)**

92. Raj is the eldest player in our team. **(X)**

93. Rani is wiser than all the students. **(X)**

94. We are pulling on well. **(X)**

95. We left the hostel at the daybreak. **(X)**

96. The criminal is charged of murder. **(X)**

97. He is good in mathematics. **(X)**

98. Ten kilometres are not a big distance. **(X)**

99. I can wait up to 4.0'clock. **(X)**

100. He looked at me from the head to the foot. **(X)**

101. Which city in India you like most? **(X)**

102. Both did not come for class. **(X)**

103. My circumstance does not permit. **(X)**

104. If he resigned, he will regret. **(X)**

105. This vehicle costs six lakhs. **(X)**

106. I said to him to leave the room. **(X)**

107. You are always finding faults with me. **(X)**

108. This word is incorrect, cut it. **(X)**

119. I will see you a few days later. **(X)**

116. When you come, take your bike. **(X)**

117. If I knew his name, I will tell you. **(X)**

109. Did you knock on my door? **(X)**

110. According to me, this is a good movie. **(X)**

78. ...by **an innings**. (✓)

79. I **gave up** smoking long ago. (✓)

80. ...had **ten days leave**. (✓)

81. I **have pain** in my neck/ my neck **is hurting**. (✓)

82. She does not **take care of**... (✓)

83. **Your** affectionate daughter. (✓)

84. Your watch is ....**slow. (✓)**

85. Maria is **becoming smarter**. (✓)

86. His tooth **is aching**. (✓)

87. ...put in **much effort**. (✓)

88. **Put** the duster on the table. (✓)

89. My father enjoys good health. (✓)

90. Both his **sons-in-law**. (✓)

91. **The whole class** was ..(✓)

92. Raj is the **oldest** player...(✓)

93. **.wiser** than all **other** students.(✓)

94. We are getting on well. (✓)

95. ..**at daybreak**. (✓)

96. ..is **charged with** ..(✓)

97. ...good **at mathematics**. (✓)

98. ...**is not a** big distance. (✓)

99. I can wait **till**..(✓)

100. ...from **head to foot**. (✓)

101. ...in India **do you like** most? (✓)

102. **Neither of them** came..(✓).

103. My **circumstances do** not..(✓)

104. If **he resigns**, he will regret. (✓)

105. ..**costs six lakh**. (✓)

106. I **told him** to leave the room. (✓)

107. ...**finding fault** with me. (✓)

108. ...incorrect, **erase it**. (✓)

119. ....**in a few days**. (✓)

116. When you come, **bring** ...(✓)

117. I **would tell** you. (✓)

109. Did you knock **at my door?** (✓)

110. **In my opinion/I think** that. (✓).

---xxx---

# 27. Spot the mistakes in the sentence

When sentences are given to spot out mistakes, the following aspects must be checked:

1. Check whether the basic order of words is correctly followed:

**Subject-verb-object/complement-modifier**

> **e.g.:** On 31ˢᵗ August, 2023 the director submitted his resignation letter to the proprietor of the company. **(X)**
>
> <u>The director submitted his resignation letter</u> to the proprietor of the company
>
> *sub      verb      object*
>
> <u>on 31ˢᵗ August, 2023.</u> **(✓)**
>
> **manner**

2. Check whether the modifiers (*words that show the manner, place and time of action*) are correctly placed. **(MPT order: *manner-place-time: specific time-general time*)**

> **e.g.:** The patient died yesterday in the general ward today due to cardiac arrest.**(X)**
>
> The patient died *due to cardiac arrest in the general ward yesterday.*✓)
>
> *manner          place          time*

3. Check whether nouns, particularly the uncountable nouns and always plural nouns, are correctly used.

> **e.g.:** i) Some of the datas mentioned in this report are wrong. **(X)**
>
> Some of the **<u>data</u>** mentioned in this report are wrong. **(✓)**
>
> ii) Every people of the country is given certain basic rights by the constitution.**(X)**
>
> **<u>Every one of the people</u>** of the country is given certain basic rights by the constitution.**(✓)**

4. Check whether the tenses are correctly used.

Check whether the following rules are strictly followed.

**a) The third person 's' rule:**

> Our company stand on the land allotted by the government **(X)**
>
> Our company **<u>stands</u>** on the land allotted by the government. **(✓)**

**b) Do not use 'ING' with static verbs:**

> I am enjoying every bit of my job as a team leader**. ((X):** (*Enjoy is a static verb*)
>
> I **<u>enjoy</u>** every bit of my job as a team leader. **(✓)**

**c) Past participle rule:**

These days the IT sector **have** innumerable job opportunities for skilled IT professionals. **(X)**

These days the IT sector <u>**has**</u> innumerable job opportunities for skilled IT professionals.(✓)

**d) Compatibility of tenses:**

The receptionist at the counter asked me whom I want to meet. **(X)**

The receptionist at the counter asked me whom I <u>wanted</u> to meet.(✓)

5. Check whether the verb agrees with the given subject.

 **e.g.:** The Chief Minister as well as the ministers are coming to inspect the new site of the State IT Mission Park. **(X)**

   <u>**The Chief Minister**</u> as well as the ministers <u>**is**</u> coming to inspect the new site of the State IT Mission Park. **(✓)**

6. Check whether the pronouns are correctly placed.

 **e.g.:** Priyanka and **me** are the joint partners of this start-up company.**(X)**

   Priyanka and **me** are the joint partners of this start-up company. **(✓)**

7. Check whether adjectives are correctly used.

 **e.g.:** Mr Mukesh Ambani, the Managing Director and Chairman of Reliance Industries, is the most richest man of India. **(X)**

   Mr Mukesh Ambani, the Managing Director and Chairman of Reliance Industries, is the <u>**richest**</u> man of India. **(✓)**

8. Check the use of articles.

 **e.g.:** The CEO of our company is <u>**an**</u> European who speaks several Indian languages.**(X)**

   The CEO of our company is <u>**a**</u> European who speaks several Indian languages. **(✓)**

9. Check the right usage of prepositions.

 **e.g.:** My nephew is so addicted with watching television that he hardly cares about his studies. **(X)**

   My nephew is so <u>**addicted to**</u> watching television that he hardly cares about his studies. **(✓)**

10. Check the right use of verb.

 **e.g.:** Today most of the young students in India are greatly interested to go abroad for higher studies.**(X)**

   Today most of the young students in India are greatly <u>interested in going</u> abroad for higher studies.(✓)

11. Check the parallel structure of the sentence.

 **e.g.:** These days a lot of youngsters spend a considerable amount of time in social networking, travelling and watch the latest movies on their laptop or mobile. **(X)**

Spot the mistakes

These days a lot of youngsters spend a considerable amount of time in social networking, travelling and watching the latest movies on their laptop or mobile.(✓)

12. Check the appropriateness of the verbs or adjectives used:

    **e.g.:** We had to cancel our trip to Kodaikanal, a hill station in Tamil Nadu, due to bad weather. **(X)**

    We had to cancel our trip to Kodaikanal, a hill station in Tamil Nadu, due to **<u>inclement</u>** weather. **(✓)**

13. Check whether any redundant word has been used:

    **e.g.:** My brother is a male nurse who currently works in Australia earning a good salary. **(X)**

    My brother is a **<u>nurse</u>** who currently works in Australia earning a good salary. **(✓)**

14. Check whether punctuation marks are correctly placed:

    **e.g.:** After I had completed my graduation in electronics from IIT Kharagpur I went to the USA for masters in the same field. **(X)**

    After I had completed my graduation in electronics from IIT Kharagpur, I went to the USA for masters in the same field. **(✓)**

# Exercise

**Spot the mistakes in the following sentences and mention the area of mistake by pinpointing the letter.**

1. The backwater sceneries of Kumarakom in Kerala/ is so mesmerizing that hundreds of
            A                           B
tourists flock to this nature's paradise every year / to enjoy its unending charms and bliss.
                                           C

2. Ms Bedi Tharakan, an alumni of IIT Kharagpur,/has been working as a senior manager in
             A                   B
a British company/ in Dubai since 2015.
             D

3. A good number of nurses from India these days moving/ to economically advanced
             A                     B
countries such as  the UK, Ireland, Australia, Canada, etc./ because of the excellent pay

and better living conditions available in those countries.
             C

4. My brother-in-law who is working in London/ had called me on my mobile a few days
             A                     B
ago/informing me about his promotion.
        C

<h1 align="center">Spot the mistakes</h1>

5. <u>Tom's younger sister has been working as a radiologist/</u> <u>in a private hospital in Saudi</u>
                     A                                               B
   <u>Arabia/for the past three years.</u>
            C

6. <u>The white-haired sheeps that were grazing/</u> <u>in the meadows below the mountains</u>
                     A                                        B
    <u>looked so charming/</u> <u>that we decided to go down near them and take some pictures of</u>
                                                    C
   <u>them.</u>

7. <u>Since Priyanka enjoyed to work in the paediatric ward,/</u> <u>she asked the nursing</u>
                             A                                B
    <u>superintendent to assign her duty all the time in this ward/</u> <u>but the former refused her</u>
                                                        C
   <u>request.</u>

8. <u>Every children born in this world whether in a rich or poor family/has certain rights such</u>
                     A
    <u>as right to living, right to education, right to religion, freedom from exploitation, etc./</u> but
                                    B
    <u>today in several parts of the world these basic rights are denied to them.</u>
                               C

9. <u>The captain ordered his men,/</u> <u>"all of you must run 10 km up the hill carrying a knapsack</u>
                A                                      B
    <u>weighing 30 kilos /</u><u>and then should come back to the barracks within 40 minutes from</u>
    <u>now."</u>                                                C

10. <u>The new botany lecturer had commenced his first lecture/by displaying a few dried</u>
                       A                                     B
     <u>leaves of some rare plants /</u> <u>soon after all the students had returned from the</u>
                                         C
   <u>science lab.</u>

11. <u>The criterias mentioned in the prospectus for the selection of office staff for the company</u>
                                  A
    <u>stated clearly/that the applicants must be proficient in English language/</u> <u>and must have</u>
                                       B
   <u>a working knowledge of computer operations.</u>
                     C

12. The director of the hospital said that he will consider my request for a higher pay/after
                                            A

   he had gone through my performance profile/ as well as the report of the ward
                                  B

   superintendent and the duty doctors of the ward.
                          C

13. 'Brain drain', a term used to refer to the migration of trained personnels from developing
                               A

   countries to developed countries/ has become an obsolete term/ as the world has become
                        B                     C

   a global village.

14. Our college has a sufficient number of labs for every department /and this has been one
                 A                            B

   of the major factors/ that have helped our college to acquire accreditation from the
                            C

   government quite fast.

15. The salary of a college principal is much higher than/ a school principal in most countries
                       A                     B

   of the world/ because the post of the college principal requires several higher academic
                          C

   degrees unlike a school principal.

16. Our college has been noted for its excellent faculties/ who are not only well-qualified
                A                       B

   but also they are well experienced in their respective fields/ which none of the nearby-
                             C

   colleges can boast of.

17. Today globalization is breaking down political boundaries/and brings people of different
                A                     B

   culture, race, religion, economy, etc./ under a single unit called the global village.
                          C

18. Maria has not yet passed OET (*Occupational English Test*) despite several attempts;/
                A

   nevertheless she plans to write the test/till she gets the required score.
        B                          C

# Spot the mistakes

19. <u>Everyone in my village knows each other</u>/ <u>as the population of the place is quite small</u>/
          A                                                B
    <u>and people interacts with each other almost every day.</u>
                              C

20. <u>The Indian constitution grants every Indian women</u>/ <u>certain rights which no government</u>
              A                                                    B
    <u>can take away</u>/ <u>even if the opposition parties support it.</u>
              C

21. <u>The police was searching for the culprits</u> /<u>who looted the passengers of the night bus</u>
              A                                              B
    <u>which was travelling from Bangalore to Hyderabad</u>/but <u>they couldn't get any trace of the</u>
                                                                        C
    <u>persons involved in the crime.</u>

22. <u>The late Abdul J Kalam was considered to be one of the finest presidents of India</u>/who
                              A
    <u>made the post of the president</u>/ <u>people-friendly and highly admirable.</u>
                  B                                    C

23. <u>Seldom our town experiences traffic bloc or congestion</u>/ <u>as there is a bye-pass outside</u>
                      A                                                B
    <u>the town centre</u>/ <u>which takes much of the traffic away from the town.</u>
                                              C

24. <u>What India need today is</u>/ <u>honest and efficient political leaders</u>/ <u>who have vision and</u>
                  A                            B
    <u>wisdom to guide this nation to greater heights.</u>
                          C

25. <u>Each of the candidates</u>/ <u>have been asked several rounds of questions by the interview</u>
              A                            B
    <u>board</u>/but <u>they couldn't get the right candidate for the post advertised.</u>
                              C

26. <u>The cash my father gave me was sufficient enough</u>/<u>to meet the travel and food expenses</u>
                          A                                            B
    <u>incurred on the way.</u>/ <u>In fact, at the end of the journey I had some amount as balance.</u>
                                                  C

27. <u>I have rung up my brother-in-law who is in London</u> /<u>and inquired about his health</u>
                      A                                              B
    <u>condition yesterday</u>/as <u>he had met with an accident recently.</u>
                                          C

Spot the mistakes

28. <u>The more we climbed up the hill,</u>/ <u>the more we can enjoy</u>/ <u>the mesmerizing scenic</u>
               A                            B
    <u>beauty of the green-capped tea garden valleys down.</u>
                   C

29. <u>After our group had visited London</u>/ <u>we decided to move to Paris to enjoy the charms</u>
             A                         B
    <u>offered by this city</u>/ <u>after which we planned a short visit to Rome.</u>
                          C

30. <u>Bob is quite fluent in many European languages such as French, German, Spanish, etc.</u>/
                        A
    <u>but his friend Sham cannot hardly utter a word in these languages</u>/ <u>although the latter</u>
                        B
    <u>speaks excellent Russian.</u>
             C

31. <u>No sooner had the patient taken some solid food,</u>/ <u>he started to vomit severely</u>/
                    A                       B
    <u>forcing the duty doctor to shift him to the ICU ward immediately.</u>
                    C

32. <u>All our friends watched the famous Hindi movie 'Pathaan' in the theatre some time ago.</u>
                    A
    <u>But Raj hasn't watched it yet,</u> <u>and I didn't either.</u>
             B                   C

33. <u>Our group is invited for Maria's birthday party.</u>/ <u>Sarita will wear a new costume for the</u>
                    A                      B
    <u>occasion</u> /and <u>her friend Janvi will also.</u>
                   C

34. <u>The city of Singapore is having excellent transport facilities</u>/<u>when compared with</u>
                      A
    <u>those of the other cities such as Mumbai, Tokyo, Beijing, Hong Kong, etc.,</u>/<u>which makes</u>
                        B
    <u>it the most sought-after city in Asia.</u>
                C

35. <u>I will definitely help you with some financial assistance</u>/<u>if you will put your heart and</u>
                      A                         B
    <u>soul in to your studies</u>/<u>and get through your graduation with flying colours.</u>
                        C

36. <u>Approximately 60 percent of the population in our country are farmers</u>/<u>who suffer</u>
                    A
    <u>a great deal of economic hardships</u>/<u>due to climatic variations as well as defective economic</u>
              B                                      C
    <u>policies of the government.</u>

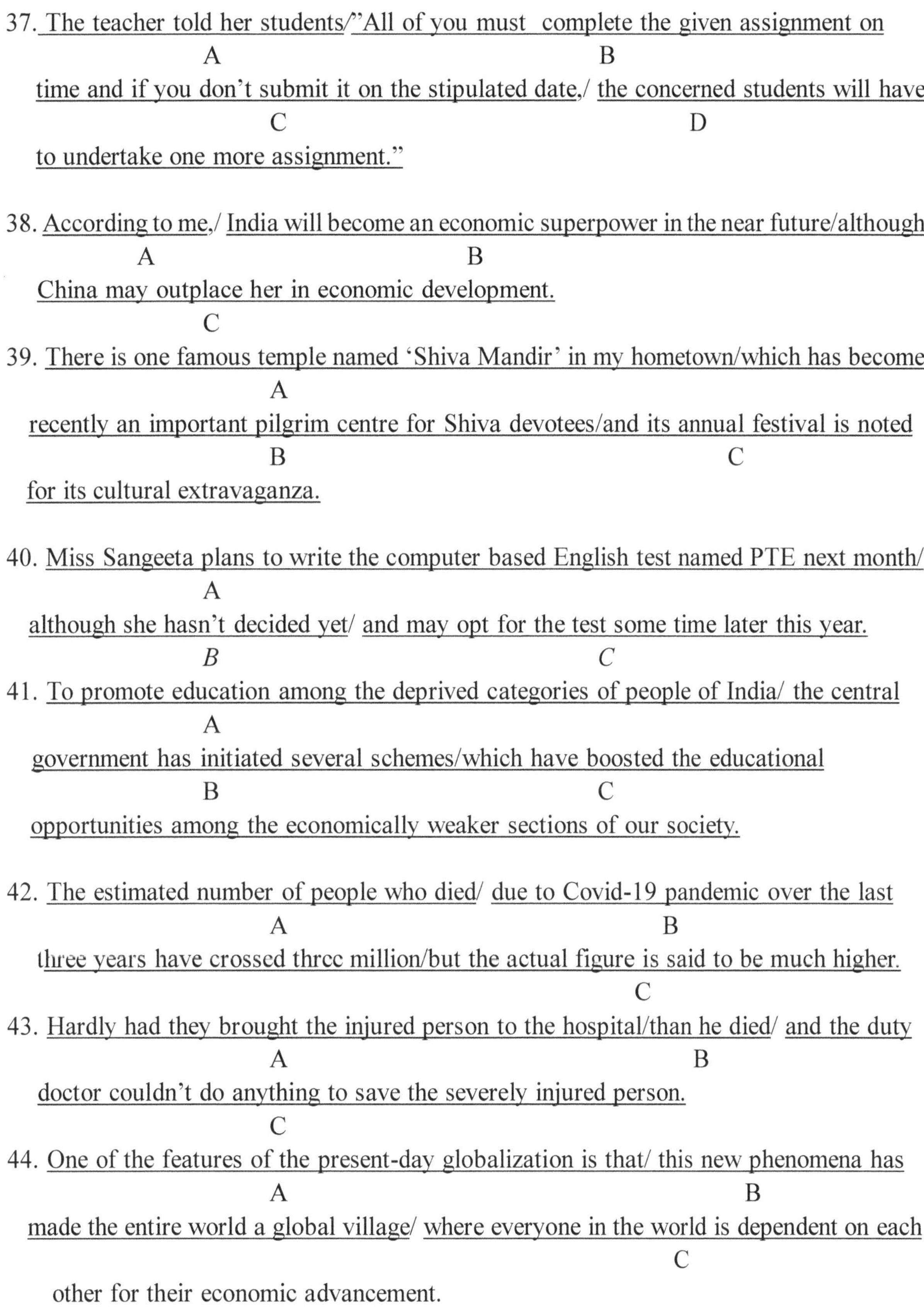

# Spot the mistakes

37. <u>The teacher told her students/"All of you must  complete the given assignment on</u>
        A                         B
<u>time and if you don't submit it on the stipulated date,/ the concerned students will have</u>
            C                          D
<u>to undertake one more assignment."</u>

38. <u>According to me,/ India will become an economic superpower in the near future/although</u>
       A                   B
<u>China may outplace her in economic development.</u>
          C

39. <u>There is one famous temple named 'Shiva Mandir' in my hometown/which has become</u>
            A
<u>recently an important pilgrim centre for Shiva devotees/and its annual festival is noted</u>
         B                          C
<u>for its cultural extravaganza.</u>

40. <u>Miss Sangeeta plans to write the computer based English test named PTE next month/</u>
          A
<u>although she hasn't decided yet/ and may opt for the test some time later this year.</u>
         *B*                        *C*

41. <u>To promote education among the deprived categories of people of India/ the central</u>
          A
<u>government has initiated several schemes/which have boosted the educational</u>
         B                 C
<u>opportunities among the economically weaker sections of our society.</u>

42. <u>The estimated number of people who died/ due to Covid-19 pandemic over the last</u>
            A                         B
<u>three years have crossed three million/but the actual figure is said to be much higher.</u>
                                    C

43. <u>Hardly had they brought the injured person to the hospital/than he died/ and the duty</u>
          A                        B
<u>doctor couldn't do anything to save the severely injured person.</u>
          C

44. <u>One of the features of the present-day globalization is that/ this new phenomena has</u>
          A                         B
<u>made the entire world a global village/ where everyone in the world is dependent on each</u>
                                  C
<u>other for their economic advancement.</u>

45. <u>These days the children spend a major part of their lives playing with their mobiles/</u>
A

<u>which in turn,/</u> <u>ruins their health, negatively affects their studies and makes them mental</u>
    B                                C

<u>wrecks in the long run.</u>

46. <u>Availability of housing, education and healthcare are considered to be  important</u>
A

<u>parameters/ to determine the actual economic status of the people/</u> <u>but many people do</u>
            B                         C

<u>not agree with this view.</u>

47. <u>The college management informed the students that/</u> <u>they regretted for the delay in</u>
      A                            B

<u>conducting the final examination on time/</u> <u>which is said to have ruined the job opportunities</u>
C

<u>of several students.</u>

48. <u>The patient is unconscious since last week/</u> <u>and all attempts to revive him have failed so</u>
       A                           B

<u>far/</u> <u>leaving the doctor who conducted the operation much puzzled.</u>
C

49. <u>The UN has played a big role in easing international tensions/</u> <u>and bringing greater</u>
A

<u>international cooperation among its member nations/</u> <u>which in turn has resulted in fewer</u>
       B                                C

<u>wars in the world.</u>

50. <u>There is no doubt to the fact that/</u> <u>if you worked hard,/</u> <u>you would have obtained better</u>
      A                    B              C

<u>marks in your final examination.</u>

**Answers:**

1. **Ans : A** (*The term 'scenery' is an uncountable noun and it cannot be used in plural form.*)

2. **Ans : A** (*'An alumna' is the correct term for a female former student.*)

3. **Ans : A** (*general information is given in present simple tense.*)

4. **Ans : B** (*When specific past time is mentioned, simple past should be used.*)

5. **Ans : C** (*past time cannot be mentioned with present perfect tense*)

6. **Ans : A** (***Sheeps*** *is an incorrect usage. The term 'sheep' is used both as singular and plural noun.*)

7. **Ans: A** (*'enjoyed to work' is a wrong usage; it should be 'enjoyed working'.*)

8. **Ans: A** (*The term 'every children ' is a wrong usage; it should be 'every child'.*)

9. **Ans: B** (*All quotations in a direct speech must begin with a capital letter.*)

10. **Ans: A** (*When there are two actions in the past, both actions cannot be in past perfect tense; the first action should be in past perfect tense and the second action should be in past simple tense.*)

11. **Ans: A** (*The noun 'criteria' is always a plural noun and so 's' cannot be added to make it plural.*)

12. **Ans: B** (*If the main clause is in past tense, the next clause cannot be in future tense.*)

13. **Ans: A** (*'Personnels' is an incorrect usage; it should be 'personnel'*)

14. **Ans: B** (*'The expression* **'one of the'** *should be followed by a singular verb; hence the verb should be* **'has'** *and not* **'have'.**)

15. **Ans: B** (*Illogical comparison; here the salary of a college principal is compared to a school principal.*)

16. **Ans: A** (*The term 'faculties' meaning staff is a wrong usage; it should be 'faculty' only.*)

17. **Ans: A** (*General information or statement is mostly given in present simple.*)

18. **Ans: A** (*'not yet' is an incorrect usage; 'yet' should be used at the end of the clause.*)

19. **Ans: C** (*The term* **'people'** *is plural and, therefore, it cannot be* **'interacts** *but only* **'interact. '**)

20. **Ans: A** (*'Every Indian women'* *is a wrong usage; it should be* **'every Indian woman'.**)

21. **Ans: A** (*The term 'police' is plural and so the verb should also be plural.*)

22. **Ans: B** (*When we speak of the great personalities of the past we should use present simple tense.*)

23. **Ans: A** (*'seldom' is an adverb and it should be placed before the main verb.*)

24. **Ans: A** (*When a sentence begins with* **'what'** *the verb is singular and so it should be* **'what India needs'.**)

25. **Ans: A** (*Each of the candidates is singular and so the verb should also be singular.*)

26. **Ans: B** (* In this sentence 'enough' is a redundant word and so it should not be used.*)

27. **Ans: B** (*The term 'yesterday' cannot be used with present perfect tense.*)

28. **Ans: B** (*The first clause being in past tense, the second clause should also be in past tense.*)

29. **Ans: A** (*Whenever a complex sentence begins with a subordinate clause, there should be a comma after the subordinate clause.*)

30. **Ans: C** (*'cannot hardly' is wrong because both terms are negative.*)

31. **Ans: B** (*The expression 'no sooner' should be accompanied by 'than'.*)

32. **Ans: C** (*In a negative statement the tense of both clauses should be the same, i.e., 'I haven't either'.*)

33. **Ans: C** (*In an affirmative agreement sentence, 'too or so' is generally used and not 'also'.*)

34. **Ans: A** (*Improper use of 'having'*)

35. **Ans: B** (*We cannot use double 'will' in the same sentence.*)

36. **Ans: A** (*The term 'population' is an uncountable noun and so the verb should be singular.*)

37. **Ans: A** (*After the first clause of the direct speech, there should be a comma:* **The teacher told her students,**)

38. **Ans: A** (*While giving personal opinion we should use terms such as* **'In my view, as far as I know, to my best of knowledge, etc.**)

39. **Ans: A** (*The article 'a' appears to be more appropriate than 'one'.*)

40. **Ans: A** ( *'write the test' is an incorrect term; use the term 'take the test/appear for the test'.*)

41. **Ans: A** (*A sentence, preferably, should not begin with a preposition.*)

42. **Ans: B** (*The term 'the number' is followed by a singular verb.*)

43. **Ans: B** (*With 'hardly' the adverb 'when' should be used and not 'than'.*)

44. **Ans: B** (*'this new phenomena' is wrong; it should be 'this new phenomenon has'.*)

45. **Ans: A** (*The article 'the' is not required as the term 'children' is spoken in a general way.*)

46. **Ans: B** (*'to determine' is an correct usage here; it should be 'in determining'.*)

47. **Ans: B** (*'regret for' is an incorrect usage. The verb 'regret' should not be followed by a preposition.*)

48. **Ans: A** (*'Since' is generally used in present perfect and not in present simple tense.*)

49. **Ans: A** (*'a big role' is an incorrect usage; it should be 'a major/significant role'.*)

50. **Ans: A** (*When the main clause is in conditional perfect tense, the subordinate clause should be in past perfect conditional tense:* **'if you had worked hard'.**)

—xxx—

## Useful data

# 16. Trinomials (*three words joined together to form a group*)

| | |
|---|---|
| mind, body and soul | healthy, wealthy and wise |
| father, mother and child | here, there and everywhere |
| deaf, dumb and blind | knife, fork and spoon |
| Tom, Dick and Harry | signed, sealed and delivered |
| faith, hope and charity | |

# 28. English terms that enhance speaking and writing

(Words are given in alphabetical order for easy reference)

| | |
|---|---|
| **Achilles' heel** | : a person's weak or vulnerable part |
| **Acid test** | : any decisive test for knowing the worth and quality of something. |
| **Adam's apple** | : the projection in front of the throat |
| **Air Force One** | : the official plane of the US President |
| **Alma mater** | : former school, college or university where one studied |
| **Aviculture** | : scientific rearing of birds |
| **Bachelor party** | : a male party given to a young man who is going to get married |
| **Back-seat driver** | : a passenger who gives unwanted advice to the driver about driving |
| **Backpedal** | : to go back on a promise or a plan of action proposed |
| **Bargaining chip** | : something which someone is willing to lose in order to gain something. |
| **Biological clock** | : an in-built mechanism which controls the physiological rhythm and cycles of organisms. |
| **Birthday suit** | : completely naked |
| **Blue chips** | : shares that sell well because of their long record of reliable earnings |
| **Blue revolution** | : leading to an increase in fish production |
| **Brain-teaser** | : a problem for which it is hard to find the answer |
| **Brain-wave** | : sudden bright idea |
| **Breathing space** | : enough rest or space to move about |
| **Bridal brocades** | : special dress worn by a bride during her marriage ceremony |
| **Bridal wear/attire:** | wedding clothes of a woman |
| **Cakewalk** | : something that is easy |
| **Calculated risk** | : a risk which you consider worth taking because the result, if it is successful, will be good |
| **Call of nature** | : a polite term to refer to the need to urinate or defecate |
| **Caparisoned elephants** | : decorated elephants for certain temple or other functions |
| **Car pooling** | : sharing of car to reach a place or an office |
| **Career woman** | : a woman for whom job is more important than looking after one's family |
| **Catch-22 situation:** | describing a no-win situation in which alternate choices are also equally bad |
| **Catwalk** | : the long, narrow stage over which models walk |
| **Chew the cud** | : to reflect about the past, to ponder over the past, etc. |
| **Clean forgot** | : forgot completely |
| **Clichéd phrases** | : a phrase which is commonly used by people and has become boring |
| **Close call/close shave :** | a miraculous escape |
| **Cloud Nine** | : to be extremely happy, a fanciful place, etc. |
| **Comfort zone** | : a situation or area in which you feel comfortable |

English terms that enhance speaking and writing

**Cosmetic surgery** : intended to improve only the appearance of something, superficial

**Crocodile tears**    : tears that you shed when you are not really sad or sorry

**Cutting-edge technology**: new technology that is faster, quicker, better, etc.

**Dalal Street**    : Indian stock-market

**Damoclean sword**: danger in the midst of prosperity or success

**Diamond wedding anniversary**: 60th anniversary of wedding

**Dog-fight**    : a close combat between fighter planes, any rough fight, etc.

**Doldrums**    : in low spirits, a period of uncertainty

**Dry run**    : a dummy run, rehearsal, a mock trial, etc.

**Dutch courage**    : the confidence some people get from drinking alcohol before doing something frightening

**Earth-shattering/shaking**: events having tremendous importance or significance

**Eve-teasing**    : making fun of ladies while standing in street corners, roadsides, etc.

**Fast buck**    : a slang for quick money

**Feign ignorance**    : pretend not to know although the person knows it

**Festooned umbrellas** : coloured umbrellas used for religious festivals or other occasions

**Fifth column**    : a group of people within a country who help an enemy country

**Finishing school**    : a school or college where young people are given training in soft skills  such as effective communication, etiquette, etc.

**Fish-plate**    : Crossbeams used to keep rail tracks strong

**Foregone conclusion** : certain conclusion, result that is definite and sure

**French leave**    : leave without permission

**Freudian slip**    : an unintentional mistake in speaking

**Fringe benefit**    : an extra benefit given in addition to salary or wage

**Gatecrash**    : to go to a party or other event when you have not been invited

**Ghost writer**    : one hired to write material for someone who will take the credit for the writing

**Globetrotter**    : someone who often travels to a lot of different countries

**Golden handshake**: usually large payments made to make someone leave the job for good

**Golden wedding anniversary**: 50th year of wedding

**Green Bench**    : a set of judges appointed to hear cases related to forests and environment

**Green fingers**    : the ability to make plants grow well

**Green paper**    : official Govt. publication containing proposals for legislation issued to interested persons for comments

**Green room**    : a room in a theatre where performers can relax and change dress

**Greenhouse gas**    : carbon dioxide and other gases which are said to be the main cause for greenhouse effect

**G-spot**    : a small area inside the vagina which increases sexual pleasure when rubbed

| | |
|---|---|
| **G-string** | : a narrow string of cloth tied around the waist covering the genitals |
| **Guinea pig** | : a person or an animal used in scientific experiment |
| **Hat trick** | : when a player scores three times in the same game |
| **Herculean task** | : a work requiring great effort |
| **Hitch ride** | : get a free ride in someone's vehicle |
| **Hi-tech** | : using the most advanced and developed machines and methods. |
| **Hocus-pocus** | : talk or behaviour designed to draw one's attention from something |
| **Holistic medicine** | : treatment which deals with the whole person, not just the injury or disease |
| **Hornet's nest** | : a very difficult or unpleasant situation |
| **Horse sense** | : practical knowledge and good judgment about ordinary life, common sense. |
| **Horse trading** | : buying off elected members to form a government |
| **Hung jury** | : jury that is unable to agree on a verdict |
| **Impeccable record:** | a record with no negative remark or action |
| **Impromptu action** | : action done on the spur of the moment without planning |
| **In camera** | : a court proceeding in which the public is excluded |
| **Inclement weather:** | bad weather |
| **Indelible imprint/mark** | : something that is not easily erased, long lasting impact, etc. |
| **Indian cuisine** | : Indian food stuffs |
| **Indian Diaspora** | : Indians who are settled abroad |
| **Informed guess** | : guessing based on facts. |
| **Inside information** | : information that is not available to others outside the company or office |
| **Intellectual property** | : someone's idea that has value or got acceptance |
| **Jacob's ladder** | : ladder in a ship usually made out of rope |
| **Judas hole** | : a peep hole in a door for identifying people |
| **Kangaroo court** | : unofficial court of law which tries people according to their law. |
| **Kick-start** | : to make something start to happen |
| **Kissing distance** | : by a very small margin, narrow escape, miraculous escape, etc. |
| **Kitchen cabinet** | : a small unofficial group of people who give advice to the Prime Minister or an important political leader |
| **Knee-jerk reaction** | : sudden reaction, doing something without thinking |
| **Know-how** | : practical knowledge in doing something |
| **Landmark ruling** | : an important court ruling |
| **Launch pad** | : something that helps someone to start an action |
| **Literary garb** | : put in nice and beautiful language |
| **Litmus test** | : test that will decide the effectiveness of something |
| **Live-in relationship:** | two unmarried people staying together. |
| **Maiden speech** | : the first formal speech made by a politician or person |

English terms that enhance speaking and writing

**Manicure** : careful treatment of fingers, nails, etc. to make them appear better

**Marching orders** : asked to leave a job or place because one has done something wrong

**Mercy killing** : the act of killing someone who is very ill or very old so that they do not have to suffer any longer

**Midas touch** : the ability of someone whose action always brings success or profit

**Modus operandi** : a particular way of doing something especially one that is characteristic or well-established

**Money laundering** : making black money*(money obtained illegally)* legitimate.

**Morning ablutions** : morning wash, activities such as brushing teeth, going to the washroom, etc. that people do in the morning

**Multi-faceted** : having many different parts

**Multitasking** : ability to do more than one task at a time

**Nanotechnology** : a technology that tries to make electronic gadgets smaller and smaller

**Netizens** : people who use the internet frequently

**Nuptial knot** : the gold chain put around the bride's neck by the bridegroom during the marriage ceremony as a sign of marriage bond

**Oedipus complex** : boy's affection for mother and jealousy and anger towards father

**One-night stand** :. a sexual relationship which lasts only for one night

**Over-the-counter** : a medicine bought from a shop without a doctor's prescription.

**Pandora's box** : something which creates a lot of new problems that you did not expect

**Panic button** : to do something quickly without thinking in order to deal with a difficult or worrying situation

**Paper tiger** : something that looks dangerous and strong but in reality it is weak and not harmful

**Pedicure** : treatment of toes and legs to make them look better

**Photo opportunity** : an occasion when a politician or famous person is photographed doing something that will make them popular with the public

**Pink slips** : forced dismissal from jobs

**Pipe dream** : an idea or plan that is impossible or very unlikely to happen

**Pyrotechnics** : a display of fireworks

**Red herring** : something that diverts attention from the real issue

**Regatta** : boat race

**Repartee** : the ability to give a quick and fitting reply to something that is said

**Ripple effect** : when one effect leads to several other effects or results

**Road Map** : a plan of action

**Ruby anniversary** : the date exactly 40 years after someone's wedding or event.

**Scot-free** : let off without receiving the deserved or expected punishment.

**Second-degree burn** : a serious burn in which the skin develops blisters.

**Senior citizen** : a polite term for an elderly person, retired individual, etc.

English terms that enhance speaking and writing

**Seventh heavens** : in extreme happiness
**Shadow boxing** : fighting imaginary enemies
**Shoplifting** : stealing from a shop by a customer
**Shouting match** : an argument in which  people shout at each other
**Silver jubilee** : 25th anniversary
**Silver screen** : film industry
**Silviculture** : scientific way of caring for forests
**Sine-qua-non** : a necessary condition without which something is not possible
**Sitting duck** : an easy target, a helpless victim
**Sixth sense** : intuitive power besides the usual five senses
**Smokescreen** : something which hides the truth about someone's intentions
**Sneezing distance** : very close, near-by
**Soft porn** : no explicit showing of sex but only suggestive talk, message, etc.
**Soft skills** : skills in communication, organization, leadership, interpersonal skill, etc.
**Sunset years** : the period after retirement, old age, etc.
**Surrogate mother** : a woman who bears a baby for a childless couple for some money
**Techno-savvy** : a person who is fond of using many technological gadgets
**The Fourth Estate** : the mass media/the press
**Think-tanks** : persons whose main job is to frame policies and find solutions
**Top-notch** : something that is good and excellent, first-rate, etc.
**Trojan horse** : disguised enemy or threat within one's own rank or group
**Uncle Sam** : US nation or government personified
**Wall Street** : American money market, American stock-market
**Watershed** : very important aspect, significant event, etc.
**Wedding Brocades** : wedding clothes of a woman who is going to get married
**Wet blanket** : a person whose lack of enthusiasm dampens the spirit of others
**Wet nurse** : a woman who breastfeeds another's child due to sickness or the death of the mother
**Whistle-blower** : a person who brings to light the illegal activities of certain important individuals, companies, government departments, etc.
**White elephant** : an expensive possession that proves to be useless
**White lie** : a harmless lie
**White paper** : official government report or policy statement on some issues
**Window dressing** : things that are said or done in order to make an attractive effect but which are of no real importance
**Window-shopping** : spending time looking at the goods on sale in shop windows without intending to buy any of them.
**Yesteryears** : past years, bye-gone years, etc.
**Zebra crossing** : areas where pedestrians are allowed to cross the road

—xxx—

# 29. Synonyms

(Words that have the same or nearly the same meanings)

| | | |
|---|---|---|
| **ability** *(n)* | : | talent/competence/proficiency/knack/skill |
| **abundant** *(adj)* | : | plentiful/ample/lavish/bountiful/teeming |
| **adequate** *(adj)* | : | enough/ample/sufficient/satisfactory/suitable |
| **admire** *(v)* | : | applaud/appreciate/esteem/value/honour/respect |
| **adventure** *(n)* | : | risk/hazard/danger/peril/quest/venture |
| **adversary** *(n)* | : | opponent/antagonist/rival/enemy/foe |
| **adversity** *(n)* | : | misfortune/ill-luck/distress/woe/mishap |
| **advice** *(n)* | : | guidance/counseling/counsel/suggestion |
| **affection** *(n)* | : | love/liking/warmth/fondness/attachment |
| **afraid** *(adj)* | : | frightened/scared/fearful/nervous/terrified |
| **agony** *(n)* | : | suffering/pain/distress/torment/anguish |
| **allot** *(v)* | : | earmark/designate/assign/allocate/apportion |
| **allow** *(v)* | : | permit/let/authorize/sanction/concede to |
| **alone** *( adj)* | : | solitary/lonely/ deserted/single/isolated |
| **alter** *(v)* | : | change/modify/transform/amend/recast |
| **ambition** *(n)* | : | desire/aspiration/longing/yearning/goal |
| **amusement** *(n)* | : | mirth/fun/merriment/gaiety/joy/delight |
| **anger** *(n)* | : | rage/fury/temper/wrath/outrage/ire/irritation |
| **anxiety** *(n)* | : | worry/concern/apprehension/uneasiness |
| **appreciation** *(n)* | : | gratitude/thankfulness/indebtedness |
| **arrest** *(v)* | : | apprehend/detain/seize/capture/catch |
| **assignment** *(n)* | : | task/job/duty/mission/chore/venture/project |
| **assist** *(v)* | : | help/support/cooperate/collaborate/augment |
| **authentic** *(adj)* | : | genuine/bona fide/legitimate/real/true/actual |
| **avoid** *(v)* | : | shun/eschew/evade/shirk/elude/avert/dodge |
| **beautiful** *(adj)* | : | lovely/attractive/pretty/charming/exquisite |
| **begin** *(v)* | : | start/commence/embark/initiate/launch |
| **benefit** *(n)* | : | advantage/gain/profit/worth/betterment |
| **blunder** *(n)* | : | error/fault/folly/mistake/slip/faux pas |
| **brave** *(adj)* | : | valiant/courageous/fearless/gallant/bold |
| **bright** *(adj)* | : | shining/brilliant/vivid/dazzling/sparkling |
| **build** *(v)* | : | construct/erect/manufacture/set up/fabricate |
| **calamity** *(n)* | : | disaster/catastrophe/tragedy/misfortune |
| **capable** *(adj)* | : | competent/able/efficient/proficient/adept |
| **career** *(n)* | : | occupation/profession/vocation/calling |
| **cause** *(n)* | : | origin/root/source/beginning/reason |
| **change** *(v)* | : | alter/modify/transform/convert/recast |

Synonyms

| | | |
|---|---|---|
| **characteristic***(n)* | : | quality/attribute/feature/trait/property |
| **charming** *(adj)* | : | delightful/pleasing/appealing/attractive/lovely |
| **cheat** *(v)* | : | deceive/trick/defraud/dupe/hoodwink |
| **cheerful** *(adj)* | : | happy/bright/merry/glad/gay/delightful |
| **clean** *(adj)* | : | unsoiled/immaculate/unstained/spotless |
| **clever***(adj)* | : | intelligent/bright/sharp/keen/astute |
| **command** *(n)* | : | order/decree/ bidding/injunction |
| **companion** *(n)* | : | partner/escort/comrade/colleague/ally |
| **conflict** *(n)* | : | fight/clash/hostility/tussle/strife/combat |
| **conquer** *(v)* | : | vanquish/subdue/subjugate/defeat/rout |
| **consequence** *(n)* | : | result/effect/outcome/aftermath/prominence |
| **consider** *(c)* | : | examine/ponder/contemplate/envisage/regard |
| **construct** *(v)* | : | build/erect/make/ set up/fabricate/create |
| **country** *( n)* | : | nation/state/realm/kingdom/domain |
| **crime** *(n)* | : | offence/misdeed/transgression/sin |
| **current** *(adj)* | : | present-day/contemporary/modern/up-to-date |
| **damage** *(n)* | : | harm/injury/hurt/impairment/loss |
| **defend** *(v)* | : | guard/safeguard/shield/protect/ward off |
| **delicious** *(adj)* | : | tasty/appetizing/mouthwatering/palatable |
| **desire** *(n)* | : | wish/want/longing/yearning/goal/ambition |
| **destroy** *(v)* | : | demolish/dismantle/raze/ravage/ruin/wreck |
| **different** *(adj)* | : | unlike/dissimilar/diverse/divergent |
| **difficult** *(adj)* | : | hard/strenuous/arduous/laborious |
| **discover** *(v)* | : | find/uncover/unearth/detect/stumble upon |
| **distinguished** *(adj)* | : | famous/eminent/renowned/prominent |
| **effect** *(n)* | : | result/outcome/consequence/repercussion |
| **eminent** *(n)* | : | great/distinguished/prominent/famous |
| **empty** *(adj)* | : | vacant/hollow/void/bare/unoccupied |
| **enchanting** *(n)* | : | charming/delightful/captivating/alluring |
| **enemy** *(n)* | : | foe/opponent/rival/adversary/antagonist |
| **enjoyment** *(n)* | : | amusement/entertainment/delight/gaiety |
| **environment** *(n)* | : | surroundings/milieu/habitat/setting/environs |
| **error** *(n)* | : | mistake/flaw/fallacy/inaccuracy/folly |
| **essential** *(adj)* | : | necessary/indispensable/vital/critical/pivotal |
| **excellent** *(adj)* | : | great/distinguished/super/superb/outstanding |
| **famous** *(adj)* | : | well-known/renowned/famed/distinguished |
| **forest** *(n)* | : | woods/wood/woodland/wilderness/jungle |
| **forgive** *(v)* | : | pardon/exonerate/absolve/acquit |
| **fortune** *(n)* | : | wealth/treasure/affluence/opulence |
| **friend** *(n)* | : | companion/comrade/soul mate/confidant |

| | | |
|---|---|---|
| **fun** *(n)* | : | amusement/entertainment/pleasure/gaiety |
| **grand** *(adj)* | : | impressive/magnificent/imposing/splendid |
| **gratitude** *(n)* | : | gratefulness/thankfulness/indebtedness |
| **handsome** *(n)* | : | attractive/pretty/elegant/beautiful/charming |
| **help** *(v)* | : | assist/aid/augment/support/collaborate |
| **home** *(n)* | : | house/abode/residence/dwelling |
| **honest** *(adj)* | : | upright/straightforward/candid/frank |
| **illness** *(n)* | : | ailment/sickness/malady/affliction |
| **importance** *(n)* | : | significance/seriousness/value/noteworthiness |
| **imprisonment** *(n)* | : | custody/confinement/detention |
| **inadequate** *(adj)* | : | insufficient/meagre/scarce/sparse |
| **intelligent** *(adj)* | : | clever/bright/brilliant/sharp/astute |
| **job** *(n)* | : | task/undertaking/chore/assignment/work |
| **journey** *(n)* | : | trip/expedition/trek/jaunt/voyage |
| **joy** *(n)* | : | delight/pleasure/gladness/mirth/happiness |
| **landmark** *(n)* | : | milestone/watershed/historic/feature |
| **liberty** *(n)* | : | freedom/independence/autonomy/sovereignty |
| **love** *(n)* | : | affection/fondness/care/warmth |
| **misfortune** *(n)* | : | bad luck/ill-fortune/mischance/adversity |
| **necessity** *(n)* | : | essential/requisite/prerequisite/sine qua non |
| **new** *(adj)* | : | modern/recent/present-day/current/latest |
| **occupation** *(n)* | : | job/work/profession/service/calling |
| **outstanding** *(adj)* | : | prominent/eminent/well-known/renowned |
| **permanent** *(adj)* | : | everlasting/perpetual/eternal/endless |
| **pollute** *(v)* | : | contaminate/adulterate/infect/spoil |
| **problem** *(n)* | : | difficulty/complication/trouble/predicament |
| **quarrel** *(v)* | : | fight/dispute/squabble/wrangle/row |
| **reason** *(n)* | : | grounds/cause/basis/motive/rationale |
| **significance** *(n)* | : | importance/import/essence/implication |
| **skill** *(n)* | : | ability/accomplishment/adeptness/talent |
| **spectacular** *(adj)* | : | magnificent/splendid/breathtaking/glorious |
| **toilet** *(n)* | : | comfort room/bathroom/rest room/washroom |
| **trait** *(n)* | : | characteristic/attribute/feature/quality |
| **treasure** *(n)* | : | riches/valuables/wealth/fortune |
| **vengeance** *(n)* | : | revenge/retribution/retaliation/reprisal |
| **wealth** *(n)* | : | treasure/capital/fortune/riches/assets |
| **whole** *(adj)* | : | entire/complete/full/total/undivided |
| **wrong** *(n)* | : | incorrect/inaccurate/error/mistake |
| **youngster** *(n)* | : | youth/juvenile/teenager/adolescent |

—xxx—-

# 30. Homonyms
### (Words similar in sound but having different meanings)

1. **adopt**     : *take up*
     **adapt**     : *change according to the situation*
   Researchers need to **adopt** scientific methodology in their work.
   Human beings have the innate ability to **adapt** to varying situations.

2. **advise**     : *to give suggestion for improvement* (verb)
     **advice**     : *points for improvements (nouns)*
   My doctor **advised** me to give up smoking for good immediately.
   The new principal's **advice** to the students to focus on their studies went
     unheeded.

3. **allusion** : *indirect reference*
     **illusion** : *deceptive vision*
   The Finance Minister's speech was full of **allusion** to hard economic
     measures.
   Mr. Krishnan is under the **illusion** that he would be made the manager of the
     firm.

4. **artiste**     : *professional singer or actor or dancer*
     **artist**     : *a person who practises one of the fine arts*
   Rajini Kant is considered to be one of the top-most film **artistes** of the Tamil
     movie world.
   Mr. Hussain is a renowned **artist** in the field of painting.

5. **antic**     : *queer behaviour, funny behaviour*
     **antique**     : *old, ancient*
   The comedian's **antic**s amused everyone present in the hall.
   Today many famous Indian **antiques** can be found in  European homes.

6. **altar**     : *table used for sacrifice*
     **alter**     : *change*
   Generally, **altars** are considered to be sacred by most Christian groups.
   The river Brahmaputra often **alters** its course creating great havoc in the
     process.

7. **ascent**     : climb
     **assent**     : agreement
   The **ascent** to Mt. Everest is so difficult that only a handful have reached its
     top.
   The manager has given his **assent** for his junior's promotion.

8. **breath** : *air taken into the lungs*
   **breathe** : *the act of taking air into and from the lungs*
   **breadth** : *distance from side to side*
   There wasn't a **breath** of air on the mountain-top.
   If we **breathe** foul air for a long time, it will greatly affect our health.
   The **breadth** of this floor is beyond the permitted limit.

9. **bridal** : *wedding feast*
   **bridle** : *that part of a horse's harness that is used for controlling, something to control*
   The **bridal** party came to the bridegroom's place on horses.
   If you do not **bridle** your temper, it may create problems for you.

10. **Britain** : *It is another name of England.*
    **Briton** : *A person who lives in Britain.*
    Once upon a time India was a colony of **Britain.**
    **Britons** are considered to be harbingers of modern civilization in many parts
    of the world.

11. **Born** : *to come into the world*
    **Borne** : *to carry or to tolerate, suffer*
    Abdul J Kalam was **born** in a poor family but he was able to become the
    President of India.
    In India, the financial burden of the family is mostly **borne** by the father
    although today this trend is slowly changing.

12. **coma** : *the state of unconsciousness*
    **comma** : *punctuation mark (,)*
    After the operation the patient fell into a **coma** all of a sudden.
    **Comma** is an important punctuation mark in English.

13. **collision** : *dash against each other*
    **collusion** : *secret agreement or understanding*
    There was a head-on **collision** between the bus and the car on the public
    road.
    There seems to be a **collusion** between the mafia and the police.

14. **canon** : *church law*
    **cannon** : *a big gun*
    The Catholic Church is noted for its strict **canon** laws which need to be
    adhered to by its followers.
    Nowadays **cannons** are no longer used in ground battles and wars.

15. **canvas** : *a kind of leather*
    **canvass** : *to seek vote during election*
    Mr Sathyan, a rich businessman, prefers to wear expensive **canvas** shoes.
    These days **canvassing** during an election is a costly affair.

16. **cite**     : *quote*

    **site**     : *a place, location*

          Our principal always **cites** some good quotations during his pep talks.

          The **site** of the new Indian parliament was chosen after a series of consultations.

17. **coward** : *a person who is frightened*

    **cowardly** : *the quality of being frightened*

          Mr Lal is a **coward** who doesn't want to take any risk in life.

          Mr Mohan's running away from the scene of the accident was a **cowardly** act.

18. **complement** : *go together*

    **compliment** : *praise, wishes*

          Rice and wheat are **complementary** food items in India and people consume both.

          Kindly give my **compliments** to your Daddy who is a good friend of our family.

19. **childlike** : *to have qualities of a small child*

    **childish** : *mischievous*

          Pt. Jawaharlal Nehru had a **childlike** spirit and he enjoyed talking to children.

          Jayan is too **childish** to be made the class leader.

20. **confidant** : *a friend who is very close*

    **confident** : *having faith in oneself or in others*

          Chanakya was a **confidant** of King Chandragupta Maurya.

          My sister was **confident** of getting through OET (*Occupational English Test*) this time.

21. **confirm** : *make firmer or stronger*

    **conform** : *to be in agreement with, comply with*

          Kindly **confirm** the appointment by an official letter.

          The director of the company asked his employees to **conform** to the rules of the firm.

22. **cemetery** : *a place where the dead are buried*

    **symmetry** : *having similarity*

          Christians bury their dead in **cemeteries** which are generally well-maintained.

          There is no **symmetry** between those two figures.

23. **corps**     : *one of the technical branches of the army*

    **corpse**     : *dead body*

          My elder sister is a major in the Indian Army Medical **Corps**.

          The unclaimed **corpses** after the violence were buried quietly.

24. **check** : *make sure*

    **cheque** : *paper leaflet used for monetary transactions*

        The duty doctor asked the nurse to **check** the blood pressure of the patient.

        Mr Sangma lost his **cheque** book while travelling in a public bus.

25. **dairy** : *milk farm*

    **diary** : *book which keeps a record*

        There is a good **dairy** farm near my house which supplies milk to the nearby town.

        Some people have the habit of maintaining a **diary** in which they write the key events of the day.

26. **dependent** : *basing on, depending on*

    **dependants** : *one who depends on another*

        The arrival of Monsoon in India is **dependent** on several factors.

        The **dependants** of the man, who died in a train accident, have claimed compensation from the government.

27. **defer** : *postpone*

    **differ** : *not same, not agree*

        The function has been **deferred** to the next month due to the sudden outbreak of flu in the campus.

        In most situations, the opposition parties and the government **differ** on many aspects of governance.

28. **decent** : *respectful*

    **descent** : *come down*

    **dissent** : *disagreement*

        The spectators during the football match did not show **decent** behaviour.

        Many mountaineers have lost their lives during their **descent** from Mount Everest.

        The manager expressed his **dissent** over the new proposal of the Director.

29. **desert** : *vast dry area full of sand*

    **dessert** : *a sweet food item served at the end of a meal*

        The Thar **desert** that lies in the western part of the country is the only desert in India.

        Europeans always take a **dessert** at the end of their meals.

30. **dying** : *ending of life*

    **dyeing** : *change colour*

        Today a lot of innocent people are **dying** in different parts of the world due to terrorist attacks.

        These days many middle-aged persons, both male and female, **dye** their hair to look younger.

31. **exert** : *put pressure or force*
    **exhort** : *advise*
    The opposition parties **exerted** pressure on the Govt. to withdraw the new bill.
    I **exhorted** my friend to quit smoking but he didn't pay heed to my advice.

22. **elicit** : *cause to come out*
    **illicit** : *unlawful, forbidden, etc.*
    The teacher tried to **elicit** correct answers from the students but none came forward with the correct answer.
    Carrying of **illicit** weapons in public has become rampant in some parts of the country.

33. **eminent** : *famous*
    **imminent** : *coming soon*
    Dr Purushotam Lal is an **eminent** cardiologist of our country.
    Since the Monsoon is **imminent,** the farmers have started sowing seeds.

34. **especially:** *in a special manner*
    **specially** : *meant for a particular person or thing*
    The theatres in India become full **especially** when new films are released.
    We prepared a dinner **specially** for our new neighbour.

35. **economic** : *of economics, connected with money*
    **economical** : *careful in spending money, time etc.*
    The **economic** condition of India is improving slowly but steadily.
    The rich are noted for their lavish spending; they are least bothered about **economical** spending.

36. **fair** : *beautiful, small market*
    **fare** : *cost of a ticket*
    Sarita is not as **fair** as Shiny, although both are equally brilliant.
    Village **fairs** in India are slowly disappearing as shopping malls have come up in every nook and corner of the country.
    What is the taxi **fare** from New Delhi to Agra?

37. **gentle** : *kind*
    **genteel** : *polite, well-bred, elegant*
    The chairman of the company was greatly impressed with the **gentle** behaviour of his new secretary.
    The captain's **genteel** behaviour during the match was well appreciated by the crowd.

38. **honorary:** *an honour given without the usual formalities*
    **honourable** : *deserving honour and respect*
    Mr Smith, the **honorary** President of our club, is no longer active in the club's activities.
    At the funeral of Caesar, Brutus said that he was an **honourable** person.

39. **hail**    : *frozen raindrops from the sky*
    **hale**    : *happy, contented*
       <u>**Hail**</u> stones are common in many parts of the country.
       Sam is always <u>**hale**</u> and spreads his joy wherever he goes.

40. **hoard**   : *to store up things to obtain a better price later*
    **horde**   : *a group of people, particularly robbers*
       Some businessmen have the habit of <u>**hoarding**</u> things to earn higher profit later.
       During the Sultanate period <u>**hordes**</u> of Mongolians used to invade India.

41. **human**  : *person*
    **humane** : *kind and generous*
       It is believed that <u>**human**</u>s are found only on the earth.
       Gandhiji was a <u>**humane**</u> person who cared for the wellbeing of others.

42. **illegible** : *handwriting which cannot be read*
    **eligible**  : *fitting*
       It is a fact that students who have <u>**illegible**</u> handwriting obtain less marks in examinations.
       The board members felt that the current manager of the company was most **eligible** for the post of the director.

43. **Industrial**   : *of industry*
    **Industrious** : *hard-working*
       The <u>**industrial**</u> town of Coimbatore is noted for its numerous small-scale industries.
       <u>**Industrious**</u> students always achieve good results in whatever they do.

44. **Jealous** : *not feeling happy with others' success*
    **Zealous** : *full of enthusiasm*
       It is useless to feel **jealous** at others' success because success often comes after a series of failures.
       The current principal of our college is <u>**zealous**</u> for making our college one of the topmost in the state.

45. **lessen**   : *to reduce*
    **lesson**   : *a part of a textbook*
       We must always try to <u>**lessen**</u> people's burdens.
       The teacher took a long time to complete her <u>**lessons**</u>.

46. **lightening** : *reducing*
    **lightning**  : *a flash of light in the sky accompanied by thunder*
       The government has done little to <u>**lighten**</u> the burden of the common man.
       Certain hills and mountains in our state are notorious for <u>**lightning.**</u>

47. **loose**   : *free, not held*
   **lose**    : *no longer in possession*
        I feel more comfortable in **loose** dresses than tight-fitting outfits.
        Some people have the devil-may-care attitude and **lose** everything they have.

48. **personal**  : *belonging to the person, private*
   **personnel** : *staff, persons employed in any work*
        The psychiatrist asked the young man to reveal all his **personal** worries to him.
        The entire office **personnel** were scolded by the director for misplacing an important file.

49. **politic**   : *prudent*
   **politics** : *science of government*
        It would not be **politic** for you to be seen here.
        Indian **politics** has lost its true spirit as caste considerations have become its foremost guiding principle.

50. **pray**   : *to talk to God*
   **prey**   : *animal or bird etc. killed and eaten by another*
        Some people **pray** to God only when there are difficulties.
        The eagle devoured its **prey** within seconds.

51. **president** : *head*
   **precedent** : *earlier happening or decision taken as an example*
        Dr Vikas has been elected **president** of the State Doctors' Association.
        Is there any **precedent** that all newly chosen ministers should touch the feet of the Chief Minister?

52. **pride**   : *a quality of being boastful about one's talents or success.*
   **proud**  : *boastful*
        Indians took great **pride** in the successful landing of Chandrayan-3 on the moon on August 23, 2023.
        Romesh is **proud** of being the first person from his district to become an IAS officer.

53. **precede** : *go before*
   **proceed** : *continue*
        The matter has been explained in detail in the **preceding** issue of the magazine.
        The hospital management decided to **proceed** with the work of adding one more block to the main building.

54. **Popular**  : *famous*
   **populous** : *having abundance of people*
        Amitabh Bachchan was considered to be the most **popular** film star in India.
        India is the second most **populous** country in the world.

55. **pail**    : *pot*
    **pale**    : *sad-looking*
        In the interior parts of Rajasthan, ladies can be seen carrying **pots** of various sizes, shapes and hues.
        After his heart operation Hari appears **pale** and anemic.

56. **persecute** : *make someone suffer*
    **prosecute** : *start legal proceedings against someone.*
        In some countries individuals are **persecuted** on account of their religion.
        Mr Chand has been **prosecuted** for his involvement in money laundering.

57. **rays**    : *streams of light*
    **raze**    : *destroy*
        The sun's ultra-violet **rays** are harmful to the body.
        Mongols **razed** to the ground several important  palaces of India.

58. **rout**    : *defeat*
    **route**    : *way*
        The Indian cricket team was badly **routed** by the South African team.
        Since the **route** to the town was a bit confusing, we asked several people for direction.

59. **recent**    : *not long before*
    **resent**    : *feel bitter*
        In **recent** times there has been a great deal of  communal violence in India.
        There is nothing to **resent** about it because it was done unknowingly.

60. **sore**    : *tender and painful part of the body, wound*
    **soar**    : *fly high*
        Our teacher has such a severe **sore** throat that he cannot speak much.
        The skylark **soared** higher and higher in the sky until it could no longer be seen.

61. **suit**    : *a set of articles of outer clothing*
    **suite**    : *a set of rooms*
        I bought an expensive **suit** for my marriage.
        A well-furnished **suite** in the hotel has been given to the minister for his stay.

62. **stationery**    : *articles generally sold from a shop*
    **stationary**    : *not moving, fixed, etc.*
        There is a **stationery** shop close to the college.
        The stars are supposed to be **stationary** heavenly objects.

63. **seize**    : *capture, catch tightly*
    **cease**    : *die, stop*
        Customs officials **seized** all the smuggled goods from the traveller.
        The government ceased LPG subsidies as part of cost-cutting measures.

64. **statues** : *man-made figures*
   **statutes:** laws
   > The <u>**statue**</u> of Liberty is a famous one in America.
   > The govt. passes many <u>**statutes**</u> in the parliament, some of which are never implemented.

65. **septic** : *a type of infection*
   **skeptic** : *a person who doubts certain beliefs or theories*
   > Wounds caused by rusty nails are likely to become <u>**septic.**</u>
   > Some scientists are <u>**skeptic**</u> about the possibility of life in Mars.

66. **temporal** : *belonging to the physical world*
   **temporary:** *lasting for a short time*
   > The Pope has certain spiritual as well as <u>**temporal**</u> powers in the Church.
   > Miss Leela was given a <u>**temporary**</u> appointment in the firm.

67. **urban** : *of city*
   **urbane** : *modern, polished in manners.*
   > The urban <u>**population**</u> in our country is rapidly increasing.
   > Mr Sam's <u>**urbane**</u> behaviour is noticed by everyone who meets him.

68. **vain** : *useless*
   **vein** : *small nerve in the body*
   > The minister spoke in <u>**vain**</u> and the agitating farmers did not allow him to proceed along the highway.
   > The silly girl cut her <u>**vein**</u> in anger as she was denied permission to go for a movie with her friends.

69. **vain** : *pride*
   **wane** : *become less*
   **vane** : *arrow or pointer which is turned by wind.*
   > The rich man was <u>**vain**</u> and spoke about the number of expensive cars he possessed.
   > These days the size of the moon is <u>**waning.**</u>
   > Holland is a country which taps power through <u>**wind-vanes.**</u>

70. **veil** : *a cloth covering the face*
   **vale** : *valley*
   > Generally, Muslim women cover their faces with a <u>**veil.**</u>
   > Switzerland is renowned for its beautiful snow-covered <u>**vales.**</u>

71. **vine** : *the tree which produces grapes.*
   **wine** : *the alcoholic drink obtained from grapes.*
   > <u>**Vines**</u> are mostly cultivated in the Mediterranean region.
   > Drinking <u>**wine**</u> regularly has a lot of health benefits.

---xxx---

# 31. Antonyms (opposites)

(Arranged in alphabetical order for easy reference)

| Word | | Opposite | Word | | Opposite |
|---|---|---|---|---|---|
| able | : | unable | assemble | : | disperse |
| absent | : | present | associate | : | dissociate |
| abstract | : | concrete | attack | : | defend |
| absolute | : | limited | attentive | : | inattentive |
| accept | : | reject | attract | : | repel |
| accidental | : | intentional | aware | : | ignorant |
| accuse | : | defend | backward | : | forward |
| acknowledge | : | deny, disown | barren | : | fertile |
| acquit | : | convict | beautiful | : | ugly |
| active | : | passive | beauty | : | ugliness |
| admit | : | deny | begin | : | end |
| admire | : | despise | belief | : | disbelief |
| advance | : | retreat | bind | : | loosen |
| adversity | : | prosperity | bitter | : | sweet |
| affirmative | : | negative | black | : | white |
| agree | : | differ | blame | : | praise |
| allow | : | disallow | blessing | : | curse |
| always | : | never | blunt | : | sharp |
| amateur | : | professional | bold | : | timid |
| ambiguous | : | clear | bravery | : | cowardice |
| ample | : | meagre | bright | : | dark |
| analysis | : | synthesis | broad | : | narrow |
| ancient | : | modern | borrow | : | lend |
| animate | : | inanimate | bottom | : | top |
| appoint | : | dismiss | buy | : | sell |
| appear | : | disappear | care | : | neglect |
| arrogant | : | humble | careful | : | careless |
| arm | : | disarm | cautious | : | reckless |
| arrive | : | depart | cheap | : | dear |
| ascend | : | descend | choose | : | reject |
| ascent | : | descent | civil | : | rude |
| clean | : | dirty | collect | : | scatter |
| clever | : | stupid | comedy | : | tragedy |
| cold | : | hot | common | : | rare |

Antonyms (opposites)

| **Word** | | **Opposite** | **Word** | | **Opposite** |
|---|---|---|---|---|---|
| compare | : | contrast | earn | : | spend |
| complete | : | incomplete | economical | : | uneconomical |
| compulsory | : | optional | employ | : | dismiss |
| conceal | : | reveal | empty | : | full |
| confess | : | deny | encourage | : | discourage |
| confident | : | diffident | enjoy | : | suffer |
| consent | : | dissent | enrich | : | impoverish |
| conquer | : | lose | enthusiasm | : | apathy |
| conspicuous | : | inconspicuous | enemy | : | friend |
| contract | : | expand | enter | : | exit |
| convex | : | concave | equal | : | unequal |
| correct | : | incorrect | eternal | : | temporal |
| courage | : | cowardice | ever | : | never |
| courteous | : | discourteous | evil | : | good |
| credit | : | debit | exclude | : | include |
| crude | : | refined | export | : | import |
| danger | : | safety | extend | : | limit |
| dawn | : | dusk | expand | : | contract |
| dead | : | alive | exterior | : | interior |
| debit | : | credit | exult | : | lament, mourn |
| debtor | : | creditor | fact | : | fiction |
| decent | : | indecent | fade | : | bloom |
| decrease | : | increase | fail | : | succeed |
| deep | : | shallow | failure | : | success |
| defend | : | attack | fair | : | foul, unfair |
| defensive | : | offensive | faithful | : | unfaithful |
| deficit | : | surplus | fame | : | infamy |
| deny | : | affirm, confess | famous | : | notorious |
| dependent | : | independent | familiar | : | unfamiliar |
| diminish | : | increase | fat | : | thin |
| disclose | : | conceal | fertile | : | barren |
| different | : | same | firm | : | infirm |
| difficult | : | easy | find | : | lose |
| do | : | undo | first | : | last |
| docile | : | stubborn | fit | : | unfit |
| dwarf | : | giant | flexible | : | rigid |
| dynamic | : | static | flourish | : | decay |
| eager | : | indifferent | fortunate | : | unfortunate |
| early | : | late | fortune | : | misfortune |

## Antonyms (opposites)

| Word | | Opposite | Word | | Opposite |
|---|---|---|---|---|---|
| freedom | : | bondage | idle | : | busy, diligent |
| fresh | : | stale | ignorance | : | knowledge |
| friend | : | enemy | illuminate | : | darken |
| front | : | back | ill | : | well |
| full | : | empty | immaculate | : | soiled, stained |
| gain | : | loss | important | : | trivial/unimportant |
| gay | : | morose, sad | import | : | export |
| general | : | particular, special | increase | : | decrease |
| generous | : | avaricious | include | : | exclude |
| gentle | : | rude | inferior | : | superior |
| genuine | : | counterfeit | inhale | : | exhale |
| giant | : | dwarf | initial | : | final |
| give | : | take | innocent | : | guilty |
| glorious | : | inglorious | inside | : | outside |
| glory | : | disgrace | intelligible | : | unintelligible |
| grand | : | mean, petty | interior | : | exterior |
| gratitude | : | ingratitude | interested | : | disinterested/uninterested |
| grant | : | refuse | join | : | separate |
| great | : | small | joy | : | sorrow |
| handsome | : | ugly | junior | : | senior |
| happiness | : | misery | just | : | unjust |
| **Word** | | **Opposite** | justice | : | injustice |
| happy | : | sad | **Word** | | **Opposite** |
| hard | : | soft | kind | : | unkind |
| harmony | : | discord | kindness | : | cruelty |
| haste | : | delay | knowledge | : | ignorance |
| heavy | : | light | labour | : | rest |
| help | : | hinder | lawful | : | unlawful |
| height | : | depth | lazy | : | industrious |
| high | : | low | laugh | : | weep |
| hit | : | miss | lead | : | follow, mislead |
| honest | : | dishonest | legal | : | illegal |
| honour | : | shame | legible | : | illegible |
| hope | : | despair | legitimate | : | illegitimate |
| hopeless | : | hopeful | lend | : | borrow |
| hospitable | : | inhospitable | lenient | : | strict |
| hot | : | cold | lessen | : | enlarge |
| humble | : | proud | liberty | : | bondage |
| humane | : | cruel | lie | : | truth |

| Word | | Opposite | Word | | Opposite |
|---|---|---|---|---|---|
| life | : | death | odd | : | even |
| like | : | dislike | old | : | young |
| light | : | darkness, heavy | oppose | : | support |
| limited | : | unlimited | optimist | : | pessimist |
| literate | : | illiterate | oral | : | written |
| liquid | : | solid | partial | : | impartial |
| living | : | dead | particular | : | general |
| little | : | much | peace | : | war |
| lock | : | unlock | perfect | : | imperfect |
| logical | : | illogical | permanent | : | temporary |
| long | : | short | permit | : | prohibit |
| loose | : | tight | pious | : | impious |
| love | : | hatred | please | : | displease |
| loyal | : | disloyal | pleasant | : | unpleasant |
| major | : | minor | please | : | displease |
| majority | : | minority | pleasure | : | pain |
| material | : | immaterial | plenty | : | scarcity |
| maximum | : | minimum | polite | : | impolite |
| meek | : | haughty | predecessor | : | successor |
| merit | : | demerit | preliminary | : | final |
| mild | : | harsh | presence | : | absence |
| minor | : | major | pride | : | humility |
| miser | : | spendthrift | proficient | : | deficient |
| moderation | : | excess | profit | : | loss |
| modest | : | immodest | profound | : | shallow |
| modern | : | ancient, old | progressive | : | regressive |
| monotony | : | variety | proper | : | improper |
| moral | : | immoral | prosperity | : | adversity |
| mortal | : | immortal | prudent | : | imprudent |
| narrow | : | broad, wide | public | : | private |
| native | : | foreign | punish | : | reward |
| natural | : | artificial | pure | : | impure |
| negative | : | positive | question | : | answer |
| noble | : | ignoble | quick | : | slow |
| normal | : | abnormal | raise | : | lower |
| novice | : | veteran | rational | : | irrational |
| numerous | : | few | raw | : | cooked |
| obedience | : | disobedience | real | : | unreal, imaginary |
| occasional | : | frequent | rear | : | front |

# Antonyms (opposites)

| Word | | Opposite | Word | | Opposite |
|---|---|---|---|---|---|
| regular | : | irregular | take | : | give |
| rejoice | : | grieve | tame | : | wild |
| relevant | : | irrelevant | theory | : | practice |
| religious | : | irreligious | thick | : | thin |
| remember | : | forget | timid | : | fearless |
| retreat | : | advance | tight | : | loose |
| reveal | : | hide | tolerance | : | intolerance |
| rich | : | poor | top | : | bottom |
| right | : | wrong | triumph | : | failure |
| ripe | : | raw | trust | : | distrust |
| rise | : | fall | truth | : | falsehood |
| rough | : | smooth | uniform | : | varied |
| rural | : | urban | unite | : | disunite |
| sacred | : | profane | unity | : | diversity |
| safe | : | unsafe | urban | : | rural |
| same | : | different | use | : | abuse |
| savage | : | civilized | vacant | : | occupied |
| secure | : | insecure | vague | : | definite |
| sense | : | nonsense | valid | : | invalid |
| serious | : | light, trifling | valour | : | cowardice |
| severe | : | mild | vertical | : | horizontal |
| shallow | : | deep | victory | : | defeat |
| sharp | : | blunt | virtue | : | vice |
| simple | : | complex | visible | : | invisible |
| sincere | : | insincere | voluntary | : | compulsory |
| smile | : | frown | vulgar | : | refined |
| sorrow | : | joy | war | : | peace |
| spiritual | : | material | well | : | ill |
| start | : | finish | weak | : | strong |
| steadfast | : | fickle | weep | : | laugh |
| straight | : | crooked | wet | : | dry |
| strict | : | lenient | whole | : | part |
| success | : | failure | wholesale | : | retail |
| summit | : | base | wicked | : | virtuous |
| superficial | : | deep | wide | : | narrow |
| surplus | : | deficit | win | : | lose |
| superior | : | inferior | wisdom | : | folly |
| sweet | : | bitter | wise | : | unwise, foolish |
| synonym | : | antonym | young | : | old |

# 32. Important phrasal verbs

**Phrasal verbs:** *A phrase that consists of a verb with a preposition or adverb or both is known as a phrasal verb.* The use of these terms can enhance the quality of one's language.

### Bear

1. **Bear with** : *to tolerate*
   I can no longer **bear with** your unkindly criticism.

2. **Bear up** : *to suffer*
   We have **to bear up** with many ups and downs in life.

3. **Bear out** : *to support*
   Your behaviour **bears out** your true character.

4. **Break out** : *to spread*
   A new type of epidemic has **broken out** in the city.

5. **Break into** : *to enter forcibly*
   A thief **broke into** our house last night and took away many valuable items.

6. **Break down** : *to collapse, decline, come down, etc.*
   My uncle's health **broke down** as a result of over-work and tension.

7. **Break news** : *to convey sad news*
   Mr Roy had **to break the news** about the accident of his friend to the latter's family.

8. **Break off** : *to stop suddenly*
   The match was suddenly **broken off** due to the unruly behaviour of the spectators.

9. **Bring up** : *to look after*
   Parents **bring up** their children with lots of affection and care.

10. **Bring out** : *to publish*
    Our college is planning to **bring out** a college magazine this year.

11. **Bring about** : *to cause*
    Lack of personal cleanliness can **bring about** several sicknesses.

12. **Bring in** : *to yield*
    Mr Sham's new job does not **bring in** sufficient income to maintain his family.

13. **Bring forth** : *to produce*
    Hard work coupled with perseverance can **bring forth** excellent results.

## Call

14. **Call on**      : *to visit*

I **called on** my friend yesterday as he was not feeling well.

. **Call in**      : *to summon*

The commander **called in** the captain to his office to explain certain matters.

16. **Call off**      : *to withdraw*

The workers have **called off** their proposed indefinite strike.

17. **Call to account:** *to scold*

The General Manager of the company **called to account** his personal assistant for her neglect of duty.

18. **Call for**      : *demand*

Success in one's life and career **calls for** hard work coupled with strong determination.

## Carry

19. **Carry out**      : *to obey*

We must always **carry out** the wishes of our elders and parents.

20. **Carry away**      : *to be influenced by*

The youth are often **carried away** by what they see and hear in the mass media.

## Come

21. **Come to light :** *to be known*

Our evil deeds will **come to light** one day or another.

22. **Come to blows:** *to fight*

The two friends **came to blows** after a few pegs of drinks.

23. **Come to a standstill:** *come to a stop*

Due to the workers' strike, the work in the factory **came to a standstill.**

24. **Come about**      : *to happen*

Would you be kind enough to explain to me how the accident **came about?**

25. **Come around :** *to agree*

Finally, my opponent **came around** to my views on the issue.

26. **Come into force:** *to become a practice*

The new timetable will **come into force** today itself.

27. **Come to pass :** *to happen*

This year the monsoon **came to pass** without causing much havoc.

28. **Come true**    : *to fulfil*

The holy man's predictions about another earthquake in India have not **come true.**

29. **Come across**  : *to see suddenly*

Suddenly I **came across** one of my close relatives at the New Delhi airport.

## Cut

30. **Cut down**    : *to bring down*

Mr Roberts was forced to **cut down** his personal expenditure as he had retired from service.

31. **Cut short**    : *to interrupt*

The chief guest was forced to **cut short** his speech due to the shouting of the unruly crowd.

32. **Cut off**     : *to die*

Rajiv Gandhi, former Prime Minister of India, was **cut off** in the prime of his life.

33. **Cut out for**  : fitting

Mr Jones is **cut out** for the post of a principal of a college.

## Drop

34. **Drop in**     : *to visit all of a sudden*

My teacher promised to **drop in** at my place sometime in the evening.

35. **Drop a line**  : *to write a letter*

My friend promised to **drop a line** at the earliest opportunity.

36. **Drop out**    : *to come away*

Many students from the rural areas **drop out** from school due to poverty.

## Do

37. **Do away with** : *to abolish*

The Govt. has decided to **do away** with certain British-made laws in our country.

8. **Done for**     : *to be ruined*

Mr Roberts is **done for** as he lost a great deal of money in the recent stock market fall.

## Fall

39. **Fall off**    : *to drop, leave*
Many friends **fall off** when adversity strikes.

40. **Fall back**    : *to retreat, to get back, etc.*
During the Kargil war between India and Pakistan, the Pakistan army was forced to **fall back** to their original positions.

41. **Fall through**    : *to fail*
The new project of interconnecting all major rivers of India **fell through** for want of political support.

42. **Fall upon**    : *to attack*
A gang of robbers **fell upon** the passengers of the bus and looted all their belongings.

43. **Fall out**    : *to quarrel*
Both the friends **fell out** on account of their political differences.

## Get

44. **Get up**    : *to rise up*
Generally, I **get up** at 5 o'clock in the morning.

45. **Get through**    : to *pass*
My friend failed to **get through** the Civil Service Examination this time too.

46. **Get into**    : *to get involved*
Mr Sharma has **got into** serious financial difficulties due to his careless spending.

47. **Get over**    : *to overcome*
Mr John cannot **get over** the loss of his son who died in a road accident.

48. **Get rid of**    : *to free from*
It is important that we **get rid of** certain bad habits early in life.

49. **Get on with**    : *to continue*
The director of the institute asked his staff to **get on with** their work.

50. **Get off**    : *to escape*
The criminal **got off** from the jail premises under cover of darkness.

## Give

51. **Give up**    : *to stop*
Mr Anand has **given up** smoking after he heard about the ill-effects of smoking on health.

**52. Give in**    : *to yield*
The proprietor of the company finally **gave in** to the demands of the workers for an increase in their pay.

**53. Give away**    : *to distribute*
The chief guest **gave away** the prizes during the school's Annual Day function.

**54. Give vent to**    : *to express*
It is not good to **give vent to** our feelings in public.

### Go

**55. Go astray**    : *to wander from the true course*
Many children **go astray** nowadays due to peer pressure.

**56. Go by**    : *to follow*
Many follies in life can be avoided if we **go by** the instructions of our elders and parents.

**57. Go into**    : *to investigate*
A panel of judges was appointed to **go into** the misuse of Govt. funds.

**58. Go up**    : *to rise up*
The prices of essential commodities are **going up** day by day.

**59. Go back**    : *to fail to keep*
Many candidates **go back** on their promises once they win the elections.

**60. Go off**    : *to explode*
The bomb was timed to **go off** at 6.00 p.m.

**62. Go on**    : *to continue*
Mr Shankar is planning to **go on** with his work despite his poor health.

**63. Go through**    : *to read*
I shall **go through** your manuscript a little later.

### Keep

**64. Keep up**    : *to maintain*
We must always try to **keep up** the honour of our family.

**65. Keep back**    : *to hide*
Some individuals always try to **keep back** their secrets even from close friends.

**66. Keep aloof**    : *to avoid*
Raja **keeps himself aloof** from his colleagues.

**67. Keep pace with:** *to be modern*

          Most educated persons **keep pace with** the times.

## Lay

**68. Lay out**     : *to organize, construct, etc.*

          Emperor Shahjahan **laid out** several beautiful gardens during his lifetime.

**69. Lay down**    : *to sacrifice*

          The greatest sign of sacrifice is to **lay down** one's life for others.

**70. Lay hands on** : *to get hold of*

          Some individuals take away whatever they **lay their hands on.**

**71. Lay waste**    : *to destroy*

          The Mongol invaders **laid waste** the entire northern India several times during the medieval period.

## Let

**72. Let into**     : *allowed*

          I was **let into** the office by the attendant.

**73. Let off**      : *punished leniently*

          The smuggler was **let off** by the Excise dept. after he paid a small fine.

## Look

**74. Look for**     : *to search*

          My brother has been **looking for** a good job abroad.

**75. Look up**      : *to become better*

          Anil's health has been **looking up** after his recent operation.

**76. Look into**     : *to enquire*

          The public asked the minister to **look into** the possibility of providing better transport facilities in the town.

**77. Look after**    : *to take care*

          Nowadays  home nurses **look after** elderly persons in well- to-do homes.

**78. Look over**    : *to examine*

          A judge has been appointed to **look over** the case of Manipur violence.

**79. Lookout for**   : *to search for*

          Mr Jayan has been on the **lookout for** a good job.

80. **Look upon**  : *to regard*

      Mr Jain **looks upon** me as his best friend.

## Make

81. **Make good**  : *make up for loss*

      Mr Raj was forced to **make good** the damage he had caused to his friend's vehicle as a result of the accident.

82. **Make out**  : *to understand*

      I could not **make out** anything from what the stranger said to me.

83. **Make up one's mind:** *to decide*

      Tom has **made up his mind** to go abroad this year itself.

84. **Make off**  : *to run away with*

      The thief **made off with** all the stolen goods in a vehicle.

85. **Make up for**  : *to compensate*

      Mr Jones tried to **make up for** the wrong he had done to his friend.

86. **Make it up with:** *to settle one's differences*

      Mr Hari tried to **make up with** his neighbour over the question of proper boundary for his property.

## Pass

87. **Pass by**  : *to go by*

      A week has **passed by** since my uncle met with a car accident.

88. **Pass through**  : *overcome*

      Satish had to **pass through** several difficulties during his school days.

89. **Pass himself off:** *to pretend*

      The terrorist **passed himself off** as a tourist visiting the various sites in the city.

## Pull

90. **Pull down**  : *to demolish*

      Mr Brown **pulled down** his old house to construct a new one.

91. **Pull up**  : *to scold*

      The manager **pulled up** his secretary for her laziness and lack of punctuality.

92. **Pull together**  : *to work in harmony:*

      All members have to **pull together** in order to achieve  peace and harmony in a family.

93. **Pull through**  : *to recover*
> Mr Ramesh managed **to pull through** after a serious heart operation.

## Put

94. **Put out**  : *to extinguish a fire*
> The firemen's main job is to **put out** the fire in private and public buildings.

95. **Put down**  : *to suppress*
> The Govt. tried in vain to **put down** the one-day token strike organized by its employees.

96. **Put off**  : *to postpone*
> The function was **put off** to another date due to inclement weather.

97. **Put up with**  : *to tolerate*
> In life we have to **put up with** people of different ideas.

98. **Put up**  : *to stay*
> Where are you **putting up** for the night?

99. **Put on**  : *to wear*
> The soldiers were ordered to **put on** their uniform and come out of their barracks.

100. **Put in**  : *to work*
> My eldest son has **put in** a great deal of work in his new job.

101. **Put forth**  : *to bring forward*
> The new manager **put forth** several ideas to the proprietor for the smooth running of the factory.

## Run

102. **Run into**  : *to get involved*
> My friend is likely **to run into** debts as he spends more than he earns.

103. **Run short of** : *to be exhausted*
> We had to stop our journey mid-way as we **ran short of** money.

104. **Run after**  : *to go after, pursue, etc.*
> Most people **run after** wealth, pleasure, and power in life.

105. **Run out**  : *to expire*
> My work contract with the foreign company will **run out** this week, and I hope that the company will renew the contract.

## See

121. **See through** : *to detect*
    I was able to **see through** the trick of the stranger.
122. **See into** : *to find out*
    It is really hard to **see into** the real motives of people.
123. **See off** : *to bid good-bye*
    My friend came to the railway station to **see me off.**

## Set

106. **Set apart** : *to reserve*
    During elections some officials are **set apart** for monitoring the election process.
107. **Set in** : *to start*
    The monsoon is likely to **set in** sometime in the first week of June.
108. **Set up** : *to start a project*
    My uncle has *set up* a new super-specialty hospital in his hometown.
109. **Set out** : *to begin a journey*
    Mr Dev has **set out** on a journey round the world on a bicycle.

## Speak

124. **Speak of** : *worth mentioning*
    There is nothing worth in this book to **speak of**.
125. **Speak out** : *to express an opinion*
    Mr Kumar, the manager of the company, spoke **out** his mind fully during his meeting with the workers.

## Take

110. **Take off** : *to remove*
    You have to **take off** your shoes when you enter a temple.
111. **Take ill** : *to feel offended*
    Mr Shah **took ill** at my friend's unkindly remark.
112. **Take after** : *to resemble*
    Gopal **takes after** his father more than his mother.
113. **Take over** : *to take charge*
    A new principal is expected to **take charge** of our college next month.

**114. Take down** : *to write down*

    The teacher asked the students to **take down** the notes.

**115. Take for** : *to mistake for*

    The villagers **took** the stranger **for** a thief and beat him up severely.

**116. Take up the cause:** *to support*

    The Local M.L.A. has **taken up** the case of the slum-dwellers against their eviction.

## Turn

**117. Turn up** : *to appear*

    Many candidates **turned up** for the interview although there was only one vacancy.

**118. Turn out** : *to appear to be*

    The stranger who was roaming around the town **turned out** to be a thief.

**119. Turn down** : *to reject*

    The Govt. **turned down** the request of the Opposition parties for a discussion on the issue of Manipur violence.

—xxx—-

**Useful data**

# 17. Collective names for a group of animals/creatures

| | | |
|---|---|---|
| a school/shoal/haul/catch of fish | an army/ a colony of frogs | a flock /gaggle of geese |
| a herd/tribe of goats | a herd of elephants | a leash of greyhounds |
| a down/hush of hares | a brood of hens | a team/pair of horses |
| a pack/mute of hounds | a troop/mob of kangaroos | a leap of leopards |
| a plague of locusts | a troop of monkeys | a colony / an army of ants |
| a herd/ pack of asses | a culture of bacteria | a sleuth of bears |
| a pack/swarm of rats | a crash/herd of rhinos | a nest of snakes |
| a host of sparrows | a dray of squirrels | a flight of swallows |
| a bevy/ herd of swans | a bale of turtles | a pack of wolves |
| a school/pod of whales | a swarm of bees | a flock/flight/of birds |
| a herd of buffaloes | an army of caterpillars | a clowder/clutter of cats |
| a herd/drove of cattle | a brood/peep of chickens | a quiver of cobras |
| a kine of cows | a sedge/siege of cranes | a float of crocodiles |
| a litter of cubs | a herd of deer | a pack of dogs |
| a dule of doves | a brace/team of ducks | a clutch of eggs |

# 33. Appropriate term for a group of words
(Arranged in alphabetical order for easy reference)

| | |
|---|---|
| **Accessible** | : That which can be approached. |
| **Accomplice** | : A partner in crime |
| **Aerodrome** | :Landing place for airplanes. |
| **Alien** | : A citizen of another country. |
| **Amateur** | : A person who does something for pleasure |
| **Amphibian** | : Animal that lives on land as well as in water. |
| **Anniversary** | : The day to celebrate an event every year. |
| **Anonymous** | : A writing whose writer is not known. |
| **Anthropology** | : The science of the development of mankind. |
| **Antidote** | : A medicine that destroys the effect of poison. |
| **Aquatic** | : Of water. |
| **Archaeology** | : The science of historical relics, monuments etc. |
| **Artisan** | : A person who practises a craft. |
| **Atheist** | : One who does not believe in God. |
| **Audible** | : That which can be heard. |
| **Audience** | : A large assembly of hearers. |
| **Auditor** | : A person who checks up accounts. |
| **Autobiography** | : The life history of a person written by oneself. |
| **Bankrupt** | : Financially ruined. |
| **Biennial** | : That which happens after every two years. |
| **Bigamy** | : The practice of taking two wives. |
| **Blonde** | : A woman who has a fair complexion and light hair |
| **Brittle** | : That can be easily broken. |
| **Bureaucracy** | : A government run by officials |
| **Calligraphy** | : Art of beautiful handwriting. |
| **Cannibal** | : The creatures that eat human flesh. |
| **Carnivore** | : An animal that lives on flesh. |
| **Catalogue** | : A list of goods, books etc. |
| **Celestial** | : Pertaining to the sky. |
| **Cemetery** | : A place where the dead are buried. |
| **Chauffeur** | : A person who is a professional driver. |
| **Chemist** | : A person who sells medicine. |
| **Colleague** | : An associate in an office or profession |
| **Colt** | : The young one of a horse. |
| **Confectioner** | : A person who deals in sweets. |
| **Contemporary** | : A person living at the same time as another. |

| | |
|---|---|
| **Coot** | : The nest of a dove. |
| **Cosmopolitan** | : A citizen of the world. |
| **Crematory** | : A place where the dead are burnt. |
| **Dead language** | : A language which is no longer in use. |
| **Deadlock** | : A situation where there is no progress |
| **Defamation** | : Causing bad name to an eminent person |
| **Democracy** | : A Govt. by representatives of people. |
| **Dentist** | : A person who cures diseases of the teeth. |
| **Despot** | : A ruler who rules with absolute powers |
| **Divorce** | : Legal separation between husband and wife |
| **Dockyard** | : A place where ships are built. |
| **Drawn** | : A game in which neither side wins |
| **Eccentric** | : A person who has strange habits and behaviour |
| **Effeminate** | : A person who has feminine qualities |
| **Eligible** | : Fit for the post. |
| **Emigrant** | : A person who left his country to settle in another |
| **Encyclopaedia** | : A book of knowledge and information. |
| **Epic** | : A long poem based on some noble theme |
| **Extempore** | : A speech delivered without preparation. |
| **Fanatic** | : A person filled with excessive religious sentiments |
| **Fauna** | : The animals of a particular place |
| **Feminist** | : A person who champions the cause of women |
| **Fiasco** | : A matter which ends in failure |
| **Flirt** | : A woman who loves men only for pleasure |
| **Flora** | : The plants which grow in a particular place |
| **Galaxy** | : A group of stars in the sky |
| **Garage** | : A shed for vehicles |
| **Geology** | : The science of the study of the earth's crust |
| **Glossary** | : A list of words with meaning and explanations |
| **Glutton** | : A person who is fond of eating |
| **Gosling** | : The young one of a goose. |
| **Grocer** | : A person who sells corns, pulses, etc. |
| **Gymnasium** | : A building for practising exercises. |
| **Herbivore** | : An animal that lives on herbs or grass. |
| **Heterogeneous** | : A combination of several different elements |
| **Hive** | : The place where bees live |
| **Homicide** | : Murder of human beings |
| **Homogeneous** | : A combination of several similar thing |
| **Honorary office** | : An office for which no salary is paid |
| **Hospitable** | : Treating guests well |

Appropriate term for a group of words

| | |
|---|---|
| **Hypothesis** | : Supposition made on the basis of reasoning |
| **Illegal** | : That which is against law |
| **Illegible** | : That which cannot be read easily |
| **Illiterate** | : One who can neither read nor write |
| **Immigrant** | :  One coming to a foreign country to settle there |
| **Immunity** | : Protection against infection |
| **Impunity** | : Exemption from punishment |
| **Inaudible** | : That which cannot be heard |
| **Incorrigible** | : That which cannot be corrected |
| **Incurable** | : That which cannot be cured |
| **Infallible** | : One who cannot make any mistake |
| **Infanticide** | : Murder of an infant |
| **Inflammable** | : That which catches fire easily |
| **Innocent** | : One who is not guilty |
| **insolvent** | : One who is unable to pay one's debts |
| **Intelligentsia** | : The class of people who have independent thinking |
| **Invalid** | : A person disabled by illness, not correct |
| **Invincible** | : That which cannot be conquered |
| **Invisible** | : That which cannot be seen |
| **Jockey** | : A professional rider of horses in a race |
| **Kennel** | : a house of dogs |
| **Kindergarten** | : A school for small children |
| **Laboratory** | : A building where scientific experiments are performed |
| **Launderer** | :  A person who washes clothes |
| **Lavatory** | : A place for washing hands and face |
| **Library** | : A place for keeping books for study |
| **Linguist** | : A scholar of many languages |
| **Lithography** | : The art of printing, drawing, and writing on stones |
| **Locksmith** | : A person who makes and repairs locks |
| **Lullaby** | : A song to put babies to sleep |
| **Lunar** | : Pertaining to the moon |
| **Mammal** | : An animal that suckles its young ones |
| **Manuscript** | : A handwritten document |
| **Martyr** | : A person who dies for a noble cause |
| **Mason** | : A person who builds houses |
| **Mercenary** | : One who fights for money |
| **Meticulous** | : A person who is particular about every minute detail |
| **Monarchy** | : Government by a king |
| **Monogamy** | : The practice of having one wife only |
| **Monotheist** | : A person who believes in one God |

218

Appropriate term for a group of words

| | |
|---|---|
| **Monotonous** | : Characterized by dull uniformity |
| **Mortuary** | : A place where the dead are kept |
| **Museum** | : A building where historical relics are kept |
| **Namesake** | : One who has same name with another |
| **Narcotic** | : A drug which brings about sleep |
| **Nepotism** | : Undue favour shown by a person in power to his relatives |
| **Non-vegetarian** | : One who eats meat, egg , fish, etc. |
| **Novice** | : A person who is new to a profession or trade |
| **Obituary** | Notice of a person's death |
| **Obsolete** | : That which is not used nowadays. |
| **Octogenarian** | : One who is between 80 and 90 years old |
| **Oligarchy** | : government by a few people |
| **Omnipotent** | : All-powerful |
| **Omnipotent** | : having infinite power |
| **Omniscient** | : All-knowing |
| **Opaque** | : A thing that cannot be seen through |
| **Ophthalmologist** | : One attends to eye diseases |
| **Optimist** | : One who looks at the bright side of things |
| **Orphan** | : A child whose parents are no more |
| **Palmistry** | : The science of reading palms |
| **Panacea** | : A remedy for all diseases |
| **Panorama** | : A complete view of surrounding region |
| **Paradox** | : A statement contradictory to a universally accepted view |
| **Parasite** | : An animal that lives on another's food |
| **Patricide** | : Murder of one's father |
| **Patriot** | : A man who loves his country |
| **Pedestrian** | : One who walks on foot |
| **Pessimist** | : One looking only at the dark side of things |
| **Pesticide** | : A medicine that kills pests |
| **Philanthropist** | : A person who loves mankind |
| **Pick-pocket** | : One who steals from others' pocket |
| **Polyandry** | : The practice of having many husbands |
| **Polygamy** | : The practice of having many wives |
| **Polyglot** | : One who knows many languages |
| **Porter** | : A person who carries luggage |
| **Posthumous** | : Coming or happening after death |
| **Pseudonym** | : A pen name used by an author |
| **Quadruped** | : A four-footed animal |
| **Red tapism** | : Excessive official formalities |
| **Republic** | : A government by elected representatives |

219

# Appropriate term for a group of words

| | | |
|---|---|---|
| **Rhetoric** | : | The art of writing figurative language |
| **Sabotage** | : | Spoil a plan or project |
| **Scapegoat** | : | A person who is blamed for the mistakes of others |
| **Scavenger** | : | A person who sweeps streets clean |
| **Skeptic** | : | One who always doubts |
| **Seamstress** | : | A sewing woman |
| **Solar** | : | Pertaining to the sun |
| **Solo** | : | A song sung by a single person |
| **Spendthrift** | : | A person who spends lavishly |
| **Spinster** | : | An unmarried woman |
| **Spokesman** | : | One who speaks for others |
| **Suicide** | : | Murder of oneself |
| **Surgeon** | : | doctor who performs operations |
| **Tableau** | : | A group of persons arranged to represent a scene |
| **Tadpole** | : | The young one of a frog |
| **Teetotaler** | : | A person who abstains from alcoholic drinks |
| **Theist** | : | A person who believes in God |
| **Transparent** | : | That which can be seen through |
| **Troupe** | : | A group of actors or drama artistes |
| **Ultimatum** | : | A final warning given by a group |
| **Unanimous** | : | All of one opinion |
| **Utopian** | : | something that is perfect and ideal |
| **Vegetarian** | : | One who lives on vegetables |
| **Verbatim** | : | The repetition of anything word for word |
| **Versatile** | : | genius who knows several things |
| **Veteran** | : | An experienced person |
| **Voluntary** | : | Without being forced |
| **Wardrobe** | : | Almirah where clothes are kept |
| **Watermark** | : | An invisible seal on an important document |
| **Waterproof** | : | That through which water cannot pass |
| **Whelp** | : | The young one of a lion |
| **Widow** | : | A woman who has lost her husband |
| **Widower** | : | A person who has lost his wife |
| **Windfall** | : | Unexpected gains |
| **Zenith** | : | Highest point in the sky |
| **Zoology** | : | The science which studies about animal life |

—xxx—-

# 34. Redundant words

(given in alphabetical order for easy reference)

**Redundant sentence:** A sentence in which some information is unnecessarily repeated is called redundant sentence. The second word, therefore, should be avoided.

    **E.g.:**  Advance ~~forward~~

           The army **advanced forward** against the invading forces.**(X)**

| | |
|---|---|
| 1. 12 midnight | 31. ~~certainly~~ true |
| 2. ~~12~~ noon | 32. chase ~~after~~ |
| 3. a.m. ~~in the morning~~ | 33. circle ~~around~~ |
| 4. ~~absolutely~~ certain | 34. ~~close~~ proximity |
| 5. ~~absolutely~~ essential | 35. combine ~~together~~ |
| 6. ~~absolutely~~ necessary | 36. compete *~~together~~* |
| 7. ~~absolutely~~ sure | 37. ~~completely~~ filled |
| 8. add ~~up~~ | 38. ~~completely~~ finished |
| 9. ~~added~~ bonus | 39. ~~current~~ incumbent |
| 10. ~~advance~~ preview | 40. ~~current~~ status quo |
| 11. ~~affirmative~~ yes | 41. ~~current~~ trend |
| 12. ~~all-time~~ record | 42. cut it ~~out~~ |
| 13. ~~alternative~~ choice | 43. descend ~~down~~ |
| 14. ~~always~~..... used to | 44. ~~different~~ kinds |
| 15. ~~anonymous~~ stranger | 45. ~~direct~~ confrontation |
| 16. ~~armed~~ gunmen | 46. ~~during~~ the course of |
| 17. assemble ~~together~~ | 47. ~~empty~~ space |
| 18. ATM ~~machine~~ | 48. ~~end~~ result |
| 19. attach ~~together~~ | 49. estimated ~~about/roughly~~ |
| 20. bald ~~headed~~ | 50. ~~exact~~ replica |
| 21. *~~basic~~* fundamentals | 51. ~~fellow~~ classmates |
| 22. ~~basic~~ necessities | 52. *~~fellow~~* companion |
| 23. besides...~~also~~ | 53. filled ~~to capacity~~ |
| 24. best ~~ever~~ | 54. ~~final~~ conclusion |
| 25. blend ~~together~~ | 55. ~~final~~ outcome |
| 26. ~~brief~~ summary | 56. footpath *~~road~~* |
| 27. browse ~~through~~ | 57. ~~frank and~~ honest exchange |
| 28. but ~~yet~~ | 58. ~~free~~ gift |
| 29. *can't ~~able to~~* | 59. ~~frozen~~ ice |
| 30. ~~careful~~ scrutiny | 60. gathering *~~together~~* |

61. *general* public
62. He is a ~~male~~ nurse
63. in addition to ...~~also~~
64. into two ~~equal~~ halves
65. ~~invited~~ guests
66. *kindly ~~please~~*
67. kneel ~~down~~
68. lag ~~behind~~
69. latest ~~modern~~ facilities
71. ~~little~~ baby
72. ~~main~~ notable feature
73. ~~major~~ feat
74. major ~~significant~~
75. merged ~~together~~
76. mix ~~together~~
77. ~~more~~ better
78. ~~more smarter~~ (*more smart/smarter*)
79. My family consists of ~~me~~
80. ~~neat and~~ clean room
81. never ~~before~~
82. ~~new~~ beginning
83. ~~new~~ innovations
84. ~~new~~ recruit
85. ~~new~~ upcoming project
86. no ~~other~~ alternative
87. ~~old~~ adage
88. ~~old~~ custom
89. oral ~~conversation~~
90. ~~original~~ source
91. ~~over~~ exaggerate
92. ~~over~~ more than
93. p.m. ~~in the evening~~
94. ~~passing~~ fad
95. ~~past~~ experience
96. ~~past~~ history
97. ~~past~~ memories
98. ~~past~~ records
99. ~~personal~~ friend
100. ~~personal~~ opinion
101. ~~personally,~~ I think/feel that

102. plan ~~ahead~~
103. plan ~~in advance~~
104. plunge ~~down~~
105. postponed ~~until~~ later
106. proceed ~~ahead~~
107. proceed ~~forward~~
108. proceed ~~further~~
109. progress ~~forward~~
110. quick ~~speed~~
111. quickly ~~hurried~~
112. reason is ~~because~~
113. reason... ~~why~~
114. reason...~~due to~~
115. recur ~~again~~
116. refer ~~back~~
117. ~~regular~~ routine
118. reiterate ~~again~~
119. repay ~~back~~
120. repeat ~~again~~
121. return ~~back~~
122. revert *~~back~~*
123. scrutinize ~~in detail~~
124. share ~~together~~
125. sink ~~down~~
126. ~~small~~ speck
127. ~~some~~ few napkins
128. sufficient *~~enough~~*
129. sufficiently ~~adequate~~
130. sum ~~total~~
131. summarize ~~briefly~~
132. surrounded ~~on all sides~~
133. ~~underground~~ sub-way
134. ~~unexpected~~ emergency
135. ~~unexpected~~ surprise
136. ~~unintended~~ mistake
137. ~~unmarried~~ bachelor
138. used to...~~often~~
139. ~~usual~~ custom
140. ~~usually...~~used to

---xxx---

# 35. Important idioms

*(arranged in alphabetical order for easy reference)*

1. **A bed of roses** : *an easy work, something that is easy,* etc.
   Life is not **a bed of roses**. We have to face many ups and downs in our life.

3. **A bird's eye-view** : *a cursory glance, an overall view,* etc.
   We can have **a bird's eye-view** of the entire town from this hill-top.

3. **A black sheep** : *an unfitting member, a member who does not support the group*
   Mr. Santhosh is considered to be **a black sheep** in our group. He always opposes whatever others propose.

4. **A burning question** : *an important issue*
   The issue of global warming is **a burning question** nowadays.

5. **A child's play** : *an easy job*
   To get through the Medical Entrance Examination is not **a child's play**.

6. **A cold reception** : *a half-hearted welcome*
   The minister was given **a cold reception** by the local people as he had not done anything worthwhile for the village.

7. **A fair weather friend** : *a friend who remains only during good times*
   Most people have many **fair weather friends**. They go away when misfortune strikes.

8. **A golden opportunity** : *an ideal chance, an excellent opportunity,* etc.
   Today nurses have **golden opportunities** to go abroad and earn high salaries.

9. **A good Samaritan** : *a person who helps others in need*
   **Good Samaritans** are seldom recognized and rewarded. Very few people come to know about their good deeds.

10. **A man of his word** : *one who keeps his word*
    My friend promised me a sum of two thousand rupees to pay my fees in the college. I trust him because he is **a man of his word**.

11. **A turning point** : *a major event which has lots of significance*
    Taking MBA in HR was a **turning point** in my life. The course gave a new direction to my career.

12. **Add fuel to the fire** : *to add more trouble*
    David, one of the brightest students in the class, failed in one of the semester examinations and was already feeling bad about it. The next day the class teacher called him and severely scolded him. It was like **adding fuel to the fire.**

13. **A stone's throw** : *close-by*

The town railway station is situated just **a stone's throw** from my school.

14. **At one's beck and call:** *under absolute control, easily available,* etc.

Today banking services are **at one's beck and call**. Most banks often go out of their way to please their customers.

15. **At the eleventh hour:** *at the last moment*

Many students think of preparing for examinations **at the eleventh hour.**

16. **Bag and baggage** : *with all belongings*

As the final examination ended, I left the hostel with **bag and baggage**.

17. **Beat about the bush** : *avoid coming to the main point*

Our local M.L.A. **beats about the bush** whenever he gives a public speech.

18. **Bone of contention** : *unsettled point of disagreement*

Sharing of the Cauvery river water between Tamil Nadu and Karnataka has been **a bone of contention** between the two states.

19. **Bring to light** : *to expose, make known,* etc.

The clerk's action of stealing money from the office has **brought to light** his true character.

20. **Bird's eye view** : *a general view from above*

We had a **bird's eye view** of the town from the tower.

21. **Burn one's finger** : *get into trouble*

If you put your money in some unauthorised private banks, you are likely to **burn your finger** sooner or later.

22. **By fits and starts** : *irregularly*

A person who does his work by **fits and starts** is not going to reach anywhere.

23. **By hook or by crook:** *by any means*

The neighbouring college team tried to win the match **by hook or by crook.**

24. **By leaps and bounds:** *to become larger swiftly*

There is no doubt that India is progressing by **leaps and bounds** in all sectors of the economy.

25. **Come into force** : *to become effective, to come into operation,* etc.

The rule regarding the compulsory use of helmet while driving two-wheelers **came into force** in our state only some time ago.

26. **Face the music**     : *to get scolding, receive punishment,* etc.
I had to **<u>face the music</u>** of the college librarian for using mobile in the library.

27. **False alarm**     : *a wrong warning*
The early rain gave a **<u>false alarm</u>** about the forthcoming monsoon in India. The monsoon came much later than expected.

28. **Fire and fury**     : *full of anger*
When the principal of the college heard that some of the senior students were involved in ragging the freshers he was all **<u>fire and fury</u>** and immediately expelled the culprits.

29. **Fire and sword**     : *cause destruction*
During the medieval period the Mongolian invaders caused **<u>fire and sword</u>** in our country on several occasions.

30. **Foot the bill**     : *to pay the bill*
Yesterday, I was forced to **<u>foot the bill</u>** for my friend's meal.

31. **Foregone conclusion** : *a sure fact, certain,* etc.
The possibility of India becoming a permanent member of the UN Security Council in the near future is a **<u>foregone conclusion</u>**.

32. **From scratch**     : *from the beginning*
Mr. Samuelson built up his exporting business **<u>from scratch.</u>**

33. **From A to Z**     : *completely, thoroughly,* etc.
Mr. Jobinson knows **<u>from A to Z</u>** of vehicles. He can immediately spot the trouble in any vehicle.

34. **Gain ground**     : *become popular*
Net banking is **<u>gaining ground</u>** these days even among ordinary people.

35. **Give a piece of one's mind**: *to scold*
The manager **<u>gave a piece of his mind</u>** to his office secretary for not completing the work on time.

36. **Good for nothing**     : *useless*
Many people consider Rajan to be **<u>good for nothing</u>**. But he has a lot of hidden talents.

37. **Hale and hearty**     : *happy, contented*
My uncle appears to be **<u>hale and hearty</u>** after his kidney operation.

38. **Hit the nail on the head**: *to do or say the correct thing, to strike the right point*
Try to **<u>hit the nail on the head</u>** while delivering a speech. People in general dislike speakers who beat around the bush.

39. **Hard and fast**     : *strict*
The rules of the army are generally **<u>hard and fast</u>**.

40. **Hue and cry**       : *make a lot of noise, loud public protest,* etc.

When Mr. Ravindran, a new member of the  party, was given the party ticket for election, there was a **hue and cry** against the decision.

41. **If the worse comes to the worst : *even under the worst situation***

I have prepared hard for the Bank Probationary Officers' Test and I hope to get through it this time. **If the worse comes to the worst**, I will opt for the bank    clerical post for which I have already received the  appointment letter.

42. **In bad books**       : *out of favour*

The Vice-Principal of our college is in the **bad books** of the college management. Most probably the management may not allow him to continue his job next year.

43. **black and blue**       : *severely*

The guards beat the shoplifter **black and blue** and threw him out of the shopping mall.

44. **In black and white** : *in writing*

I asked my director to give me my transfer order **in black and white**.

45. **In full swing**       : *in full capacity, moving quickly forward,* etc.

The construction work of the new stadium in our town is going on **in full swing.**

46. **In high spirits**       : *to look happy and cheerful, full of joy,* etc.

My uncle who has had an open heart surgery recently is **in high spirits** these days.

47. **In the nick of time** : *just in time, at the right time, etc.*

The crowd wanted to beat up the thief who was just caught. However, **in the nick of time** the police arrived and the man was whisked away.

48. **Ins and outs**       : *in detail*

Would you mind explaining to us the **ins and outs** of the project that you intend to undertake in our village?

49. **It goes without saying** : *to be taken for granted, understood*

Robert has secured the first rank in the State Medical Entrance Examination. **It goes without saying** that he can get an MBBS seat in any government medical college of his choice.

50. **Kith and kin**       : *blood relatives*

Many of my **kith and kin** are settled in Mumbai.

51. **Like fish out of water** : *in a strange situation, doesn't know what to do,* etc.

When I went to college for the first time I felt like **a fish out of water**. I did not know what to do on such a huge campus.

52. **Maiden speech** : *first speech*

I made my **<u>maiden speech</u>** during a college function and it was an unforgettable experience.

53. **Make up one's mind:** *to decide*

Many youngsters find it difficult to **<u>make up their minds</u>** with regard to the choice of career in their life.

54. **Neither head nor tail** : *cannot understand anything*

I could understand **<u>neither head nor tail</u>** of what the teacher taught us today in the class.

55. **Null and void** : *no longer in practice*

Sati which existed for many years in India is **<u>null and void</u>** today.

56. **Part and parcel** : *essential part*

Etiquette is **<u>part and parcel</u>** of a well-groomed personality.

57. **Pie in the sky** : *unreachable promises, unrealistic aims,* etc.

During the time of elections most politicians woo voters by offering **<u>a pie in the sky</u>**.

58. **Pros and cons** : *points for and against, the good as well as the bad aspects*

My teacher asked me to think well about the pros and cons of not taking the final examination this year.

59. **Put heart and soul** : *earnestly, to put in all efforts possible,* etc.

My father advised me to **<u>put my heart and soul</u>** into my studies.

60. **Safe and sound** : *quite safely*

We all reached the top of the mountain **<u>safe and sound</u>** after three hours of tough climb.

61. **Scot free** : *to go unpunished*

The High Court left Madhavan **<u>scot free</u>** although the lower court had found him guilty of murder.

62. **Sitting on the fence** : *not decided, delay in taking a decision,* etc.

Hariharan is **<u>sitting on the fence</u>** with regard to his joining the army.

63. **Slip of tongue :***an error committed unknowingly while speaking*

Most people make **<u>slips of the tongue</u>**. Nothing to feel bad about it.

64. **Speak volumes** : *to reveal a great deal of information*

The high marks that Raj got in his examination **<u>speak volumes</u>** about the hard work he might have put into his studies.

65. **Spread like wild fire:** *spread very fast*

The news of the plane crash near our town **<u>spread like wild fire</u>**.

66. **Square meal** : *full meal*

There are hundreds of people in our country who cannot afford a **<u>square meal</u>** a day.

67. **Stood his ground**  : *maintain one's position or view*
Tom **stood his ground** when the teacher accused him of stealing his neighbour's lunch box.

68. **Strained every nerve:** *used one's utmost effort*
I **strained every nerve** to see the popular film actor who had come to inaugurate the new textile showroom in our town.

69. **The fair sex**  : *womenfolk, women in general,* etc.
Today **the fair sex** faces a lot of sexual harassment in work places and on public transport systems.

70. **The lion's share**  : *the major share, the main part,* etc.
My eldest brother got the **lion's share** of our ancestral property.

71. **The rank and file**  : *common people*
**The rank and file** failed to see the rationale behind the government's move to reduce the number of LPG cylinders to six per household.

72. **Through thick and thin** : *in misery and prosperity*
Only genuine friends remain **through thick and thin**.

73. **Time and tide**  : *time or opportunities*
Grab all opportunities that come your way. **Time and tide** waits for none.

74. **Tit for tat**  : *take revenge in the same way*
Some people always follow the policy of **tit for tat**.

75. **To and fro**  : *to and from*
What is the train fare **to and fro** Delhi and Chennai?

76. **Tooth and nail**  : *with all might and power*
The slum dwellers fought **tooth and nail** against the eviction order of the municipality

77. **To be born with a silver spoon in one's mouth:** *to be born rich*
I was not **born with a silver spoon in my mouth**. I had to struggle a lot to reach this position in life.

78. **To be in the good books of :** *to find favour*
My colleague is **in the good books o**f the director. He is likely to get a promotion this year.

79. **To be up and doing**  : *to be active/busy*
In spite of being eighty years old my grandfather is **up and doing.**

80. **To blow one's own trumpet:** *to praise oneself*
My friend likes to **blow his own trumpet.**

81. **To break the news**  : *to give bad news*
Mr. David did not know how **to break the sad news of** the accident of his friend to his family.

82. **To bring disgrace to** : *bring bad name*
     When my little brother was caught copying in the examination, it **brought disgrace** to our family.

83. **To bring to light** : *to bring to the open, to come to know,* etc.
     The investigation has **brought to light** several new facts about the case.

84. **To bring to book** : *to punish the offender, to rebuke,* etc.
     One of the main functions of the courts in any country is **to bring offenders to book.**

85. **To bring home** : *to make one realise or understand something*
     The speaker was able **to bring home** the point that unless we take care to protect our environment, we shall all perish in the long run.

86. **To build castles in the air** : *to make imaginary schemes*
     Many youngsters spend their precious time **building castles in the air.**

87. **To burn the midnight oil** : *to work till late night*
     My father used **to burn the midnight oil** to keep his business going and worthwhile.

88. **To burn the candle at both ends**: *spend all money lavishly*
     There are always some people who **burn the candle at both ends.** They spend very fast whatever they earn.

89. **To bury the hatchet** : *to settle all differences*
     The party leader asked the various sub-groups in the party **to bury the hatchet** and work for the party's success in the elections.

90. **To carry the day** : *to get victory, to win*
     In the last Football World Cup, Germany couldn't **carry the day.**

91. **To catch red-handed**: *to catch while doing a crime*
     The foreign terrorist was **caught red-handed** while attempting to cross over to India.

92. **To come off/out with flying colours**: *to succeed well, achieve success,* etc.
     I am sure that my friend will **come off with flying colours** in the interview for the bank officers' post.

93. **To cry for the moon**: *an impossible dream, something that is not possible*
     Raj's desire to do MBA in London is **to cry for the moon** as he is extremely poor.

94. **To end up in smoke**: *to come to nothing*
     The opposition parties' plan to pass a non-confidence motion against the government in the parliament **ended in smoke**.

95. **To fish in troubled waters** : *to take advantage of other's difficulties*
> America often tries **to fish in troubled waters** of the Middle East.

96. **To follow suit** : *to do the same, copy,* etc.
> The religious leader asked his followers to **follow his suit** in rejecting worldly pleasures.

97. **To get into hot water:** *to get into trouble*
> Today if you hurt religious feelings of individuals by your comments in the social network, you will **get into hot water**. The police can take action against you.

98. **To go hand in hand** : *to go together, to be related*
> Hard work and success always **go hand in hand.**

99. **To hang fire** : *to remain undecided, to delay or wait,* etc.
> The question of constructing an Express Highway in the state has been **hanging fire** for some time.

100. **To hang in the balance** : *to be uncertain, to be in a critical situation,* etc.
> After the open heart surgery my uncle's life was **hanging in the balance** for one or two days.

101. **To hold one's tongue:** *to be silent*
> It is sometimes good **to hold one's tongue** in certain situations. Your silence can speak volumes.

102. **To hold out the olive branch :** *to offer peace*
> The central government's efforts in **holding out the olive branch** to the north-eastern underground groups is starting to bear fruit.

103. **To hold water** : *to have some strong logical point*
> Your arguments on state funding of elections in India does not **hold water**.

104. **To keep body and soul together:** *to keep from starving, enough money to survive*
> The poor family living next to my house finds it difficult **to keep body and soul together**.

105. **To kill two birds with one stone:** *to have two advantages*
> I went to Bangalore a few months ago to appear for an interview as well as to meet my uncle who works over there. It was like **killing two birds with one stone**.

106. **To keep your head above water:** *just be able to manage*
> Rajan's father earns just enough to **keep his family's head above water**.

107. **To keep one in the dark** : *to keep uninformed, not to tell*
> The manager kept the director of the company **in the dark** regarding the notice of the workers for a flash strike in the factory.

108. **To keep pace with** : *to be modern, to be up with the times,* etc.
> Young people always try **to keep pace with** the times.

109. **To leave no stone unturned :** *to try all means possible*
> Ms Savita **left no stone unturned** in getting back her money when the bank made a mistake in transferring her money to someone else's account.

110. **To lend a hand** : *to help*
> My friend requested me **to lend him a hand** in his project work as he was already late to submit the work.

111. **To lend one's ears to**: *to listen*
> Kindly **let me your ears**; I have something important to tell you.

112. **To let the cat out of the bag:** *to reveal a secret*
> The rustic expletives used by the politician against his opponent **let the cat out of the bag** about his true character.

113. **To live a hand to mouth existence:** *to have just sufficient money to survive*
> The common people in India today are forced **to live a hand to mouth existence** due to the sky-rocketing prices of essential commodities.

114. **To make both ends meet:** *to meet the needs of oneself or family*
> With my salary remaining static for several years, I find it difficult **to make both ends meet.**

115. **To make a clean breast of** : *to confess*
> The surrendered terrorist **made a clean breast of** his terrorist activities in the country.

116. **To nip in the bud** : *to stop something at the very beginning*
> Children's habit of telling lies must be **nipped in the bud**. Such a habit can have disastrous consequences in the future.

117. **To play second fiddle to** : *to be subservient*
> In India, the President **plays second fiddle** as the major decisions of the government are taken by the Cabinet headed by the Prime Minister.

118. **To play with fire** : *to play with danger*
> When politicians arouse communal passions to get votes, they are **playing with fire.**

119. **To pick holes in** : *to criticize, to find fault,* etc.
> The opposition parties always **pick holes** in whatever the ruling party does.

120. **To put an end to** : *to stop*
> The Supreme Court of India has ordered the government **to put an end** to manual scavenging in the country.

121. **To put heads together :***consult together, discuss together,* etc.

           If the ruling party and the opposition parties **put their heads together** many of the country's problems can be solved.

122. **To put one's heart and soul:** *to do one's best*

           Only those who **put their heart and soul** into their work succeed in whatever they do.

123. **To read between the lines :** *to catch the hidden meaning*

           Some people are good at **reading between the lines**.

124. **To rain cats and dogs :** *to rain heavily*

           For a few days it **rained cats and dogs** in our area. The entire town was fully flooded within a short time.

125. **To sell like hot cakes :** *to have a good sale*

           The book that gave details of the US secret attack on Osama Bin Laden's hideout in  Pakistan was **sold like hot cakes.**

126. **To smell a rat** : *to suspect something is wrong*

           The opposition parties **smelled a rat** when the government offered them the post of the Vice-President without any conditions.

127. **To step into someone's shoes:** *to take over charge from someone*

           Many young people in India would like to see Rahul Gandhi **stepping into Dr. Manmohan Singh's shoes.**

128. **To toe the line** : *to conform under pressure*

           I was asked **to toe the line** of the boss' point of view on the proposed factory site  which I blindly refused.

129. **To take to heels** : *to run away*

           The stone-pelting students **took to their heels** when they saw the police coming towards them .

130. **To throw cold water on** : *to discourage*

           The Municipal Chairman **threw cold water on** the suggestion of the members to construct one or two free eco-friendly toilet facilities in the city.

131. **To turn a deaf ear to :** *not to listen to*

           I **turned a deaf ear to** my son's request to buy him the latest sports bike costing over a lakh rupees.

132. **To turn over a new leaf** : *to start anew*

           Realizing that the main cause of failure in his profession was his drinking habit, Mr. Mathews **turned a new leaf** by giving up drinking.

---xxx---

# 36. Commonly used foreign words in English

1. **Ad hoc** *(Latin)* : for the special purpose, temporary arrangement
2. **Ad interim** *(Latin)* : in the meantime
3. **Aficionado** *( Spanish)* : a devoted supporter of a sport, a fan
4. **Aegis** *(Greek)* : patronage, under the banner of
5. **Alma mater** *(Latin)* : Mother institution
6. **Al fresco** *(Italian)* : in the open air, outside
7. **Alter ego** *(Latin)* : closest friend
8. **Alumni** *(Latin)* : ex-student of an institution
9. **Amnesty** *(Greek)* : an official pardon granted by the authorities
10. **Au revoir** *(French)* : good-bye
11. **Bete noire** *(French)* : a person or thing that are particularly disliked, a leader disliked by another
12. **Blitz** *(German)* : concentrated military attack or great show
13. **Bonanza** *(Spanish)* : good fortune, sudden increase of wealth
14. **Bonhomie** *(French)* : good nature, new friendship
15. **Bona fide** (Latin) : genuine, in good faith
16. **Bon Voyage** *(French)* : happy journey, happy voyage
17. **Carte blanche** *(French)* : complete freedom to act as one thinks best
18. **Communiqué** *(French)* : an official announcement
19. **Chauffeur** *(French)* : a professional driver
20. **Corrigendum** *(Latin)* : correction in a newspaper or in a book
21. **Coup d'état** *(French)* : capture power by force
22. **Cuisine** *(French)* : particular type of food preparation of a place
23. **Debacle** *(French)* : an utter failure, fiasco
24. **Deja vu** *(French)* : a feeling of having experienced the situation before
25. **Debut** *(French)* : first appearance
26. **De facto** *(Latin)* : Real, original
27. **De jure** *(Latin)* : by right
28. **Dei gratia** *(Latin)* : by the grace of God
29. **Detenu** *(French)* : a prisoner
30. **Deo Volente** *(Latin)* : God willing
31. **El Dorado** *(Spanish)* : the golden land of dreams
32. **En block** *(French)* : all together, in a body
34. **En masse** *(French)* : all together, in a big group
35. **En route** *(French)* : on the way
36. **Entourage** *(French)* : people who accompany and assist important persons
37. **Entente** *(French)* : understanding

Commonly used foreign words in English

38. **Etiquette** *(French)* : good manners, correct behaviour
39. **Ex-officio** *(Latin)* : in virtue of one's office, an official post
40. **Ex-gratia** *(Latin)* : by the grace of God
41. **Fait accompli** *(French)* : something done and for this reason, not worth arguing about
42. **Faux pas** *(French)* : a noticeable blunder
43. **Factotum** *(Latin)* : a person employed to do all types of work.
44. **Glasnost** *(Russian)* : openness, having freedom from Govt. control
45. **Gaffe** *(French)* : an embarrassing blunder or mistake
46. **Gusto** *(Spanish)* : vigour, spirit, great enthusiasm
47. **In cognito** *(Italian)* : in disguise
48. **Ipso facto** *(Latin)* : by that very fact, virtually
49. **Imbroglio** *(Italian)* : a complicated problem
50. **Incommunicado** *(Spanish)*: without any means of communication, having no contact
51. **In situ** *(Latin)* : in its original place, in position
52. **In toto** *(Latin)* : as a whole, in all
53. **In camera** *(Latin)* : proceedings held in a private room
54. **In memoriam** *(Latin)* : to the memory of
55. **Largesse** *(French)* : generosity, showing great kindness
56. **Impasse** *(French)* : a deadlock
57. **Lingua franca** *(Italian)* : main language of a place
58. **Locus standi** *(Latin)* : a right to interfere
59. **Malafide** *(Latin)* : acting in bad faith
60. **Mandarin** *(Chinese)* : a high-ranking official or leader
61. **Modus operandi** *(Latin)* : a particular way of doing something
62. **Mogul** *(Persian)* : a powerful person or authority
63. **Nouveau riche** *(French)* : people who became rich very recently
64. **Paparazzo** *(Italian)* : a journalist or photographer who trails famous people
65. **Par cxcellence** *(French)* : better or more than all others of the same kind
66. **Per se** *(Latin)* : by or itself, intrinsically
67. **Parole** *(French)* : released from jail before stipulated time
68. **Persona non grata** *(Latin)* : an unwelcome person, person not wanted
69. **Prima donna** *(Italian)* : the main person, chief female singer
70. **Prima facie** *(Latin)* : based on the first impression
71. **Perestroika** *(Russian)* : economic liberalization initiated by Mikhail Gorbachev in former Russia
72. **Post-mortem** *(Latin)* : examination of the body after death to find the cause of death, careful examination of events
73. **Pundit** *(Hindi)* : an expert in a particular subject
74. **Pro tem** *(Latin)* : for the temporary period

| | | |
|---|---|---|
| 75. **Raison d'etre** *(French)* | : the most important reason | |
| 76. **Rendezvous** *(French)* | : a place where people agree to meet | |
| 77. **Realpolitik** *(German)* | : politics based on the circumstances and needs of the people | |
| 78. **Sine qua non** *(Latin)* | : an essential condition | |
| 79. **Status quo** *(Latin)* | : existing state of affairs, as it is now | |
| 80. **Sine die** *(Latin)* | : without date, indefinitely | |
| 81. **Sub judice** *(Latin)* | : under judicial consideration | |
| 82. **Tempo** *(Italian)* | : spirit, rate of movement | |
| 83. **Tete-a-tete** *(French)* | : a private conversation between two persons | |
| 84. **Tycoon** *(Japanese)* | : a wealthy person | |
| 85. **Tableau** *(French)* | : representation of a scene by people. | |
| 86. **Versus** *(Latin)* | : against | |
| 87. **Via media** *(Latin)* | : middle course | |
| 88. **Vice versa** *(Latin)* | : in the opposite way or manner | |
| 89. **Viva voce** *(Latin)* | : oral test | |
| 90. **Volte-face** *(French)* | : complete turnabout, reversal of policy | |

—xxx—

**Useful data**

# 18. Commonly used Latin abbreviations in English

| 1. a.m. | ante meridiem | before noon |
|---|---|---|
| 2. A.D. | Anno Domini | in the year of our Lord |
| 3. ad lib., | ad libitum | to any extent that is desired |
| 4. D.V. | Deo Volente | God willing |
| 5. e.g. | exempli gracia | for example |
| 6. et seq., | et sequentia | and what follows |
| 7. etc. | et cetera | and the rest |
| 8. i.e. | id est | that is |
| 9. N.B. | Nota Bene | note carefully |
| 10. ob., | obit | died |
| 11. p.m. | post meridiem | after noon |
| 12. pro tem., | pro tempore | for the time |
| 13. q.v. | quod vide | which see |
| 14. R.I.P. | requiescat in pace | May he/she rest in peace |
| 15. viz., | videlicet | namely |

# 37. Slang and rhyming words

(Most rhyming words are slang terms. Such terms often add beauty and richness to the
language.)

1. **Airy-fairy** : not practical, utopian ideas, etc.
2. **Bigwig** : VIPs, highly influential persons, etc.
3. **Block buster** : publicly acclaimed, highly popular, etc.
4. **Brain drain** : emigration of highly skilled or qualified persons into another country.
5. **Brick-bat** : using some broken pieces as a missile
5. **Bric-a-brac** : a collection of miscellaneous items having little value
6. **Chit-chat** : informal and friendly conversation
7. **Claptrap** : empty talk or writing, showy, etc.
8. **Culture vulture** : a person who is much interested in culture and arts
9. **Dilly-dally** : vacillate, waste time in deciding
10. **Die-hard** : very strong supporters
11. **Ding-dong** : a fierce argument or fight
12. **Downtown** : towards the central or main area of town or city
13. **Dribs and drabs** : in small amounts, little by little
14. **Dum-dum** : an unintelligent person
15. **Flip-flop** : frequent reverses in policy or action
16. **Flotsam and jetsam**: floating parts of a wrecked ship, poor people whose lives have been wrecked
17. **Hanky-panky** : improper behaviour, underhand dealings
18. **Helter-skelter** : in confusion or disorder
19. **Higgledy-piggledy** : confused, disorderly fashion
20. **Hillbilly** : an unsophisticated rural person, people who are rather unsophisticated in their behaviour
21. **Hobnob** : have friendly talk, mix socially with those of higher social status
22. **Hocus-pocus** : meaningless talk to draw one's attention away
23. **Hotchpotch** : jumble, number of things mixed together without order
24. **Hoity-toity** : supercilious and haughty, arrogant
25. **Horse-trading** : change of parties by elected members due to financial benefits
26. **Hair-trigger** : ready to attack or to do something evil
27. **By hook or by crook**: by any means, anyhow and somehow
28. **Hubbub** : uproar, tumult, chaotic noise
29. **Huff and puff** : blow out noisily, breathe heavily
30. **Humdrum** : lacking variety, monotonous, boring, etc.
31. **Humpty-dumpty** : a short fat person, a person who is not much agile to do simple tasks.

| | | |
|---|---|---|
| 32. | **Hunky-dory** | : good, excellent, fine, etc. |
| 33. | **Hurly-burly** | : busy, confusion, great deal of activity, etc. |
| 34. | **Hush-hush** | : secret dealing, confidential |
| 35. | **Hustle and bustle** | : hurried activities, excited, hectic life, etc. |
| 36. | **Itsy-bitsy** | : very small, in small amounts, etc. |
| 37. | **Jet set** | : people who constantly travel by air |
| 38. | **Leap-frogging** | : jumping quickly, rising fast, etc. |
| 39. | **Knick-knack** | : small unimportant ornaments, articles of dress, pieces of furniture, etc. |
| 40. | **Kowtow** | : to be subservient towards someone |
| 41. | **Mayday** | : an international radio distress signal used by ships and aircraft |
| 42. | **Mishmash** | : a confused mixture |
| 43. | **Nitty-gritty** | : important aspects of a problem |
| 44. | **Nitwit** | : a silly or foolish person |
| 45. | **Pin-drop** | : absolute silence |
| 46. | **Pell-mell** | : confused, in disorderly manner |
| 47. | **Powwow** | : a meeting, gathering for the purpose of discussion |
| 48. | **Pot-shot** | : a nearby shot, an excellent shot |
| 49. | **Ragtag** | : made up of mixed or ill-sorted elements |
| 50. | **Razzle-dazzle** | : cause attraction, shine brightly |
| 51. | **Riff-raff** | : disreputable persons, ill-behaved people |
| 52. | **Sanctum sanctorum:** | most holy place, a place of utmost privacy |
| 53. | **Shilly-shally** | : unable to make up one's mind |
| 54. | Spic **and span** | : very neat, absolutely clean |
| 55. | **Think-tank** | : intellectuals, people whose main job is to frame future plans and work out strategies |
| 56. | **Ticky-tacky** | : inferior quality |
| 57. | **Topsy-turvy** | : upside- down, in confusion, etc. |
| 58. | **Willy-nilly** | : haphazardly, without planning, etc. |
| 59. | **Wishy-washy** | : weak, feeble, lacking in spirit or vigor, etc. |
| 60. | **White paper** | : a report given by the Govt. to give clear-cut information |

—xxx—

# 38 . Interview strategies (Job interview/examination interview)

Most of us have to attend job interviews or examination interviews. International English examinations such as IELTS (*International English Language Testing System*) and OET (*Occupational English Test*) test candidates' speaking proficiency in English. Interview whether as part of job application or examination interview examines your proficiency in the language which is expressed through appropriate use of vocabulary, correctness of grammar and variety of sentence structures.

## Tips to enhance your speaking at interviews & speaking tests

1. Before you enter the interview room, knock thrice gently and say *'Could/May I come in, Sir/Ma'am?'* (*'Can I come in?' is slightly informal*)
2. Enter the room only after you hear *'Come in.'*
3. Before you go in, make sure that you have normal breathing and your clothes are in correct order.
4. Do not rush into the room. Take a deep breath and control your breathing and then enter.
5. Try not to show your back to the interview board/examiner. Take a step forward and close the door from your back with your hands.
6. As soon as you close the door, stand near the door and wish the members of the interview board/examiners with a slight genuflection of the neck saying, *'Good Afternoon...Good Evening.'* according to the time of the day. The wishing should be done with a smile on your face and should be done in a lively manner.
7. Move forward only when the examiner says 'Please take your chair.'
8. Walk briskly towards the chair, and sit comfortably adjusting the distance of the chair from the table in such a way that you are able to move your hands freely. But do not drag the chair. Lift it and adjust.
9. Do not extend your hand for a handshake. Extend your hand only if the examiner extends his hands.
9. Look at the eyes of the examiner/examiners and talk even if the examiner is a person of the opposite sex. Talking without looking at the face of the person is not a British way of talking.
10. If there are several persons in the interview board, turn your eyes from the centre towards the sides gradually. In this scenario, do not look at one person only.
10. Do not rest your hands on the table. Keep them free to move as you speak.
11. Make sure your dress looks neat and clean; it should be ironed. Ladies' shawls must be properly pinned. Do not wear casual dress. Interviews are formal occasions and, therefore, the dress must also be fitting to the occasion.

12. Use extensively body language such as eye contact, hand gestures, nodding of the head, various expressions on the face, etc.

13. Always present an optimistic view of things around. Reduce your negative statements.

14. Use emphatic **Yes** or **No. Oh Yes, Definitely yes, Definitely not, Certainly yes,** etc.

15. Speak with confidence, enthusiasm and gusto.

18. If the question is not clear to you,

> say *'Could you be kind enough to repeat the question?'*
> *'I didn't get the question correctly.'*
> *'Would you mind repeating it?'*

19. Try to avoid all kinds of filler/killer sound...Ah...Ah...Um ...Um ..er...er...etc. while talking. Close your mouth fully after each sentence.

20. Do not tell the examiner that you are nervous.

21. Do not blink your eyes during your talk.

22. Do not look at the roof or the window during interviews.

23. Do not move too much on the chair.

24. Do not snap your fingers, play with a pen,

25. If you want to blow your nose, wipe your face or cough, turn to one side and do it politely.

26. Never murmur to yourself if the examiner asks you a tough question. Never speak to yourself in your mother tongue.

27. When a difficult question is asked, do not show displeasure, anger or bitterness on your face. Keep your cool.

28. Do not speak with downcast /wandering eyes.

29. Do not beat around the bush if you do not know the answer. Acknowledge your deficiency and say:

> *'I'm afraid I do not know the answer.'*
> *'Sorry, I am not sure of the answer.'*
> *'Sorry, I don't think I will be able to answer that question.'*

30. If you realize that you made a mistake say immediately.

> *'Sorry, I would like to repeat what I am trying to say.'* (*now say it correctly*)

31. Do not think back on the exact words or figures you said. There may be mistakes. It will confuse your present talk. You cannot talk with a distracted mind. Focus only on what is being talked about.

32. If you cannot think of what else to say:

> *'I think that is all I can tell you.'*
> *'I'm afraid this is all what I know.'*
> *'I can't think of anything else now.'*

33. Make sure to thank the examiner sincerely:

> *'Thank you so much... It was a pleasure meeting you...'*
> *'I enjoyed talking to you...I was happy to meet a person like you...'*

34. While coming away from the room, do not look back to see the score that is being written by the examiner.
35. Close the door gently.

# Job interviews

**Types of personal interviews:** The main types of personal interviews are the following:

**i) Structured interview:** In this type of personal or one-on-one interviews, the questions are predetermined both in topic and order. The interviewer asks from an already pre-prepared list of questions related to the topic one by one as provided to him. Generally, he does not ask any question which is not given to him or her.

**ii) Semi-structured interview:** In the second category of personal interview, the interviewer asks a few pre-prepared questions as well as some unplanned questions. Here, the interviewer  may ask a number of questions as he/she thinks best.

**iii) Unstructured interview:** In this category of interview,  the questions are not prepared beforehand. The interviewer asks the questions from any topic depending on the situation.

Sometimes the company or organization may provide the interviewer a range of topics to ask questions from. Generally, they are free to ask questions of their choice.

**Chief objectives of  personal interview:** The main objectives of one-on-one interviews are the following:

i) to obtain additional information about the interviewee's skills, experience and knowledge.

ii) to check the candidate's suitability for the job in terms of their personality and attitudes.

iii) to get an idea about the candidate's rational thinking process, communication skills and creativity.

iv) to evaluate your genuine interest in the company and your ability to add value to the company, etc.

# Important tips for job interview

**A. <u>Before the interview:</u>**

1. **Know your resume well:** Be prepared to talk about any point mentioned in the resume. Do not embellish your achievements and exaggerate your skills which may come to haunt in the form of tough questions related to the aspects mentioned in the CV.

2. **Know the company well:** You should make a thorough study about the company, its origin, development over the years, its market value, annual turn-out, achievements of the company, etc. Knowing the name of the founder or the present director will give an impression that you are a well-read individual genuinely interested in being part of the company's workforce.

**3. Practise interview questions beforehand:** While you can't predict every question that may be asked at the personal interview, there are some commonly asked interview questions that you should be prepared to answer. Therefore, prepare your answers to these common questions in accordance with your skill, experience and knowledge. However, make sure not to memorize the answers but rather speak normally as if you are getting the question for the first time.

**4. Have proper sleep and rest:** It is highly recommended that you get a proper sleep the previous night because a worn-out body and exhausted mind can ruin your performance the next day. A good sleep and a relaxed mind will sharpen your ability to listen as well as concentrate on the topic that is being talked about.

**B. At the time of interview:**

**5. Be punctual:** Punctuality is a quality of a gentleman. It is a sign of personal discipline and the mark of a well-groomed individual. Therefore, reach the venue of the interview at least 20 minutes ahead of the scheduled time. Reaching late or after the interview has begun will  only increase your already existing tension and this may affect negatively your performance at the interview.

**6. Dress professionally:** Wearing a suit isn't always required for most job interviews in India. Nevertheless, if the company is a multi-national or a major Indian company or you are being interviewed for a senior post, you may be required to follow certain dress code. In such a situation, contact the HR manager and try to know the type of dress you are expected to wear. However, what is important is that your dress must look neat and clean, well ironed, properly buttoned and in tune with your physique. The dress that you wear can speak volumes about your personality.

**7. Use a good deal of body language:** It is said that in effective communication more value is attributed to non-verbal communication than verbal communication and, therefore, use a good deal of body language expressions such as effective hand movement, nodding of the head, shrugging of shoulders, eye contact, various facial expressions, etc. Paralanguage signs such as pitch variations, intonation, pause, rhythm, voice quality, etc. too can greatly reinforce what you intend to say through words.

**8. Talk to everyone present:** Generally, there is more than one interviewer in most personal interviews. Therefore, it  is important that you talk not only to the person who asked you a question but to everyone present. Gently move your eyes towards the right and left making an eye-contact with all the interviewers present.

**9. Natural flow of words:** The sentences that you utter should flow naturally. There shouldn't be too long pauses or sudden stop though short pauses can enhance the quality of your speaking. One should not speak too fast or too slow. Keep a medium pace with every word said clearly.

**10. Listen before answering**: Do not rush to answer the question. Wait for the examiner to complete the question. Take your time to digest the question. For this, one has to listen very carefully. Interviewers are impressed with candidates who listen carefully, think a bit and then answer the question. Moreover, it is important to speak only what is relevant, and needed.

**11. Be truthful:** Don't speak of achievements that you cannot claim. Do not lie when asked about something you haven't done. Exaggerated narration of talents and skills can get you into trouble as the interviewers may want more explanation about them. Therefore, be truthful in what you write in your resume as well as in what you utter.

**12. Never criticize your previous employer:** Never say anything negative about your previous employer or the company where you may have had a tough time. Try to say the negative aspects in a positive manner without any personal attack or blunt criticism. When you are asked to state the reason for leaving the former job, say something positive such as *'greater educational opportunities for children', 'improved pay', 'better working environment', 'greater promotion prospects'*, etc.

**13. Learn to ask proper questions:** The interviewer may conclude the session by asking if the candidate has any question to ask. Never say that you don't have any question to ask. This is your opportunity to get more details about the position offered. In this context, you can ask about the salary offered, the responsibilities associated with the post, the promotion avenues available once you are in the job, etc. all of which will show that you are truly interested in the opportunity.

**14. End the interview on a positive note:** When the interview comes to an end, thank the interviewer/interviewers sincerely and express your interest in the position. This is a great opportunity to reiterate why you're the best candidate for the job and saying as you get up from the chair, ***'it was nice to talk to you', 'I enjoyed talking to you', 'it was a pleasure meeting a person like you',*** etc. can boost your chances of getting a better score in your interview.

# Most commonly asked interview questions

**<u>Point to note:</u>** Preparing precise and clear answers to the following most commonly asked questions, no doubt, can enhance your performance at the interview. However, make sure that you don't speak as if the answers have been memorized. The answer should appear spontaneous and naturally flowing on the basis of the question asked.

1. Tell us about yourself.
2. What are your strengths and weaknesses?
3. What is your greatest strength?
4. Why do you want to work with us?
5. Where do you see yourself in five years?
6. Why are you leaving your current company or organization?
7. What can you offer us that other candidates cannot?

8. Tell us about a time you made a mistake and how you dealt with it.

9. Describe a time you dealt with a difficult colleague and how did you resolve it.

10. What do you know about our company/organization?

11. What is your greatest achievement?

12. What kind of working environment do you prefer to work in?

13. Why have you switched jobs so many times?

14. Are you a team player?

15. Are you a risk-taker?

16. How do you deal with work pressure or stressful situations?

17. How quickly do you adapt to new technology?

18. What do you think our company could better?

19. Give an example of how you have handled a challenge in the workplace before.

20. Give an example of when you performed well under pressure.

21. Give an example of when you showed leadership qualities.

22. What do you like to do outside your work?

23. What are you passionate about?

24. What is your dream job?

25. Do you have any question for us?

—xxx—

## Useful data

# 19. Tongue-twisters

1. She sells seashells on the seashore.
2. Rain in Spain mainly stays in plains.
3. Peter Piper picked a peck of pickled peppers.
4. Bitter is better where better is not better.
5. The baker in the bakery bakes the bread brown.
6. Don't trouble a small bubble, because the bubble can trouble you, like a big trouble.
7. Betty Botter bought a bit of butter to put it in her batter, but the bit of butter which Betty Botter bought was bitter, so Betty Botter bought again better butter to make the bitter butter better.
8. I wish to wish the wish you wish to wish but if you wish the wish the witch wishes, I won't wish the wish you wish to wish.
9. A tutor who tooted the flute, tried to tutor two tutors to toot.
   Said the two to the tutors: Is it easier to toot or to tutor two tutors to toot?

# 39. Reading strategies for comprehension passages

**(How to answer the questions of comprehension passages easily and quickly)**

**Main methods used in reading:**

**i) Skimming**:

Skimming is a selective reading method in which you focus on the main ideas of a text. When we do skimming, we deliberately skip details, stories, irrelevant information and all types of elaboration of the data. Instead of closely reading every word, the focus is on the introduction, chapter summary, first and last sentences of the paragraph, bold words, etc. In simple words, skimming is extracting the essence of the author's main arguments rather than the finer points. To skim, you will have to move rapidly through the pages. You don't need to read every word. You will pay special attention to typographical cues such as headings, bold words, bulleted and numbered lists, phrases, the names of people and places, dates and unfamiliar words. In general, follow these steps:

    i. Read the title.

    ii. Read the introduction or the first paragraph.

    iii. Read the first and last sentences of every paragraph.

    iv. Read any headings and sub-headings.

    v. Notice any pictures, charts or graphs.

    vi. Notice any italicized or boldface words or phrases.

    vii. Read the summary or last paragraph.

    viii. Chapter summary/review points or questions.

**ii) Scanning:** Scanning is a reading technique to be used when you want to find specific information quickly. In scanning you have a question or an idea in mind and you read a passage to find the answer to that point, ignoring unrelated information. In simple words, scanning is a process of extracting a point through fast search. While skimming is concerned with finding general information, namely, the main ideas, scanning involves looking for specific information. The following steps will help you to scan better.

    i. First think of the specific information you want and then search of it in the paragraph.

    ii. Think of the synonyms of the keyword of the question you are looking for.

    iii) Think of the possible answer to the question and search for it in the concerned paragraph.

    iv) Looking at the signpost words such as *dates, names, numbers, capitalized and italicized words,* etc. may help you in this task.

**Types of questions**

    i) short-answer questions

    ii) multiple choice questions

    iii) sentence completion

    iv) notes/ summary/diagram/flow chart completion

v) choosing a heading for a paragraph
vi) identification of writer's views-Yes, No, and Not given questions
vii) identification of information-True, False and not given questions
viii) classification
ix) matching lists/phrases

## Important tips for solving questions of comprehension passages

1. Before you commence your task of reading, remind yourself of the total time allotted for reading as per your exam schedule. Skim over the passage very quickly, count the number of paragraphs, look at the number of questions, and then  mentally calculate the time for each question.

2. If there is more than one comprehension passage to be done, mentally calculate the time for each passage.

3. If there are several passages, skim over the passages very quickly and select the **easy-hard-very hard** passages writing no. 1, 2, 3, etc. respectively. This can be done by looking at the title, first lines of the different paragraphs, etc.

4. Do not begin with any passage; always choose the easy passage. Trying to complete the very difficult passage first may discourage you. Therefore, select first the easy passage and start the work.

5. After having selected the first passage, read through the questions carefully, underlining the keywords of the questions.

6. Now skim over the passage very quickly in a zigzag way. Use your fingertips or pencil tip as you skim over the pages.

7. As you skim over the passage, underline the important key words, names, dates, places, etc.

8. Write the main topic of each paragraph in the margin. Generally, the first sentence is the topic sentence. Writing the main top in the margin will greatly help you to locate your answers easily.

9. When you skim through the passage try to answer the question-Who? What? Where/ How?, etc.

10. When you go through the passage, take a special note of the following:
    a. Instructions
    b. Headings
    c. First line of each paragraph
    d. Examples
    e. Bold printed words
    f. Pictures and diagrams

11. After skimming you may be able to answer one or two questions straightaway without going back to the passage. Write the answer in the allotted place and thereafter give a tick mark over the question so as to know that the question has been completed.

12. Read the introductory paragraph carefully. The first sentence of the introductory paragraph is usually the topic sentence of the whole passage.

13. Read carefully the concluding paragraph. This paragraph summarizes the main points of the passage.

14. Read the glossary and footnotes if given.

15. Stick to the time allotted for each question. If you are not able to get the answer within this time, jump to the next question. Do not panic. Put a cross mark at the side of the question and move to the next question.

16. Generally, the questions follow the order of the text. So don't go back to the paragraphs already completed i.e., answer of question no.5 is likely to be in paragraph 5 or it could be in  paragraph 3/ 4 or 6/7. The answer is likely to be somewhere here.

17. Never leave any question unanswered unless there is minus mark for wrong answers.

18. Be concerned about spelling as well as articles-'**a**, **an** and **the.**'

19. Words in the question may not be exact words in the text; it is mostly synonyms.

    E.g.: Look at this question:

    *Which is the most significant global problem today?*

    The two key words of the question are **'global'** and **'problem'**; in the text you may have to look for their synonyms:

    **Global:** *'universal, international, the whole world, inter-continental*, etc.

    **Problem**: *issue, problem, threat, concern, hurdle, trouble*, etc.

20. Ignore anything you already know about the topic. You are asked to write answers on the basis of the data given in the text and not based on your previous knowledge.

21. Accept the fact that some questions are really tough and you may not be able to answer. Do not panic. It is almost impossible to do all the questions correctly. Some answers are likely to go wrong.

22. Do the question of *'arrange the headings of the paragraph'* last because it is really tough; besides it entails going through all the paragraphs which will take a lot of time.

23. Strictly follow the instruction on the number of words of the answer. If the instruction says *'an answer not in more than two words'* , then write two words or one word.

    **e.g.:** if the answer asks for two words and the answer is **'red and yellow'**.

    You should write' **red, yellow'** and not *'red and yellow'* because it is three words.

24. One word means just one word only.

    **e.g.:** If the question says only one word and the answer is **'an earthquake'**, you should write **'earthquake'** only.

25. One of the chief reasons for low score in reading is distractions.
<u>Distraction is of two types:</u>

> a) personal distractions such as mental tension, financial problem, family problem, broken love affairs, deep hurt feelings, undue worry, etc.
>
> b) distractions of the surroundings such as the novelty of the building, hall arrangement, window curtains, or any new thing you see at the exam centre, etc.

Reduce to the maximum level both the above-mentioned types of distractions. It can enhance your score in reading.

26. Remember, you haven't come to evaluate the place. Moreover, it would be advisable to visit the place of your exam a day or two before so as not to be distracted by things you see at the exam place.

26. Best recommendation for a better score in reading :

*Never take more than the allotted time for each question.*

**Quick methods to get the answers of the comprehension passages:**

# a) Keyword approach method

**Step 1** : Look at the no. of questions and number of paragraphs and accordingly fix the time for each question.

**Step 2** : Thereafter, read all the questions of the given passage or selected passage underlining the key words of the questions.

**Step 3** : Then take the first question, read it carefully two or three times, think of the synonyms of the keyword of the question and then scan for the answer in the respective paragraph.

<u>**Remember**</u> : Questions generally follow the order of the paragraphs i.e., answer of question no. 5 will be in paragraph 5/ or it could be in paragraph 3/ 4 or 6/7.

**Step 4** : If you cannot get the answer within the allotted time, move to the next question, putting a cross mark at the question number.

**Step 5** : In this manner, complete all the questions taking only the allotted time.

**Step 6** : After completing all the questions, go back to the unanswered questions one by one and try again for answers. If you still cannot get an answer, write some answer if there is no negative mark for wrong answers.

---xxx---

# 40. Letter writing

## Kinds of letters:

1. Personal letter
2. Business letter
3. Official letter

## 1. Parts of a letter

1. Writer's address and date
3. Salutation
4. Body of the letter
5. Subscription or complimentary close
6. Signature
7. Name of the writer/ designation
8. Enclosures and postscript, if any

**1. Writer's address and date:** The writer's address and date may be written at the top right-hand corner or left-hand corner depending on the type of writing format one uses.

**Different forms of dating are:**

15th May, 2020

May 15, 2020

Monday, 15th May, 2020

The form of dating such as **5-5-2020 or 5/6/2020** is not in favour  these days.

<u>**Important Note:**</u> In American English they write the month first followed by the day, while in British English the day is written first.

    **e.g.:** 10 02 2020

is the second of October in the US while in British English it is the tenth of February. Hence most people prefer to write one of the following forms:

10th October, 2020

October 10, 2020

Wednesday, 10th October, 2020

**2. Salutation:** Salutation is the formal way of beginning a letter or an application. The type of salutation to be used depends upon the relationship or the degree of acquaintance the writer has with the person addressed.

Different forms of salutation are the following:

*i) To close relatives and intimate friends*:

    My dear Papa, Dear Papa, My dear son, My dear Hari, etc.

*ii) To a less familiar friend or an acquaintance*:

    Dear Mr. Rajan, Dear Tom, Dear Ms. Sangeeta, etc.

*iii) To a stranger or a superior*:

    Sir, Dear Sir,

*iv) To an officer in an official letter*:
> Sir,

*v) To a firm*:
> Dear Sirs, Gentlemen,

*vi) To a manager of a firm, head of institution, etc.*
> Dear Sir, Dear Madam,

**Sir:** 'Sir' is used mostly in official letters and applications and writing to strangers, whether superior or inferior in position. It is purely formal.

**Dear Sir:** It is the usual form of address in business letters and letters of a general type.

**3. Body of the application:** All three types of letters *(personal/ business/official)* generally have the following parts. However, the style and the number of words or lines used in each part vary according to the type of letters used.

> a) Introduction
> b) Content
> c) Conclusion

**4. Subscription or complimentary close:** It can be written at the right-hand corner or left-hand corner below the body of the letter.

**Common ways of writing subscription:**

*1) To relatives*:
> i) Your affectionate son,
> ii) Your loving son,
> iii) Yours affectionately,
> iv) Affectionately yours,
> v) Affectionately,

*2) To friends*:
> i) Your most affectionate friend,
> ii) Your sincere well-wisher,
> iii) Your sincere friend,
> iv) Yours sincerely,
> v) Sincerely yours,

*3) To superiors*:
> i) Yours respectfully,
> ii) Yours obediently,

*4) To a stranger*:
> i) Yours faithfully,
> ii) Yours truly,

**5) *To a firm*:**
  i) Faithfully yours,
  ii) Yours faithfully,

**6) *In official letters*:**
  i) Faithfully yours,
  ii) Yours faithfully,

**<u>Special Note</u>:** *Subscription is always followed by a comma.*

**5) Signature:** The signature should follow right below the subscription. Sign your name as you normally sign. Short forms of signatures should not be used.

**6) Name:** Name should be written below the signature. Write full name. Never write short forms of your name. Generally, initials are placed before the name. (e.g.: *Miss C J Anu* and not *Miss Anu C J*) The designation of the writer is written in brackets below the name.

1. Mrs Sangeeta Bedi M.Sc. (Nursing)
      (Principal)
2. Shri. Mathews Tharakan
      (Executive Engineer)

**7) Enclosures:** Whenever you are enclosing some documents or certificates with your application, you should mention it after the name. Enclosures can be given in the following two ways.

Enclosures: Copies of documents and testimonials.
**OR**
Enclosures:
  i) ————————————-
  ii) ————————————
  iii) ————————————

**8) Postscript** (*Normally written as P.S.*): Postscript is allowed when something has been forgotten. This is generally used only in letters of a personal and business nature. It should not be used in official letters or applications. This is written on the left-hand corner after the name and it should not exceed 3 lines.

## ii. Forms of writing letters

### i) Block Form

This is the most commonly used form of writing. In this type of writing form, the date, the introductory address, salutation, paragraphs of the letter, complimentary close or subscription, signature, name, etc. begin at the left-hand margin.

**ii) Indented Form**

The introductory address and date are written at the right-hand corner of the letter while the lines of the letter are indented, i.e., begin some distance from the margin. The subscription or the complimentary close, signature and name are placed at the right-hand margin.

**iii) Semi-Block Form**

In this form the introductory address and the date are written at the right-hand margin as in the indented form. But the lines of the letter are placed close to the left-hand margin like the block form. The complimentary close, signature and name are also written at the right-hand margin.

## 1. Format of the Block Form

Address of the sender—————————

——————————————————

Date ——————————————

Address of the addressee—————————————

——————————————————

——————————————————

Sub: —————————————————

Salutation————,

——————————————————————
——————————————————————
—————————————————
——————————————————————

——————————————————————

—————————————————

——————————————————————

—————————————————

Subscription

Signature
Name/Post

## 2. Format of Indented Form

Address of the sender————

————————————-

Date————————————

Address of the addressee————

————————————-

————————————

sub:————————————

Salutation————,

—————————————————————————

—————————

—————————————————————

————————————

—————————————————————

————————————

—————————————————————————

—————————————————

________________________________________________

______

________________________________________________

_________________________

_____________________________----------------------______

_______________________________________________

___________________________________________

Subscription

Signature

Name/Post

## 3. Format of Semi-Block Form

Address of the sender————

————————————————

Date————————————————

——

Address of the addressee————

______________________________________

______________________________________

Sub: ————————————————————

Salutation————,

________________________________________________

_______________________________________

_______________________

_______________________________________

_______________________________________

_______________________

Subscription

Signature

Name/Post

# ii. Format of Letters

## A. <u>Format of personal letter</u>

*(You can use any of the writing forms: block /indented/semi-block forms. The form used here is the indented form.)*

**I.** *Address* of the sender——

_______________________

_______________________

**II.** *Date.*————————

**III.** *Salutation* ——,

**IV.** *Body of the letter*

a) introduction

_______________________________________

_______________________

b) contents

c) conclusion

*V. Subscription*

**VI. Signature**

**VII. Name/designation**

Letter writing

## Model Personal Letter

**Write a letter to your daddy informing him that you have been selected to go to New Delhi to take part in the National Science Exhibition.**

Mount Zion Hostel,
Market Road,
Shillong-4
5th May, 2023

Dear Daddy,

How are you? How is everyone at home? Thanks for the letter you sent me a month ago. I am really glad to know that eldest brother got a good job in an IT company in Hyderabad.

I am writing this letter to tell you something that will certainly make you happy. I have been selected to go to New Delhi to take part in the Annual Schools' National Science Exhibition which is to be held in the last week of August, 2023. Our school has been selected to join this exhibition as we had won the first prize in the state level science exhibition held in Shillong last January. I was a member of the group which participated in this exhibition. We had presented a cheap solar cooking gadget for this exhibition. Our principal has asked us to put up a better model of this gadget in the forthcoming national exhibition.

Our team with the support of our science teacher is working on it. We hope to complete the work by the end of July. I have to contribute 2,000 rupees towards the making of this gadget. Last month, elder brother had given me 2,000 rupees as a birthday present. I shall use this amount for this purpose and, therefore, I shall not trouble you regarding my share for the preparation of the gadget.

We will be booking our train tickets by next week. The hotel rooms for our team have already been booked by the Asst. Principal who has been put in-charge of the trip. Once everything is finalized, I will let you know.

Currently classes are going on in full swing. The Third Term Examination will commence by first week of October. This will be followed by ten days of Puja holidays. When I come home in October, I shall enlighten you further about my forthcoming trip to New Delhi. I am eagerly longing to see our national capital with its majestic buildings and monuments.

Give my love and regards to everyone at home, particularly to mummy. I do remember you all in my prayers and I am sure you do the same for me as well.

With lots of love,

Your loving son,
*Signature*
David Syiem

## B. <u>Format of a Business Letter</u>

*(You can use any of the writing forms: block /indented/semi-block forms. The form used here is the **indented form**.)*

**I.** *Address* of the sender————

———————————————-

**II.** *Date* —————————

**III.** *Address* of the addressee

.....................

.....................

**IV.** *Salutation*—————,

**V. Body of the letter**

**VI.** *Subscription*

**VII.** *Signature*

**VIII.** *Name/designation*

Letter writing

## <u>Model Business Letter</u>

**Write a letter to Toms Publications, New Delhi, ordering 10 copies of English Grammar for High School Students.**

St: Mary's High School,
Wellington Street
Chennai-10
July 10, 2022

Toms Publications,
Prem Nagar,
New Delhi-18

Dear Sir,

  I shall be much obliged if you can send us ten (10) copies of your '**English Grammar for High School Students**' by registered post in the address given above. Once we receive the parcel, we shall send you the due amount by way of bank money transfer. Kindly send us also the bank details along with the registered post.

Expecting your kind cooperation,


 Yours sincerely,


   (*signature*)

Mrs Jane Edison
(Principal)

## C. <u>Format of an official letter</u>

**I.** *Date*————————————

**II. From**

————————————————

————————————————

**III. To**

————————————————

————————————————

————————————————

**IV.** *Sub:* —————————————

**V. Sir,**

**VI.** *Body of the letter* ——————————————————————————————
————

————————————————————————————————
————

————————————————————————————————
——

**VII.** *Subscription*

**VIII.** *Signature*

**IX.** *Name/designation*

Letter writing

**Model Official Letter**

**Send an invitation letter to the District Deputy Commissioner requesting him to be the chief guest for your school's Sports Day function.**

Kochi
4th July, 2022

From
Principal,
St. Joseph's College,
Akbar Road,
Kochi-5

To
Shri Warlong Marbah IAS
Deputy Commissioner
Kochi-2

Sub: An Invitation to be the Chief Guest

Sir,
 With reference to the subject cited above, we would like to invite you to be the chief guest for our College Annual Day function. The aforesaid function will be held in the college auditorium at 10.30 am., on 25th August, 2022. Since you are busy with your official responsibilities, you can inaugurate the function and leave at your convenience. I am sure you would be kind enough to accept our invitation and grace the occasion by your esteemed presence.

Expecting a favourable reply to our invitation,

Yours faithfully,
(*Signature*)
 Shri Ashok Kumar  M.A., B.Ed.
     (Principal)

## Common errors in writing letters and applications

| <u>Incorrect</u> | <u>Correct</u> |
| --- | --- |
| Dear Sir *(To a firm/company)* | Dear Sirs, |
| Dear sir | Dear Sir, |
| Dear Gentlemen | Gentlemen, |
| Yours Faithfully | Yours faithfully, |
| Your's faithfully | Yours faithfully, |
| your affectionately | Yours affectionately, |
| Your truly | Yours truly, |
| Yours affectionate son | Your affectionate son, |
| Faithfully Yours | Faithfully yours, |
| Dr. Mrs. A. Rajan | Dr (Mrs) A. Rajan |
| Miss. Maria P.K. | Miss P.K. Maria |

# Important points to keep in mind while writing letters

1. Never send carbon copies of letters and applications.
2. Use good paper for writing letters and applications.
3. Use good envelopes for sending letters.
4. Complaints should be in the mildest of words.
5. Never use ambiguous words.
6. Avoid repetition of ideas and sentences.
7. Never send any letter or application without revising it.
8. Make sure of spelling and punctuation.
9. Applications should be preferably typed or computer-printed unless specifically asked for handwritten applications.
10. If handwritten, it should be neatly written and in good handwriting.
11. There should be no cutting or over-writing. There should not be any correction with correcting fluid. It gives a poor impression.
12. The folding of the letter should be properly done and the letter should be placed within the envelope in such a way that the top part of the letter should appear first when it is taken out from the envelope.

—xxx—

# 41. Job application letter

**Job application letter:** A job application letter is a document that is submitted along with the resume to an employer to express your interest in the position which a particular company/organization has advertised. It is also known as 'cover letter'. The main objective of this letter is to tell the employer or the hiring team that you have all the necessary requirements for the post and therefore should be called for an interview. While the resume describes the candidate's personal details, work experience , skills and achievements, the cover letter focuses particularly on the candidate's skills and experience which are fit for the position advertised.

## Important tips to be kept mind while writing job application letters

1. **Understand the job posting well:** The first task that you as a job aspirant for the job advertised is to go through the job posting well. Follow the instructions mentioned exactly. For example, if they ask you to send the letter as an email attachment or type it directly into their online application system, then you cannot send a physical application letter. Moreover, you have to use certain keywords of the job posting in your application letter which will tell the employer that you have carefully gone through the job opening mentioned.

2. **Customize your application letter:** It is important that you customize every job application letter you write. You cannot send the same application letter to every job vacancy you apply for. Each job offer has certain unique requirements and condition. In this backdrop each application must be specific to each job opening. An employer will easily recognize such general type of application letters and may reject it straightaway without even going through it.

3. **Use formal business letter format:** It is important that your letter be written following formal business letter format which is marked by writing important data such as your name, address, employer's contact information, subject in the beginning of the letter itself. Moreover, the letter is generally written in block form i.e., all words and lines close to the left margin.

4. **Use standard margin, space and font:** Application letters should not exceed more than one page with three to four paragraphs. Your employer or hiring team may not look at a lengthy application letter as they have hundreds of such letters to go through. The letter should be single-spaced with a space between each paragraph. Use 1-inch margin with the text aligned to the left. The most commonly used font consists of fonts such as Times New Roman, Arial or Calibri and the font size should between 10 and 12 points.

5. **Use polite tone:** The application letter must be marked by a polite tone. Use of polite expressions and respectful terms boost your chances of being called for an interview. Express your skills and achievements without arrogance and over-exaggeration. Details of past experience must be authentic and genuine.

**6. Give a personal touch to your letter:** It is really good to give a personal touch to your job application letter by writing a personal salutation such as *'Dear Mohan Kumar, Dear Tom Mathews,* etc., although the most commonly used format is 'Dear Sir/Madam'. If you know the name of the interviewer or the chief hiring officer, use their name in the salutation. Such an action will definitely enhance your chance of being called for an interview.

**7. Keep it brief:** As mentioned earlier your letter should not exceed more than one page. Be brief and write only what is asked for. The language used should be n precise and concise. An employer is more likely to read a brief job application letter than a lengthy one.

**8. Use keywords of the posting:** It is really important to include certain keywords mentioned in the job posting regarding qualification, experience and skills, etc. Use of these terms will tell the employer that you have gone through the posting carefully and that you are really interested in the job offer.

**9. Use quality paper and envelope:** It is also important that write the application on a good quality paper as well as use a quality envelope to send the letter. Never send carbon copies or write the application on an organization's letter pad. Application should be neatly typed or computer printed or handwritten when asked for. There should not be any over-writing or crossing out or correction with correcting fluids.

**10. Proofread the application:** Employers are likely to overlook an application with a lot of errors. Therefore, check your letter for errors with regard to punctuation, spelling, grammar and vocabulary used. Incorrect language can stand as a major impediment in getting you called for interview.

# Main parts of a job application letter

**<u>Important details:</u>**

**Length:** A job application should not be more than one page long and the ideal number of paragraphs should be three to four. Lengthy application letters are hardly looked into by employers or hiring teams.

**Format and Page Margins:** A letter of application should be single-spaced with a space between each paragraph. Use about 1-inch margin and align your text to the left. Use block form of writing i.e., all texts aligned to the left margin.

**Font:** Use a traditional font such as Times New Roman, Arial, or Calibri, and the font size should be between 10 and 12 points.

**Name:** The first part of a job application consists of the candidate's name. Generally, the first and the last name are written.

    **e.g.:** John Mathews

**Address:** The applicant's address should be written on the left margin side. The address should be complete with flat no., street no., city, name of the country, pin code, etc. Currently no comma is put after each word although formerly there used to be comma after each word.

**Email ID:** It is important to provide your email id before the main body of the letter. Although you may have sent a physical letter, the employer may prefer to contact you via the email ID to save time.

**Date:** The next part of the job application letter is date. The following are some of the ways of writing dates:

> i) April 25, 2023
> ii) 25th April, 2023
> iii) 25.04.2023

The practice of writing date as 25-04-2023 or 25/04/23 is not much used nowadays in application letters. The date should be written beneath the email id.

**Employer's name and address:** Next comes the employer's or the hiring manager's name and contact information. Write the person's name if you know, position, company name, and company's complete address.

**Salutation:** This is your polite greeting of the employer. If you do not know the name of the person to whom you are writing, use *'Dear Sir/Madam'*. If you know the person's name, use their name which gives a personal touch to your letter. E.g.: *'Dear Mr Ravi Shankar, Dear Ms Maria Jones*, etc. Remember, nowadays full stops are not used after *Mr, Mrs, Miss,* and *Ms*.

**Subject :** It is really important that you clearly state the purpose of your letter by writing the appropriate subject title. It should be short and precise.

> **E.g.**: *an application for the post of teacher/content developer/sales manager,* etc.

**Body of the letter:** This part has generally three sub-parts:

**1st paragraph:** Mention the job you are applying for and where you saw the job listing. Details of the advertisement can be written as follows:

> i) *This is with reference to your job requirement on the MNC Job Portal for the position of ....*
>
> ii) *This is regarding your advertisement in the job portal (name of the portal) for the post of ...*
>
> iii) *This is with reference to the job posting on LinkedIn...*
>
> iv) *This is regarding your call for a Sales Manager as advertised on Naukri job portal...*
>
> v) *I am writing to apply for the position of (name of the post) in your job posting on ( name of the portal or source)*
>
> vi) *This is regarding your advertisement on (name of the portal or source) about a vacancy in your company for the position of ( name of the post)...*

vii) *I came to know about a job opening in your company from my former colleague...*

viii) *This is with reference to your advertisement in the 'Times of India ' dated May 20, —— for the post of junior lecturer....*

**2ⁿᵈparagraph:** Next, you should talk about your suitability for the role. Show that you understand what the job and the company require of you, and provide a series of further professional achievements that prove you're an ideal candidate for the job.

**3ʳᵈparagraph:** Explain your past experience and some of the achievements you have made in your field of work. You can mention what you could do for the company if given an opportunity.

**Concluding paragraph:** Here you should thank the employer for sparing his or her time to go through the letter. You can also offer follow-up information such as the phone number of your contact person or their email id.

**Complimentary close:** Sign off your letter with a polite close such as 'Sincerely', 'best regards', etc.

**Signature:** When you are sending or uploading a printed letter, end with your signature which should be handwritten followed by your name. If this is an email, simply include your typed name, followed by your contact information.

**Name:** Write the name once again as written before. You may also write your designation in brackets below the name.

**Enclosures:** If you are enclosing some attachments along with your application, you should make a mention of this fact by writing: **enclosures**:. Thereafter provide the various attachments you want to send along with the application letter at the bottom of your letter serially.

## Format of job application letter

**Candidate's name:** ——————

**Address:** ————————————

————————————————

**Email Id:** ————————————

**Phone Number:** ——————————

**Date:** ——————————————

**Employer's address**

————————————————

————————————————

**Subject:** ——————————————————————————————

Job application letter

**Salutation** : Dear Sir/ Madam, Dear Mr Mathew John, Dear Mrs Sangeeta Nair, etc.

**1st Para** : Mention the job you are applying for  and where did you get the information about the job vacancy.

**2nd Para** : talk about your suitability for the role. Mention your professional achievement. Mention some of your qualifications which match the job requirement.

**3rd Para** : Explain your past experience and some of the achievements you have made in your field of work and what you can do for the company.

**Concluding para:** Thank the employer for taking time to go through the letter and offer some follow-up information.

**Complimentary close:** Sincerely/ Best regards, etc.

**Candidate's signature**

**Candidate's name**


## Model application letter-1

### 1. Application for the post of a Lecturer

John D Martin
Bosco Villa,
Anand Marg,
Kolkata-10
Email ID: martin1969@gmail.com
Mob: 91xxxxxx767

Date: 20 August, 2023

The Principal,
St. Francis de Sales College,
Dalhousie Street,
Kolkata-5

<u>Subject</u>: Application for the post of a junior English lecturer

Dear Sir,

This is with reference to your job requirement on the Sakhi Job portal for the position of a junior English lecturer in your college. I would like to apply for the post offered as I believe that I have all the necessary requirements as mentioned in the job posting. My skills, qualifications, and experience make me a suitable candidate for the post.

I am happy to state that  I completed both graduation and post-graduation degrees with distinction from Christ College, Bangalore, one of the best colleges in South India. I have  also passed NET in the subject of English language, further making me suitable for the post of lecturer in this subject.

I have been working as a junior English language lecturer in a college in my native city, Kolkata, since 2020. These two years have been wonderful years of experience as I have been able to instill in my students greater love for the study of English language; so much so that during the year 2022 the number of students who opted for English for graduation tripled as never before.  I have come to know that your college is one of the best in Kolkata noted for academic excellence and progressive trends in education. Therefore, I would be really happy to join and serve an institution of such repute and fame.

I am confident that my skills and experience make me an ideal candidate for the post offered. Please find the attached CV in the email for further reference.

Thank you for sparing your precious time to go through my application. I do hope that you will favourably consider my candidature and call me for an interview.

Please feel free to contact me for any queries or any other information.

Sincerely,

Signature

John D Martin

# 42. E-mail job application letter

It is important to note that sending an email job application letter is slightly different from sending a fully written job application via email. In the latter, the letter is send as an attachment while in the former you send the letter directly to the concerned person through the person's email account. Moreover, in the ordinary job application letter you have to have a handwritten signature while in the email version, there is no such signature. Besides, email job application letters are more concise than normal application letters.

## Format of e-mail job application letter

**To:** Email address of the recipient

**Subject:** Application for the post (*name of the post*)

**Salutation** : Dear Mr/Ms/Mrs (*Recipient's name*)

**Content of the letter:**

1$^{st}$**para** : State the source of reference where you found the job posting and request a consideration of your candidature.

2$^{nd}$**para** : Explain the details of your study, work experience, and achievements in the sector.

3$^{rd}$**para** : Briefly explain your suitability for the post.

**Concluding para:** Thank the person for sparing their time to go through your letter and offer follow-up information.

**Complimentary close:** Sincerely,

**Candidate's name**

**Mobile no:** 91xxxxxx566

**Email Id:**xyz@gmail. com

# E-mail job application letter

## Model email application letter

### Application for the post of Graphic Designer

**To:** bestdesignsfirm@gmail.com

**Subject:** Application for the position of Graphic Designer

Dear Mr Hariprasad,

This email is in response to your job posting in the MNC job portal regarding the post of a Graphic Designer in your firm. I am interested in the offer as I feel that I have all the necessary skills, qualification, and experience as mentioned in the job posting.

I have been working as a graphic designer for a film studio in Hyderabad over five years after my post-graduation in graphic designing. I am happy to state that a lot of my work has been utilized in several new films that have come to the market recently. Now I wish to utilize my expertise in some other field where I can further expand my knowledge in the field.

I am confident that you will find my experience in the field highly beneficial to your firm and, therefore, I believe that you will take a close look at my CV and call me for interview.

Looking forward to hearing from you,

Yours faithfully,

Reethesh Singh

Mob: 91xxxxx4567

Email id: reetheshindia@gmail.com

—xxx—

# 43. Writing Biodata/Curriculum Vitae/Resume

## Importance of Biodata

The term 'resume' (*pronounced rezjumei*) is mostly used in the UK while 'Curriculum Vitae' is generally used in the US. 'Biodata' is the term that is mostly used in India and in other South Asian countries. Biodata is a document that presents your personal, educational, and professional information to a potential employer. It is an essential part of the job application process as it helps an employer to know you better and determine if you are fit for the job. It is your first contact with a potential employer. It is said that 'the first impression is the best impression'.

Therefore, your biodata should be such that it draws the attention of the employer immediately. An employer gets hundreds of resumes for a post advertised, and he has to pick the good ones out of the numerous ones he gets. If it has to be selected or taken note of, it should have certain eye-catching features which will force the recruiter to take a look at it. In this context, make sure that the following basic elements are appropriately included in the biodata.

# Basic elements to be included in a biodata

1. **A professional photo:** A photo on your biodata, though optional, gives a personal touch to your resume. It, however, should be professionally taken with your face clearly visible. The dress should preferably be formal. Avoid wearing casual dresses, trendy outfits, excessive jewellery and too much make-up, all of which create a negative impression about you.

2. **Personal information:** Your biodata should start with your name, date of birth, gender, nationality, and contact information which must include mobile number and E-mail address. You may provide this information as a bulleted list so as to enable the employer to have a quick scan of the information.

3. **Career objective:** The resume must have a clear objective or summary statement of what exactly you hope to do in this job. It will clearly tell the employer your aims in seeking the job. It should, therefore, state clearly your relevant skills in the field. A clear and concise career objective can work wonders. It is a good custom to start a resume with a career objective stated in precise terms.

4. **Education background:** Next, you should list your educational qualifications including studies such as Class X, Class XII, degree/degrees, names of the institutions where you studied, and the years of completion of the studies. It may be given in a table format for

a quick grasp. The latest educational qualification should appear on top, followed by others in chronological order.

**5. Work experience (if any):** Employers give greater weightage and importance to this section of the biodata. List your work experience, starting with your most recent job, mentioning the companies you worked for, dates you worked, etc. Also mention the job responsibilities you handled in previous companies and any achievements you may have won in your field.

**6. Achievements:** Potential employers also pay special attention to this section. Hence you should highlight your achievements in a noticeable manner. The inclusion of achievements such as an innovative idea introduced in a former work place, the promotion that you won over the years, awards and certifications received, etc. can boost your chance of being called for interview.

**7. Skills:** Make a separate list of your hard and soft skills. Hard skills are those which you have acquired through training in some software or job-related program. Certification courses in software programs such as Tally, Java, Coding, Cloud Computing, etc. fall under this category. You also should mention your level of expertise in each of these fields. On the other hand, soft skills refer to those innate qualities which you have developed over the years through personal efforts. It could include skills such as being a good communicator, smart leader, successful motivator, creative thinker, etc.

**8. Hobbies and interests:** Though this section is optional yet it can grace your biodata. However, be careful not to provide false information which may prove counter-productive later if called for an interview. Therefore, be honest and cite only those hobbies and interests which you are genuinely interested in and perform in your free time.

## Important tips to keep in mind while writing biodata

**1. Write only relevant information:** Your resume is not an autobiography. Employers have to skim through hundreds of resumes and select the best. Your resume shouldn't contain every detail. Only include information that will help you to be called for an interview.

**2. Writing style:** Use a telegraphic writing style: Eliminate personal pronouns and minimize the use of articles such as a, an, the, etc. Avoid long sentences and complicated construction. Give much of the information in bulleted form to grab the employer's attention quickly.

**3. Language:** Language should be friendly, simple, and clear. Do not use vague phrases, difficult terms and words which are redundant. Using terms and expressions from the company's website or job posting will indicate your interest in the post and this may help your biodata to be selected.

**4. Customize the resume for your job target:** Many individuals use the same resume for every job they apply for. Resume should be tailor-made to suit the job advertised. Include only information relevant for that particular job.

**5. Keep it brief:** A good resume should be as concise as possible. One who skims through your resume should notice your credentials at the first glance. Long resumes may not catch the eye of the employer. Ideally, a resume should be of one page or maximum two.

**6. Experience section should be precise and clear:** Most employers consider the experience section the most important part of a biodata. Therefore, make this section clearer, mentioning how long, in what capacity, and your accomplishments in your previous organizations. It has to be specific, action-oriented and realistic.

**7. Do research on the company:** It is important to do a research on the company, particularly its market share, area of specialization, goals, achievements, etc. Knowing it may help you write what the employer may be looking for. Therefore, use terms and expressions found in their website or job posting.

**8. Proofread your resume:** A biodata riddled with grammatical errors or spelling mistakes create a negative impression about the candidate ; and, on this ground, your biodata might be rejected outright. Therefore, make sure you proofread the contents carefully before submitting it. It should be absolutely error-free.

**9. Decent presentation:** Write or type the resume on a clean paper. The envelope in which you send it should also be of good quality. Resumes are generally typed or computer-printed unless they asked for handwritten ones. The biodata as well as the covering letter should be placed in the envelope in such a way that when it is opened the top part of the letter appears first.

**10. Send a cover letter along with the biodata:** Never send a biodata alone for a  post advertised. It should be accompanied by a cover letter which mentions  the source of your information regarding the job, the reason for your application, and briefly mention your suitability for the job. The letter should be brief and precise, written in the official application letter format.

## <u>Some important do's of writing biodata:</u>

1. The paper on which you write/type should be of good quality.
2. The resume as well as the covering letter should be neat and presentable.
3.  If it is computer-printed, make sure that the print is of good quality.
4. Your resume should be as concise as possible.
5. Experience section should be clear and precise.
6. The language of the biodata as well as the application should be simple, precise, and appealing.
7. Highlight what you can do for the company rather than what you did in the past.
8. Send only the required number of photos. The photos should be well taken.
9. Revise your application letter as well as the biodata before mailing them.

10. Resumes should be preferably typed or computer-printed unless specially asked for handwritten applications.

## Some important don'ts of writing biodata

1. Avoid lengthy resumes.
2. Never send resumes alone. A covering letter should be sent along with the resume.
3. Resumes should not be longer than two pages.
4. There shouldn't be spelling or grammatical errors.
5. Avoid difficult terms, confusing phrases and complicated sentence construction.
6. Do not send carbon copies of resumes prepared long ago.
7. Do not use letterheads of institutions for the purpose of writing applications.
8. Avoid information which has no relevance to the post advertised for.
9. The covering letter should not be lengthy. It should also be as concise as possible.
10. There should not be any striking-out or over-writing. It creates a negative impression.

## Sample biodata format

It is to be noted that there is no uniform or single format for writing biodata or resume. The format may vary depending on the nature of the job offered, the status of the candidate who applies for the post, whether the company is a multi-national or local establishment, etc. The one given below is one of the formats that is generally used in writing biodata.

Affix
passport
size photo

### Personal details

| | |
|---|---|
| Name | : ———————————— |
| Mobile No. | : ———————————— |
| E-mail Id | : ———————————— |
| Date of birth | : ———————————— |
| Gender | : ———————————— |
| Father's name | : ———————————— |
| Nationality | : ———————————— |
| Religion | : ———————————— |
| Languages known | : ———————————— |
| Address | : ———————————————————— |
| | ———————————— |

Writing Biodata

## Career objective

1. —————————————————————————————

—————————————————————————————

—————————————————————————————


## Educational background

1. —————————————————————————————
2. —————————————————————————————
3. —————————————————————————————

## Work experience

1. —————————————————————————————
2. —————————————————————————————
3. —————————————————————————————


## Skills

**Hard skills**

1. —————————————————————————————
2. —————————————————————————————


**Soft skills**

1. —————————————————————————————
2. —————————————————————————————


## Achievements

1. —————————————————————————————
2. —————————————————————————————


## Hobbies and interests

1. —————————————————————————————
2. —————————————————————————————


## Declaration

I hereby declare that all the information provided above is true to the best of my knowledge.

Signature

Place : —————————
Date  : —————————

Writing Biodata

## Sample biodata

*(There are many bio-data formats among which this appears to be the most commonly used.)*

### Personal details

| | |
|---|---|
| Name | : Krishna Kumar |
| Mobile No. | : 91xxxxxxx59 |
| E-mail Id | : xxxxx@gmail.com |
| Date of birth | : 01/05/1998 |
| Gender | : Male |
| Father's name | : Kumar Raj Singh |
| Nationality | : Indian |
| Religion | : Hinduism |
| Languages known | : English, Rajasthani, Hindi and Marathi |
| Address | : Mandi Village, Jodhpur (Dt) |
| | Rajasthan-342004 |

### Career objective

To secure a Senior HR position in a reputed organization like yours where I can utilize my skills, knowledge and experience to improve its management of manpower resources by enhancing their motivation, commitment and productivity level. I am confident of achieving success in this venture in your company as I have achieved considerable success in the present company in establishing a robust human resource management system leading to greater satisfaction among the employees, which in turn, has led to greater performance by the employees.

### Educational background

| Coursse | School/College/university | Year | Percentage of marks obtained |
|---|---|---|---|
| 1. MBA | Christ University, Bangalore | 2020 | 91% |
| 2. B. Com | St. Xavier's College, Mumbai | 2018 | 90% |
| 3. Class XII | St.Paul's Higher Sec. School, Jodhpur | 2015 | 89% |
| 4. Class X | St. Paul's Higher Sec. School, Jodhpur | 2013 | 90% |

Writing Biodata

## Work experience

1. Currently working as Senior HR Manager in a job portal named 'New Job Paradise', based in Pune since January, 2022.
2. Worked as Junior HR Manager in an IT company named 'Horizon Endeavours' based in Mumbai, from February 2020 to December 2021.

## Skills

### Hard skills

1. Got trained in Excel, MS Word and Adobe.
2. Attended a month's programme on creative thinking.
3. I am a certified English Language Trainer.

### Soft skills

1. Good at public speaking and singing.
2. I have an in-born talent of leadership.
3. I have developed over the years excellent social networking skills.

## Achievements

1. Got several prizes in the college for public speaking and singing during the period of graduation.
2. Represented my college for state quiz competition and won $2^{nd}$ prize in 2020.
3. I have been able to provide 3-month English Language Enhancement Training to more than 200 Govt. school students free of cost.

## Hobbies and interests

1. I enjoy reading novels and watching movies.
2. I like to travel by bike and I am part of an association named 'Enfield Champions' which undertakes periodic bike trips to different parts of India on Enfield bikes.

## Declaration

I hereby declare that all the information provided above is true to the best of my knowledge.

Signature

Place : Pune
Date  : 25$^{th}$ August 2023

—xxx—

# 44. Essay writing strategies for competitive examinations

Writing a general essay on a given topic has become an integral part of the present-day competitive examinations in our country. Although the nature of the essay, its length, criteria used for evaluation, etc. may vary, most essays generally follow a general pattern such as a proper introduction, well-structured body paragraphs and a befitting conclusion. Writing a good essay for a competitive examination requires a combination of several skills such as critical thinking, logical reasoning, time management, ability to use appropriate grammar and vocabulary and so on. In this context let me propose a few tips that can enhance your chances of getting excellent mark for essay writing.

## Important tips for essay writing

**1. Preparation before examination:** Well before the date of the examination, the candidate must prepare for it in the following ways:

*i) Know the topics and the time allotted for essay writing*: The first thing that the candidate must do is to go through the examination syllabus, understand fully the instructions given with regard to essay writing, comprehend the type of topics generally asked, the stipulated word count and the exact time allotted for essay writing during the examination.

*ii) Go through previous question papers:* It is good if the candidate can go through the previous questions on essay writing and take note of the type of topics generally asked. Writing down the commonly asked essay topics as well as preparing ideas on these topics well before the actual examination can do you a world of good.

*iii) Practise mock tests:* Practise writing essays in the form of mock tests and this can definitely boost your preparation. Getting the essay examined by your tutor or trainer can further enhance your writing skill.

*iv) Get to know current events:* Being  conversant with the major recent events or incidents that have happened within and outside the country will help you greatly in substantiating your points with facts and evidences.

**2. Read the question carefully:** When you are in the exam hall, the first thing to do is to take a minute or two to read and comprehend the question. You may have to read twice or thrice the question and the topic to understand what exactly the question asks for. Also, read the instructions given before the question statement. It states clearly the word limit as well as the time allotment, both of which must be strictly adhered to.

**3. Keep the word limit:** Every competitive essay writing has certain word limit. One must stick strictly to the limit stipulated. Writing less will invite penalty in most cases and writing  well beyond the limit mentioned doesn't speak well of the writer. Besides, the more you write, the more possibility of errors. Therefore, write only a little more than the given word limit.

4. **Effective time management:** Equally important is the issue of effective time management. It is often seen that many students are unable to complete the task of writing an essay within the allotted time. This folly will not happen if you make a writing plan and write according to this plan. Undertaking a series of mock tests in essay writing before the test can sharpen your skill of time management.

5. **Know well the criteria used for evaluation:** It is a fact that each competitive examination has a list of criteria to evaluate the candidates' essay. Understand these criteria well and keep them in mind while writing the essay. This will definitely help you to be on track while developing the points of the essay. Writing an essay without knowing the criteria is like jumping into a river without knowing how to swim across it.

6. **A captivating introduction:** Generally, the first sentence of the introduction is the topic sentence which acts as a curtain-raiser. It introduces the topic and gives a roadmap of what is going to be discussed in the essay. Therefore, the introduction should captivate the reader immediately. Adding an intriguing statement, a thought-provoking quote, a startling fact, etc. may help in this task.

7. **A clear thesis statement:** A good essay is always marked by a clear-cut statement of the thesis which is written immediately after the topic statement in the introduction. It provides a roadmap for the essay. The entire essay attempts to explain, discuss, and prove the above-mentioned central point. This core issue must be outlined in the beginning itself in clear and precise language.

8. **Well-structured paragraphs:** Each paragraph should address a specific point. The first sentence of the paragraph must constitute the topic sentence which explains the main point that is going to be discussed in the paragraph. The sentences that follow the topic sentence aim to expand the idea and make it clearer to the reader.

9. **Support your arguments with evidence and examples:** Another significant quality of a good essay is that the topic sentence of each paragraph is adequately substantiated with examples and evidences. Just writing or making a general statement doesn't suffice. The candidate needs to prove the point by quoting statistics, figures, examples, and evidences.

10. **Use clear and concise language:** Avoid using jargon or complex language structures that may confuse the reader. Your language should be clear, precise, concise and to the point. Beating around the topic may prove counter-productive and the examiners will notice it immediately, and this can lower your score in writing.

11. **Appropriate use of vocabulary:** The usage of the right word at the right place in the essay is another significant feature of an excellent essay. Lack of appropriateness in using vocabulary is a common lacuna in essay writing. Moreover, the vocabulary that one uses must be characterized by variety and quality. Usage of collocations (*words that go together*) enhances the beauty of your language and avoiding clichéd words and commonly used terms can get you better score in essay writing.

**12. Do not waste your time counting:** A lot of students commit the mistake of counting words after writing each paragraph or at the end of the writing to be certain that the essay is above the given word limit. This is a folly. You do not need to count the words to know the number of words you have written. Before you go for examination you should know how many words you generally write per lines by counting several of your essays and dividing it by the number of lines. For example, if you write 10 words per line and the essay's word limit is 300 words, you should write 30 lines (*30 lines x10 words*). Counting words many times distracts you from the main topic as well as takes a lot of your time.

**13. A memorable conclusion:** Ending an essay on a memorable note leaves a lasting impression on the examiner or the reader. A good conclusion consists of the concise summary of the points raised above. A conclusion can be made a memorable one by a befitting statement, a call to action, a heart-touching quotation, a fantastic thought, etc. It indicates a candidate's creative thinking ability.

**14. Proofread the essay:** It is a fact that most candidates do not get enough time to proofread the essay written by them. This is a serious lacuna. Due to tension of the exam and the pressure of time limit you may have committed serious errors with regard to vocabulary, grammar, punctuation, spelling, etc. Hence, going through the written matter quickly before you hand it over might help you to take note of the mistakes, rectify them and to make your essay relatively error-free.

# Five qualities of a good essay

**1. Focus:** A good essay is characterized by its focus on the central idea which is introduced by the topic sentence in the introduction and expanded further through the paragraphs. The chief objective of every sentence of the essay starting from the topic sentence to the last line of the conclusion is to make the central point clear to the reader.

**2. Development:** Each paragraph supports or expands the core point or idea introduced in the introduction. Each paragraph develops one aspect of this central issue further by the use of supporting sentences, evidences and examples. Thus, the whole essay is marked by a gradual progression in making the issue clearer to the reader.

**3. Unity:** The entire essay from the first line to the last has unity of thought. The central idea is stated clearly in the introduction, expanded in succeeding paragraphs and summarized in the conclusion. The whole process is marked by a logical unity of thought.

**4. Coherence:** A good essay is also characterized by coherence, i.e., ideas and points raised in the essay flow naturally and logically. The sentences within a paragraph as well as among the various paragraphs of the essay are inter-connected with one idea leading to the other.

**5. Correctness:** An ideal essay is also marked by correctness in the use of sentence structures, vocabulary, grammar, punctuation, spelling, etc. Such essays are characterized by right focus, gradual development, proper inter-connectivity and logical conclusion. It should be relatively error-free in all aspects.

# Most commonly used criteria for evaluation of essays

The following are some of the important aspects that the examiner keeps in mind while examining the essays of candidates for various competitive examinations. There is no uniform set of criteria for all the competitive examinations held in India. In fact, each examination has its own set of evaluation yardsticks. But the most common ones are the following.

1. **Task response:** One of the first points that the examiner who looks at a competitive essay is whether the candidate has fully responded to the given question or topic. In this respect he may look into the following aspects:

   a) Has the candidate clearly stated the thesis point in the introduction?

   b) Has he/she written the topic sentence of the introduction in clear and precise language?

   c) Has he/she written the paragraphs following a uniform style- topic sentence, supporting sentences, evidences and conclusion?

   d) Has he/she been able to complete the task within the allotted time and within the stipulated number of words?

2. **Cohesion and coherence:** Another key aspect that most examiners search for in an essay is whether the candidate has followed cohesion and coherence. Cohesion means unity among the sentences of the same paragraph while coherence refers to the inter-link among the various paragraphs. In this respect the following questions are pertinent:

   a) Has the candidate written sentences cohesively, one sentence leading to the others in the same paragraph?

   b) Has he/she used a good number of linking terms or connectives to link sentences and ideas?

   c) Has the concept of the central idea been maintained throughout the essay?

   d) Has he/she inter-connected the various paragraphs of the essay?

3. **Appropriate use of vocabulary:** The use of appropriate vocabulary adds charm to the essay. In this regard the examiner may look at the following points:

   a) Is the vocabulary used appropriate to the situation?

   b) Is there repetition of vocabulary?

   c) Is there a variety of vocabulary?

   d) Are there too many informal terms and mis-fitting words?

4. **Grammatical accuracy:** Grammatical inaccuracies easily catch the attention of examiners. In this regard the following aspects are checked:

   a) Are there too many errors with regard to various aspects of grammar?

   b) Has the person used appropriate tense and subject-verb agreement?

   c) Are there too many punctuation errors?

    d) Are there too many spelling mistakes?

**5. Clarity of language:** A clear language is indispensible for the proper understanding of a written matter. In this regard, the following aspects may be looked into:

    a) Are there many incomprehensible sentences?

    b) Has the person used vague terms, complicated words and unclear ideas?

    c) Is the language written clear, precise and to the point?

    d) Is the core point of the issue clear from the beginning till the end?

**6. Depth of analysis:** A good writer always dives deep into the matter and explains the various points connected to the core issue in a simple and understandable manner. In this regard, the following aspects may be examined:

    a) Has the candidate really understood the core issue in its totality?

    b) Has he /she analyzed the issue or topic in depth?

    c) Has he/she looked at the topic from different angles?

    d) Has he/she given a clear picture of the various viewpoints associated with the core issue?

**7. Originality and creativity:** A good writer through his writing exposes his originality and creative thinking ability. In this regard, the examiner may look at the following aspects:

    a) Has the candidate presented the core issue in his own words?

    b) Has he/she paraphrased the topic in proper topic sentence?

    c) Has he/she given a personal touch to the ideas and points raised?

    d) Do the ideas and views expressed depict the person's creative thinking abilities?

**8. Critical and logical thinking:** The ability to look at an issue critically and logically is an important trait of a good writer. In this regard, the examiner may examine the following aspects:

    a) Has the candidate been able to present the ideas critically without any bias or prejudice?

    b) Has he/she been able to develop the central issue logically from the introduction to the              conclusion?

    c) Has he/she given a critical and logical analysis of the core issue?

    d) Has he/she been able to look at the topic critically and present his/her views logically?

**9. Focus and development:** A good essay is characterized by a clear-cut focus and gradual development of ideas. In this regard, the following questions are relevant:

    a) Is there a focus on the central theme throughout the essay?

    b) Has the focus been side-tracked anywhere in the essay?

    c) Has the essay been gradually and progressively developed?

    d) Is there unity of thought throughout the essay?

**10. Originality and genuineness:** Originality and genuineness of the matter written constitute two major yardsticks for evaluation of essays. In this regard, the following aspects may be looked into:

    a) Are the ideas and concepts developed in the essay original and truly personal?

    b) Is there anything that has been memorized?

    c) Is there anything that has been plagiarized?

    d) Are the figures, statistics, data etc. provided authentic?

# Steps involved in writing an essay

**Step 1** : Read the question/topic twice or thrice slowly and carefully and underline its key words.

**Step 2** : Think of ideas, evidences and examples related to the topic for one or two minutes.

**Step 3** : Make a writing plan with short points for introduction, body paragraphs and conclusion.

**Step 4** : Take the exam paper and put a small mark on the line upto which you need to write the expected number of words. This depends on how many words you generally write per line and the number of words you are expected to write.

**Step 5** : Follow strictly the writing plan and write the essay keeping in mind the time limit.

**Step 6** : Proofread the essay for errors.

# Some important do's of essay writing

1. Read the topic or the question carefully. Read it again and again and try to understand its central point.
2. Analyze every part of the question and answer every part.
3. Make a writing plan and write according to this plan.
4. State your opinion clearly in the beginning.
5. Stick to your view throughout the essay. Do not contradict yourself.
6. Use a wide range of sentences and vocabulary.
7. Be concerned about spelling and punctuation.
8. Write only one idea in each paragraph.
9. What you write must be supported by examples and evidences.
10. Use extensively linking terms/connecting words.
11. Conclusion should be short, precise and summary of all the main points.
12. Always proofread what you have written.

# Some important don'ts of essay writing

Be careful to avoid the following in competitive essay writing. These can definitely lower your score or marks. Therefore, knowing these don'ts can enhance your performance in essay writing.

i) Extreme views and controversial issues

ii) Personal religious views

iii) Degrading any belief or opinion with regard to religion, politics, society, etc.

iv) Incorrect data and statistics

v) Too many abstract or philosophical concepts

vi) Lengthy sentences with multiple ideas

vii) Writing all that you know about the topic

viii) Beating around the bush about the topic

ix) Repetition of ideas and points

x) Writing points which are totally irrelevant to the topic

xi) Illegible handwriting or a handwriting that is difficult to read

xii) Too many cuttings, over-writings and jammed writing

xiii) Not leaving a space after each paragraph.

xiv) Lack of alignment of the text (*the text should be aligned to the left margin*)

xv) Writing well beyond the given word limit(*possibility of more mistakes)*

xvi) Incomprehensible sentences and unfitting vocabulary

xvii) Writing less than the given word limit

xviii) Unable to complete the writing within the allotted time

xix) Handing over the essay without proofreading

xx) Lack of coherence among the paragraphs.

# Normal structure of an essay

**Introduction**

Topic sentence (*paraphrasing the question, keeping the same meaning*).

Writer's opinion or thesis statement.

The purpose of the essay. It indicates what is going to be discussed in the essay. (*This essay describes/analyzes/ discusses...*)

**Body**

**Paragraph 1**

Topic sentence.

Supporting sentences.

Evidences/examples.

Conclusion of the paragraph.

**Paragraph 2**

Topic sentence.

Supporting sentences.

Evidences/examples.

Conclusion of the paragraph

**Paragraph 3**

Topic sentence.

Supporting sentences.

Evidences/examples.

Conclusion of the paragraph.

**General Conclusion**

Write a summary of the views expressed.

Reiterate your point.

# Method of writing an essay

## Example

### 1. Importance of nutritious diet in bringing about good health

## Introduction

### Topic sentence

*Today many people think that nutritious food intake alone is the most significant factor that leads to good health among people.*

### Personal opinion (*thesis statement*)

*I tend to disagree with this opinion. Although a balanced diet is important, there are other factors which also contribute their share in keeping people healthy.*

### Purpose of the essay

*This essay wishes to analyze both sides of this argument and tries to reach a conclusion on the basis of the points discussed.*

## Paragraph 1

### Topic sentence

*There is no denying the fact that a nutritional diet plays a role in bringing about good health in individuals.*

### Supporting sentences

*A balanced meal provides essential nutrients such as proteins, carbohydrates, minerals, fat, etc. The main organs of the body and their activities are sustained by these elements. These nutrients keep the body mechanism in its proper order and rhythm. These elements provide immunity and resistance power to the body enabling it to withstand the onslaught of the various disease-causing viruses present in the environment.*

### Evidences and examples

*In fact, malnutrition which is nothing but lack of adequate nutrients has been responsible for the high incidence of various diseases in many developing and underdeveloped countries of the world. On the other hand, high intake of nutritional meals is said to be one of the significant contributing factors for the longer life-span seen in developed countries.*

## Conclusion of the paragraph

*Thus, it is seen that people who take balanced meals, in general, are found to be healthy.*

**Paragraph 2:**

### Topic sentence

*However, nutritious diet cannot be considered as the only key factor that brings about good health among people.*

### Supporting sentences

*Factors such as lack of stress, proper rest, adequate exercise and relaxation, happy family life, healthy work environment, etc. too play a significant role in bringing about good health. Several scientific studies conducted on the  health status of various nationalities, races and people of different regions in the world reveal the fact that health is the result of several factors which are no less important than a nutritious diet.*

### Evidences and examples

*For instance, the Eskimos who live in the Arctic region survive on fish alone for several months in a year. Nevertheless, they are considered to be one of the most healthy people on earth. Even though people in the past did not always have a balanced diet yet they lived a healthy life and had higher longevity primarily due to factors such as peaceful mind,  a lot of physical activities, contented family, etc.*

### Conclusion of the paragraph

*Therefore, it is evident that many factors other than a nutritious diet play a major role in maintaining good health among people.*

**General conclusion**

### Summary of the points discussed above

*To cap the above discussion, it is clear that balanced diet is a major contributing factor of good health all over the world. Nevertheless, there are a number of other factors which are as important as balanced diet in bringing about good health among people.*

### Re-statement of personal opinion

*Therefore, I am of the opinion that good health is the result of a series of factors such as nutritious diet, stress-free life, proper exercise, and relaxation, a satisfying home and work environment, etc.*

# Full Essay

## 1. Importance of nutritional diet in bringing about good health

Today, many people think that nutritional food intake alone is the most significant factor that leads to good health among people. I, however, tend to disagree with this opinion. Although a balanced diet is important, there are other factors which also contribute their share to keeping people healthy. This essay wishes to analyze both sides of this argument and tries to reach a conclusion on the basis of the points discussed.

There is no denying the fact that a nutritional diet plays a vital role in bringing about good health in individuals. A balanced meal provides essential nutrients such as proteins, carbohydrates, minerals, fat, etc. The main organs of the body and their activities are sustained by these elements. These vital nutrients keep the body mechanism in its proper order and rhythm. These elements provide immunity and resistance power to the body, enabling it to withstand the onslaught of the various disease-causing viruses present in the environment. In fact, malnutrition which is nothing but lack of adequate nutrients, has been responsible for the high incidence of various diseases in many of the developing and underdeveloped countries of the world. On the other hand, high intake of nutritional meals is said to be one of the significant contributing factors for the longer life-span seen in the developed countries. Thus it is seen that people who take balanced meals, in general, are found to be healthy.

However, nutritious diet cannot be considered as the only key factor that brings about good health among people. Factors such as lack of stress, proper rest, adequate exercise and relaxation, happy family life and healthy work environment too play a significant role in bringing about good health. Several scientific studies conducted on the health status of various nationalities, races and people of different regions in the world reveal the fact that health is the result of several factors which are no less important than a nutritious diet. For instance, the Eskimos who live in the Arctic region survive on fish alone for several months in a year. Nevertheless, they are considered to be one of the most healthy people on earth. Even though people in the past did not always have a balanced diet yet they lived a healthy life and had higher longevity primarily due to the above-mentioned factors. Thus, it is evident that many factors other than a nutritious diet play a major role in maintaining good health among people.

To cap the above discussion, it is clear that balanced diet is a major contributing factor of good health all over the world. Nevertheless, there are a number of other factors which are as important as balanced diet in bringing about good health among people. Therefore, I am of the opinion that good health is the result of a series of factors such as nutritious diet, stress-free life, proper exercise and relaxation, a happy home and work environment, etc.

## 2. Use of animals for medical research

People have different views on how medical research should be conducted and tested. While many people think that animals have to be used for medical research, there are a lot of individuals who think otherwise. I belong to the latter category and think that testing on animals is morally wrong and unacceptable in modern society where every living creature is part and parcel of our ecosystem.

The chief argument in support of using animals for medical research is that animal testing has contributed substantially to developing many life-saving cures and treatments. It is true that nearly every medical breakthrough in the last 100 years has resulted directly from research using animals. For example, experiments in which dogs had their pancreases removed led directly to the discovery of insulin, critical to saving the lives of diabetics. Furthermore, it is impossible to release new drugs to the market before proving that it does no harm to animals. The case of new vaccines against Covid-19 is a perfect example of this fact. The quickly-developed drug was tried on animals first and then on human beings. It is in this context that the newly discovered medicines are tried first on mice because they are quite similar to human beings in many ways. Thus, it is evident that discovery of new drugs and medicines is nearly impossible without the use of animals in medical research.

However, I agree with people who consider medical development that involves the use of animals is cruel, morally wrong and, therefore, unacceptable. Scientific research has proven beyond doubt that animals too have feelings and  emotions and they express their pain and suffering in various ways like human beings. Moreover, I believe that the lives of all creatures should be respected and we, humans, have no right to let animals suffer for our own benefits. In this backdrop, governments should invest in developing alternative methods that can replace animal experimentations when doing medical research. For instance, a software program can be developed to model a human immune system and new drugs can be tested on the software rather than animals. In this way, no animals will suffer from the medical tests and the society can still benefit from such medical development.

In conclusion, although it is undoubtedly true that animal testing has helped scientists in drug developments and medical discoveries over the years, I believe that the benefits offered by it to humans do not justify the suffering caused to animals. Hence I am of the opinion that medical research using animals must be stopped forthwith and it is high time that we invented some alternative ways of testing new drugs rather than trying on the animals first.

---xxx---

# 45. Group discussion

Group discussion, or GD as it is popularly known, has become an integral step in selecting suitable candidates for admission to various higher courses or jobs. Today most companies use this method as part of their selection procedure of suitable candidates since this method provides adequate inputs regarding candidates' listening skill, communicative qualities, inter-personal skills, leadership capabilities, adaptability, etc. A group discussion reveals how a candidate participates, behaves and contributes in a group, all of which are important in today's professional world.

**Types of group discussion:** There are three main types of group discussion.

**i) Topic-based GDs:** In this type of GD the participants are asked to discuss certain common topics such as environmental pollution, child abuse, drug menace, alcoholic addiction, etc. This category can be further sub-divided into the following three groups:

**a) Factual GDs:** The discussion in this category revolves around some important comprehensive subjects like, for example, the future of democracy, relevance of the G-20 group, Ukraine War, etc. The discussion indicates participants' awareness of current events, depth of understanding and communicative skills.

**b) Controversial topics:** This type of GDs involves discussing a controversial topic which may arouse passion, anger, divergent opinion, etc. and how these are adequately managed. Topics such as governmental funding of political parties, presidential form of government, arranged marriage vs. love marriage, etc. belong to this category.

**c) Abstract GDs:** In this category, participants discuss certain conceptual topics which call for analytical skill, reasoning abilities and logical thinking. For example, the future of democracy, scope of space exploration, modern warfare, etc.

**ii) Case-based GDs:** In this type of group discussion, participants are given a case study to read, analyze and discuss. The main purpose is to gauge their problem-solving ability, analytical skill, critical thinking capacity, creative thinking skills, etc.

**iii) Article-based GDs:** In this category, participants are presented with an article on any field such as sports, movies, industry, international trade, UN, etc. The main objective is to assess participants' general knowledge, quick grasping ability, effective communication skills, etc.

**<u>Objectives of group discussion:</u>** The main objective of group discussion is to assess whether the candidate has the following skills and aptitudes which are essential for success in any organization:

    i) Communication skills
    ii) Interpersonal skills
    iii) Critical thinking
    iv) Analytical skill
    v) Problem-solving abilities

vi) Leadership potential

vii) Listening skill

viii) Flexibility and adaptability

ix) Clarity of thought and expression

x) Persuasion and convincing skills

xi) Ability to work in a team

xii) Creativity

**Organization of group discussion:** The number of participants in a group discussion range from 7 to 12 in a group. If the strength is low, the number of participants in a group may vary from 5 to 7. The average duration of a GD is 15 to 30 minutes and in certain cases it may go up to 45 minutes. The assessors or moderators sit where they can clearly see and hear all candidates. As the group discussion begins in each group, the assessors take a video of the proceedings. When the group discussion gets over, they watch the recordings and evaluate each candidate's performance. On the basis of this evaluation a shortlist is prepared and presented to the management for the next step of the selection process.

**<u>Steps involved in group discussion</u>:** A group discussion normally involves the following steps:

i) At first, all the candidates are asked to sit in a common place.

ii) Thereafter, the entire group of candidates is divided into groups consisting of 7 to 12 members.

iii) The moderator or the assessors give a pre-prepared topic to discuss in groups.

iv) The moderator may briefly explain the topic and highlight its various aspects. He also asks the groups to select someone as leader to jot down the main points discussed in the group.

v) Then the candidates of each group are asked to sit around and face one another.

vi) Generally, 3 minutes are given for personal reflection on the topic and once that period is over, the moderator gives the go-ahead signal for beginning the discussion.

vii) Once the signal is given, anyone can begin the discussion, explaining his/ her points on the given topic.

viii) The leader of each group jots down all the important points spoken by different members of the group.

ix) Once the discussion time is over, all the groups are asked to come together once again in one place.

x) The leader of each group briefly presents the main points discussed in the group.

xi) After all the group leaders have made their presentations, the chief moderator may give some time for common discussion on the points raised by different groups.

xii) Finally, the chief moderator concludes the discussion by summarizing the main points put forward by various groups.

# Main criteria used for evaluating candidates' performance in a group discussion

1. **Depth of knowledge on a given topic:** Generally the topics given for GD are common topics, current events or relevant issues. Hence, the candidates must have a thorough knowledge about what is happening in one's country and in other parts of the world. Assessors take notice of such individuals.

2. **Active listening:** The ability to listen attentively when others speak constitutes a major criterion for selection of candidates in a GD. Only an active listener can effectively participate in a group discussion. Listening skills allow people to understand different perspectives, recognize valid points and build or counter arguments effectively.

3. **Effective communication skill:** The ability to articulate one's views clearly, distinctly, and convincingly is a mark of an efficient employee or leader. The points must be explained in such a way that it is understandable to everyone present. Presenting your points in a simple and clear way will enhance your chance of being selected.

4. **Appropriate body language:** It is said that people speak more through non-verbal clues than actual words. Therefore, appropriate use of gestures, facial expression, eye-contact, nodding of the head, a smile, a pat, etc. will be taken note of by the assessors.

5. **Inter-personal skills:** Assessors also observe very carefully how each participant interacts with the others in the group. They assess their ability to agree, disagree, and to compromise when required, as these skills are essential in modern business and professional world.

6. **Analytical skill:** Another criterion that is seriously assessed in the candidates is their ability to analyze and evaluate the given data and thereafter present them logically. It involves making well-reasoned judgments and analyzing issues critically. This is particularly essential in abstract and case-study GDs.

7. **Leadership skills:** Leadership qualities can be manifested in different ways during a GD. Leaders emerge when they lead the discussion without being overly dominant or imposing. When the discussion moves away from the track, such individuals try to steer it back to the normal course. They make sure that all participants have an opportunity to express their views and try to resolve conflicts if they arise.

8. **Team work:** Most organizations look for team players. Therefore, you should not be monopolizing the talk. Give everyone an opportunity to talk. Learn to contribute to the given points. Appreciate or praise when someone adds a novel or a unique idea. The ability to accommodate others' ideas and thereby reach a consensus in a group discussion will indicate your spirit of team work.

9. **Problem-solving skills:** In GDs such as case-study GD or abstract GD, you need to show your problem-solving skills. This skill involves analyzing the various aspects of the issue, and providing innovative solutions. A good problem-solver thinks creatively, identifies the core issue, and proposes practical solutions.

**10. Creativity:** The assessors also evaluate candidates' creativity. When you present a fact or a piece of data in a different way than what others have done, you are noted by the assessors. The ability to think differently, look at things with an open mind and present the issues in a logical manner are essential in any work environment.

**11. Polite behaviour:** It is important to be polite while participating in a group discussion. If something is said that is not palatable to your tongue, do not express your anger, bitterness, or dislike. If someone in the group opposes your views, you should not be aggressive towards him/her but express your disagreement in a gentle way. Making fun of others or criticizing another participant directly will diminish your chances of being selected.

**12. Flexibility and adaptability:** Sometimes someone in the group may bring in a bright idea which no one has spoken before. Do not oppose him/her; instead, show flexibility and adaptability by accepting his/her views if you find them good and worthwhile. Make sure to appreciate such individuals by praising their innovative thinking abilities. Assessors will definitely take note of candidates who are able to appreciate others' contributions.

**13. Time management skill:** GDs have a set time limit and so participants cannot afford to speak for long on a topic. Therefore, candidates have to prioritize relevant facts, allocate time for opinions and avoid unnecessary diversions or off-topic speaking. Talking too much as well as talking too often may bring you less grades in group discussion.

**14. Persuasion and convincing skills:** Participants are also evaluated on their ability to be persuasive while maintaining a rational and objective approach. To positively influence others' opinion in supporting your view or standpoint shows your convincing skill which is quite important in present-day professional life. To be able to provide convincing arguments and solid proof in support of your viewpoint is an indication of your persuasive skill.

**15. Managing stress and pressure of GD:** Group discussion is a stressful affair as the candidates know that only a few among them are going to be selected. Hence, everyone is out there trying to outdo others in the GD, and this can be highly stressful. Hence, assessors will take note of individuals who buckle under pressure and are unable to speak coherently and logically.

Thus it can be said that your success in a GD depends on how well you play the role of initiator, listener, information seeker, information giver, supportive team player, compromiser, leader, persuasive speaker, etc.

Group discussion

<u>**Important do's of group discussion**</u>

1. Listen carefully to the topic being proposed or outlined by the group discussion moderator.
2. Carry a piece of paper and a pen to jot down your points as well as those of others.
3. When you speak, be brief and go straight to the point you want to express.
4. You should talk to all members of the group, making eye-contact with all.
5. If some member has already mentioned the point, support or add to the points mentioned.
6. Show flexibility in your views. Accept others' views if you find them good and worthwhile.
7. Use polite terms while expressing opposing views.
8. Be attentive to the person who is speaking and make sure that you are looking at him.
9. If the discussion strays from the given topic, try to steer it back to the original topic.
10. Try to be clear, energetic and forceful as you speak. Be assertive without being a bully.

<u>**Important don'ts of group discussion**</u>

1. Do not interrupt when someone speaks.
2. Do not argue with participants who oppose your views.
3. Do not monopolize the discussion.
4. Do not bring in any point which is not connected with the topic.
5. Do not talk to anyone in particular but talk to the entire group.
6. Do not correct a mistake or inaccurate statistics provided by other members.
7. Do not use humour when serious discussion is on.
8. Do not speak in a monotonous tone. Use a variety of high and low pitches.
9. Do not repeat the statements made by others.
10. Do not talk quietly or whisper among the members.
11. Do not talk too long or too frequently.
12. Do not make any personal attack or cutting remark.

# Terms and expressions that can be used during group discussion

**1) When you want to join a discussion:**
    i) Could I add a point here...
    ii) May I say something here...
    iii) I would like to say that ...
    iv) I would like to add that ....
    v) I believe I have a solid point to add here...

**2) Asking for clarifications:**
    i) I am sorry, I didn't get your points clearly.
    ii) Would you mind repeating that point?
    iii) I think it would be nice if you can substantiate that argument, please.

iv) I am afraid that the point you have raised is not very clear.

v) It would be really nice if you can clarify that point again.

**3) Expressing agreement:**

i) Well, I perfectly agree with that point.

ii) I think you are absolutely right.

iii) Definitely, you have stated the point well.

iv) I believe it is a convincing argument.

v) I cannot disagree. Nevertheless, your point is worth considering.

**4) Expressing disagreement:**

i) I am afraid I have to disagree with you on this point.

ii) Well, I cannot exactly support your argument.

iii) I am afraid your last point cannot be accepted.

iv) I am afraid we may have to reconsider the point again.

v) I am sorry, this particular point does not hold water.

**5) Answering disagreement:**

i) Yes, I see your point.

ii) Definitely yes, you have a strong point here.

iii) I am afraid I didn't make myself clear.

iv) I think my friend expressed a solid point here.

v) Yes, your line of thought seems to be right.

**6) Ways of conceding a point:**

i) Definitely I must agree with your point.

ii) I think you seem to be right.

iii) I think there is some truth in what you say.

iv) Perhaps you are right.

v) Oh yes, you are right.

**7) Expressing personal opinion:**

i) To the best of my knowledge.......

ii) If I am not wrong,........

iii) Personally, I tend to think that......

iv) In my humble view ....

v) If I may say ....

vi) As far as I know...

xxx—